INCULTURATION OF THE JESUS TRADITION

INCULTURATION OF THE JESUS TRADITION

THE IMPACT OF JESUS ON JEWISH AND ROMAN CULTURES

GRAYDON F. SNYDER

TRINITY PRESS INTERNATIONAL
Harrisburg, Pennsylvania

Trinity Press International, P.O. Box 1321, Harrisburg, PA 17105
Trinity Press International is a division of the Morehouse Group.

Cover design by Corey Kent
Cover art by Jeanine Wine, photographed by Ron Gould Studios / Chicago
Photographs by Graydon F. Snyder, digitally enhanced by Jeanine Wine

Library of Congress Cataloging-in-Publication Data
Snyder, Graydon F.
    Inculturation of the Jesus tradition : the impact of Jesus on
Jewish and Roman cultures / Graydon F. Snyder.
        p. cm.
    Includes bibliographical references.
    ISBN 1-56338-295-4 (alk. paper)
    1. Christianity and culture – History – Early church, ca. 30–600.
2. Jews – Civilization – Christian influences. 3. Rome – Civilization –
Christian influences.   I. Title.
BR166.S58 1999
232.9′04 – dc21   99–29803

Printed in the United States of America

99   00   01   02   03   04   10 9 8 7 6 5 4 3 2 1

To Irene

IN PACE

Contents

Preface

This project has been en route for many years, always there, but never quite finished. Those who know me, and even those who do not, will recognize the layers produced by time and location: Göttingen, Princeton, Oslo, Rome, Cambridge, and Chicago. Along the way some aspects of this study have been made public. My interest in *martyria* and covered cemeteries can be found in "Survey and 'New Thesis' on the Bones of Peter" (*BA* 32 [1969]: 1–24). Over a period of time that interest led to the publication of my study of early Christian nonliterary evidence, *Ante Pacem: Archaeological Evidence of Church Life before Constantine* (Macon, Ga.: Mercer University Press, 1985). More recently interests in inculturation and inscriptions resulted in a chapter entitled "The Interaction of Jews with Non-Jews in Rome," in *Judaism and Christianity in First-Century Rome* (ed. Karl P. Donfried and Peter Richardson [Grand Rapids: Eerdmans, 1998], 69–90). Forays into the topic of early Christian architecture can be found in "Early Christian Meeting Places, Constantinian Basilicas, and Anabaptist Restorationism," *Mennonite Quarterly Review* 20 (1999): 1–7; and "The Aesthetic Origins of Early Christian Architecture," in *Text and Artifact* (Waterloo, Ont.: Wilfrid Laurier University Press, 1999).

Through the years many people have encouraged me and assisted me in this project. I would like to express appreciation to all of them individually, but that is impossible. I would like to thank David Frantz for transposing a difficult part of the manuscript, Bryan Miller for critical computer assistance, and Jeanine Wine for "digital enhancement." Indeed, most of the figures and photographs have been altered in order to elucidate the text.

Finally I would like to thank Robert Maccini, John Eagleson, and Laura Hudson for a remarkable job in editing my manuscript and preparing it for publication. And, of course, there might not have been a book without the encouragement and support of friend and colleague Harold Rast of Trinity Press International.

GRAYDON F. SNYDER

Chicago, Illinois

Abbreviations

BA	*Biblical Archaeologist*
BJS	*Brown Judaic Studies*
BR	*Biblical Research*
BZAW	Beihefte zur *ZAW*
CBQ	*Catholic Biblical Quarterly*
EEC	*Encyclopedia of Early Christianity*
EvT	*Evangelische Theologie*
HTR	*Harvard Theological Review*
JAAR	*Journal of the American Academy of Religion*
JBL	*Journal of Biblical Literature*
JTC	*Journal for Theology and Church*
JTS	*Journal of Theological Studies*
NBAC	*Nuovo bulletino di archaeologia cristiana*
NTS	*New Testament Studies*
RHPR	*Revue d'histoire et de philosophie religieuses*
SICV	*Sylloge inscriptionem cristianorum veterum musei vaticani*
TLZ	*Theologische Literaturzeitung*
VC	*Vigiliae christianae*
ZNW	*Zeitschrift für die neutestamentliche Wissenschaft*
ZTK	*Zeitschrift für Theologie und Kirche*
ZWT	*Zeitschrift für wissenschaftliche Theologie*

1

Introduction

In 1991 Canaan Banana, first president of Zimbabwe, made the assertion that the Bible should be rewritten in terms of Shona history and mythology.[1] At first glance the suggestion might seem ludicrous and impossible. Upon further reflection, however, Banana's proposal contains considerable merit. As with many other African nations, Christianity came to Zimbabwe by means of Western missionaries who based their own faith on the Western canon. The concerns, the faith, the symbols of that canon — and its subsequent development — have little to do with the traditional life and faith of East Africa.

Banana correctly argued that acceptance of the Western Bible entailed acceptance of another culture, whether or not the Bible was introduced by Westerners or Africans. In other words, the canon of the Bible as we know it does not represent, ipso facto, the Christian faith, but rather, the Greco-Roman adaptation of the Christian faith. Had the initial Jesus tradition infiltrated a culture other than the Greco-Roman, our canon would indeed have been formed in quite another way, and the culture it carried could have been vastly different.

If Banana has correctly described the situation, then Christians of the twentieth century, or any other time, need to determine the nature of the Jesus tradition and the means by which it enters any given culture. It is the intent of this study to describe the missionary style of Judaism at the time of Jesus, to propose a basic Jesus tradition, to show how two New Testament writers (Paul and John) handled that Jesus tradition, and then to demonstrate how the Jesus tradition entered the Mediterranean culture.

But first, it is important that we define the variety of ways in which, over the course of Christian history, the Christian faith has approached other cultures.[2]

---

1. See Canaan S. Banana, "The Case for a New Bible," in 'Rewriting' the Bible: The Real Issues, ed. Isabel Mukonyora, James L. Cox, and Frans J. Verstraelen (Harare, Zimbabwe: Mambo Press, 1993), 17–32.
2. Works consulted on inculturation and interaction: David J. Bosch, Transforming Mission (Maryknoll, N.Y.: Orbis, 1991); Ruy O. Costa., ed. One Faith, Many Cul-

Assimilation and Acculturation

Assimilation and acculturation are opposite sides of the same coin. When two cultures meet, one may assimilate the other, or at least assimilate its heretofore unknown worldview. From the perspective of the invasive culture / worldview, when assimilation occurs it has become acculturated. As we shall frequently note, the process can be one of mutual, though seldom equal, assimilation and acculturation.

Assimilation occurs within a specific social matrix that, by definition, must manifest at least some cultural characteristics. A social matrix must care for its own sense of community and for families within that community. It must look to a common authority to guide the community and the individual's participation. It must develop common times and styles of celebration. Finally, it must define, in some way, the relationship of community to nature (specifically, land). For the purpose of this study, a *social matrix* will be defined as a community or series of communities that share a common ethos in regard to community, family, authority, celebration, and nature. In that sense we will, with some trepidation, speak of a Palestinian social matrix, a Roman social matrix, a Jewish social matrix, and a budding early Christian social matrix. If necessary, we will determine cultural encounter by means of artifacts.[3] In any case, *culture* then will be defined as the commonly accepted manner in which a specific social matrix expresses itself. *Myth* will be understood as the religious or philosophical conviction that holds together the component parts.

By no means have social scientists agreed on these much discussed terms.[4] One might understand the process of acculturation in three ways: (1) acceptance, where one culture takes on another; (2) adaptation, where

---

tures: Inculturation, Indigenization, and Contextualization (Maryknoll, N.Y.: Orbis, 1988); Mariasusai Dhavamony, *Christian Theology of Inculturation* (Rome: Editrice Pontificia Università Gregoriana, 1997); Bolaji Idowu, *Towards an Indigenous Church* (London: Oxford, 1965); Robert Redfield, *The Little Community* (Chicago: University of Chicago Press, 1955); Lamin Sanneh, *Translating the Message: The Missionary Impact on Culture* (Maryknoll, N.Y.: Orbis, 1989); Peter Schineller, *A Handbook on Inculturation* (New York: Paulist Press, 1990); Robert Schreiter, *Constructing Local Theologies* (Maryknoll, N.Y.: Orbis, 1985); Aylward Shorter, *Toward a Theology of Inculturation* (Maryknoll, N.Y.: Orbis, 1988).

3. *Culture* may be defined as a social network for dealing with common structural realities (Clifford Geertz, *The Interpretation of Culture* [New York: Basic Books, 1978], 89), or, in a more archaeological way, as occupants of archaeological sites with like artifacts (Bruce G. Trigger, *Gordon Childe, Revolutions in Archaeology* [New York: Columbia University Press, 1980]; Gordon Childe, *The Dawn of European Civilization* [New York: Knopf, 1958], vi).

4. Melville J. Herskovits, *Acculturation: The Study of Cultural Contact* (Gloucester, Mass.: Peter Smith, 1958).

the elements of the two cultures combine to produce a culture that expresses both; (3) reaction under pressure, where one culture acquiesces to another simply in order to survive.[5]

Enculturation

Within the social matrix there must be a method for establishing the validity of the dominant culture and its mythology. Children born into the matrix will be formed and educated to accept the dominant system. We call that enculturation. More complicated than the formation of children would be the enculturation of adult converts. Once Christian communities were established, how did they enculturate non-Christians? Obviously, Paul addresses this question when he advises the Corinthian Christians not to eat meat offered to idols (1 Cor. 10). Some new converts needed to know that their paradigm shift also entailed a cultural shift.

Cultural Domination

Though destruction of another culture was not an option for either Jews or Christians in the early centuries of the Roman Empire, eventually, and especially in the nineteenth century, it became the rule. The procedure is well known and widespread. A more dominant culture forces a less dominant culture to give up its characteristics and its method of enculturation. The Christianity of the more powerful culture then replaces the "pagan" culture of the oppressed group. Cultural domination normally occurs in situations where the Christian power holds a military or political advantage. However, there are other possibilities. A superior patronage system can make it advantageous for persons in the disadvantaged culture to "convert." Though less obvious, there are, of course, historical moments when the infrasystem of the dominant culture — intellectual clarity, moral superiority, or linguistic universality — make it advantageous for the less useful system to be discarded.

In Zimbabwe, Christian missionaries discouraged the function of the ancestral spirits and created, consequently, a more Western individuality. Western missionaries also introduced a calendar, as a system of celebration, that functioned well in the north (Christmas at the winter solstice), but did not utilize the Shona tribal calendar. The list of "dominations" seems endless!

---

5. Herskovits, *Acculturation*, 135–36.

Liberation

Starting in 1971, with the publication of Gustavo Gutiérrez's *Theology of Liberation*, much of Christian action in developing countries has been to free people from domination either by outside powers or within the country. For those who might be designated "liberation theologians," theology is a "critical reflection on Christian praxis in the light of the Word."[6] Liberation has the opposite intent of domination: it calls for freedom from all forms of colonial oppression. For over thirty years liberation theology has been the guiding perspective for thinkers from developing countries. Insofar as it calls for a shift in political and economic power, it tends to have a Marxist sociological base. Consequently it does wish for people from developing countries to discard those cultural patterns that might be susceptible to domination by an aggressive outside power. Understood this way, liberation theology does not engage the primary culture — if anything it encourages its demise. Liberation theologians do not speak extensively of a replacement culture. They do, however, strongly encourage popular cell groups called "base communities."[7]

Inculturation

In recent years a new term has surfaced to describe a style of mission that allows for an aggressive promotion of the Jesus tradition without seeking to dominate or destroy another culture. Pedro Arrupe, of the Society of Jesus, has defined inculturation as "the incarnation of the Christian life and of the Christian message in a particular cultural context, in such a way that this experience not only finds expression through elements proper to the culture in question, but becomes a principle that animates, directs and unifies the culture, transforming and remaking it so as to bring about 'a new creation.'"[8] Although Arrupe moves more toward an intentional result than is appropriate, the perception is correct. The Jesus tradition enters a social matrix, uses the cultural elements, and *may* in an undetermined way create a new culture that expresses the Christian faith for that matrix.

6. Gustavo Gutiérrez, *A Theology of Liberation: History, Politics, and Salvation* (Maryknoll, N.Y.: Orbis, 1973), 13. See Priscilla Pope-Levison and John R. Levison, *Jesus in Global Contexts* (Louisville: Westminster/John Knox, 1992), 186–88; David B. Batstone, *From Conquest to Struggle: Jesus of Nazareth in Latin America* (Albany: State University of New York Press, 1991), 20.

7. Batstone, *From Conquest to Struggle.*

8. Pedro Arrupe, "Letter to the Whole Society on Inculturation," *Aixala* 3 (1978): 172–81. Mariasusai Dhavamony says that "the message ought to be embodied in the soul of the people as it relates to their culture" (my translation) ("Problematica dell'inculturazione del Vangelo oggi," in *Evangelización de la cultura e inculturación del Evangelio* [Buenos Aires: Editorial Guadalupe, 1988], 145).

We look primarily to the New Testament for the way Christian inculturation operates. The Jesus tradition, lacking specific cultural components, infiltrated the Mediterranean world in such a way that eventually a Christian civilization was formed out of Greco-Roman ingredients. The New Testament canon reflects, then, that process of fusing the Jesus tradition with the culture(s) of the Mediterranean social matrix.

Mutual Culturation and Interaction

Of course, any cultural interchange must result in a mutual influence. The charismatic revelation of the prophet will need to be adapted to any given social matrix, and that social matrix will be altered in the process. At the same time, the revelation itself may be permanently modified. Thus, the Jesus tradition so altered the Greco-Roman culture that a Christian empire was formed, but at the same time the Jesus tradition became a creedalistic formulation that we have to come call "Christian orthodoxy" — an orthodoxy that did not exist in the first centuries of the faith. On the positive side, when two disparate cultures share their understanding of a common text (e.g., the Bible), they serve to correct and enrich one another's understanding of the original source. In fact, despite Western emphasis on the objectivity of history, there may be no other way to grow in understanding than through cultural interaction.

Part 1

Inculturation in the New Testament

2

The Jesus Tradition

The mission of Jesus must relate, in some sense, to the mission of contemporary Jews. One supposes the validity of that presupposition, but admittedly it may not be important. In isolating the Jesus tradition we are not asking about the historical Jesus, but only what the earliest followers considered important. The earliest followers of Jesus may well have come from a specific segment of Judaism (e.g., apocalypticists) or may even represent a more Hellenistic viewpoint than what we think of as Palestinian Judaism. Nevertheless, the first followers were Jews, and what they found most important must reflect also their sense of mission. So the question of inculturation in the Jewish sense of mission ought not to be overlooked.

Jewish Missionary Activity

In recent years few issues have attracted more attention than the nature and scope of Jewish missions in the period around the first century C.E.[1] One is hard put to explain why the issues of proselytes and God-fearers have grown in importance. Certainly one reason would be demographic: how does one explain a seeming phenomenal growth of Judaism in the Diaspora? Or was there such a growth? Another reason would be the continuing discovery of synagogues and inscriptions that point to the presence of God-fearers in Diaspora Jewish communities. Or, for some, the explosion of Christianity, a form of Judaism, requires an explanation.

The major argument for a Jewish mission derives from demographic data. The expansion of Judaism in the Diaspora was indeed phenomenal,

---

1. Louis H. Feldman, *Jew and Gentile in the Ancient World: Attitudes and Interactions from Alexander to Justinian* (Princeton, N.J.: Princeton University Press, 1993); see the critical review by Collins in *JBL* 113 (1994): 716–18. A minimalist view of Jewish missions can be found in Martin Goodman, "Jewish Proselytizing in the First Century," in *The Jews among Pagans and Christians in the Roman Empire*, ed. Judith Lieu, John North, and Tessa Rajak (London: Routledge, 1992), 53–78. Note also J. Goldstein, "Jewish Acceptance and Rejection of Hellenism," in *Aspects of Judaism: Jewish and Christian Self-Definition*, ed. E. P. Sanders (London: SCM, 1981), 2:64–87.

even if Baron and Feldman have overestimated.[2] But lacking clear evidence regarding proselytes, one can still explain the growth as increased emigration from Palestine (Philo, *Moses* 2.232 [42]) or as general growth among Jewish families, who surely did not practice infanticide, or even otherwise did not attempt to control the birth process (Tacitus, *Hist.* 5.5). Buttressing this latter explanation is the lack of evidence for missioners who attempted to convert Gentiles to Judaism. On the other hand, there are some pieces of literature that seem to have been written to attract Gentiles to Judaism (e.g., *Joseph and Aseneth*).[3] Yet, even if such literature did exist for that purpose, to what extent would that account for large numbers of conversions? Who had access to such expensive, unique literature, or, lacking wide distribution, under what circumstances would it have been read to large audiences? A social context for missionary literature, sans missioner, seems totally lacking.

If it were not for a few literary notices, one would never suspect that Judaism at the time of the New Testament was involved in missionary activity to any great extent. One such passage, "Woe to you, scribes and Pharisees, hypocrites! For you cross sea and land to make a single convert, and you make the new convert twice as much a child of hell as yourselves" (Matt. 23:15), has been taken to demonstrate a missionary movement. But such passages are rare. This one more likely reflected the attitude of the Matthean community toward Judaism. The Matthean Christian community, presumably not far distant from an Antioch synagogue, used Septuagintal language of persecution and division to indicate why they, as a Jewish sect, ought to be distinguished from other Jews. This Matthean saying, using language of the Exodus, differentiates the mission of the Christians from that of the Jews, and indeed may, with irony, refer to *one* Jewish proselyte, perhaps even a well-known convert (as in the case of Eleazer's conversion of Izates, king of Adiabene[4]).

For this study, the demographically accurate growth of Judaism is not in itself important. The nature of inculturation is. Can we determine, from the fairly sparse evidence, what cultural impact the Jewish mission had and/or what impact Jewish leaders intended to have? Judaism apparently attracted persons who sought a more "reasonable" faith; persons who, distraught over current morality, sought a more life-affirming ethic; and persons who married into the Jewish community.[5] Not all of

---

2. Salo Baron, *A Social and Religious History of the Jews* (New York: Columbia University Press, 1937); Feldman, *Jew and Gentile.*

3. P. Dalbert, *Die Theologie der Hellenistich-Jüdischen Missionsliteratur unter Ausschluß von Philo und Josephus* (Hamburg-Volksdorf: H. Reich, 1954). See Goodman, "Jewish Proselytizing."

4. Goodman, "Jewish Proselytizing," 76.

5. Soonyeol Song, *The Portraits of God-Fearers in Acts of the Apostles: Its Histori-*

those attracted became converts or, if the term applies, proselytes. Jews apparently were, for the most part, willing, or even eager, to accommodate such sympathizers. As for the sympathizers, they attended meetings, participated in some parts of the worship (prayer), and contributed to welfare programs as well as the upkeep of the synagogue. One presumes that they may have represented the concerns of the Jews to the local town council. In that capacity, the sympathizers could serve as a buffer between Jews and non-Jews.

There is little reason to suppose that sympathizers held to the specific laws of Judaism, especially dietary laws. Although they must have met on the Sabbath with the congregation, and would have heard the reading of the Septuagint and the recitation of prayers, there is no reason to suppose that they kept Sabbath rules. And the men were not circumcised. We cannot use the book of Acts as a valid source for Jewish inculturation, but the above observations do fit well with the picture given us by Luke. The sympathizer Cornelius, Luke's first Greco-Roman non-Jewish Christian, "was a devout man who feared God with all his household; he gave alms generously to the people and prayed constantly to God" (Acts 10:2). The first Greco-Roman woman, Lydia, also a God-fearer, attended prayer regularly at the riverside outside the city gate (Acts 16:13–14).

Because Jewish sympathizers did not follow dietary and ceremonial laws, social contact with birthright Jews must have been limited. And, indeed, non-Jewish writers frequently noted the antisocial behavior of Jewish people.[6] In order to create the possibility of Jewish and non-Jewish table fellowship, much of the book of Acts describes the way in which the new Christian commensalism was made possible.

Cornelius (Acts 10:1–11:18)

In Acts the narrative of Cornelius plays a critical role. The God-fearing centurion had already been attached to Judaism, but is told of a new possibility for sharing in Judaism (10:4–6). At the same time, Peter is prepared for the meeting with Cornelius by means of a vision regarding clean and unclean food (10:9–16). It seems probable that Luke has wrapped a story regarding Peter and Jewish dietary laws into a table fellowship narrative. Indeed, the point of the Cornelius story rests in 10:23–29. Cornelius, with his Gentile friends, awaits the unknown Peter. The point is made when Peter enters the house of Cornelius: Cornelius is so overwhelmed by the dissolution of racial boundaries that he falls down and

---

cal Background and Literary Function (Ph.D. diss., Chicago Theological Seminary, 1995); Goodman, "Jewish Proselytizing"; Menahem Stern, *Greek and Latin Authors on Jews and Judaism,* vol. 1 (Jerusalem: Israel Academy of Science and Humanities, 1974).

6. Song, *Portraits of God-Fearers.*

worships Peter. Responding to that action, Peter says, ἀνάστηθι· καὶ ἐγὼ αὐτὸς ἄνθρωπός εἰμι. (10:26) — that is, he, Peter, is a human being just like Cornelius. The wall between Jew and Gentile has been abolished! Peter summarizes the situation with what God showed him: he should not call any person κοινὸν ἢ ἀκάθαρτον (v. 28). So the distinction in 10:14 actually applies to humans not animals. Nevertheless, it is the abolition of the dietary laws that makes it possible for Peter ἐπιμεῖναι ἡμέρας (10:48, note also v. 23). After accepting the hospitality of Cornelius and his faith community, Peter begins his speech with the declaration that any one who fears God and does what is right will be acceptable to God. Peter has articulated what is minimally expected in order for table fellowship to occur: ὁ φοβούμενος αὐτὸν [θεὸν] καὶ ἐργαζόμενος δικαιοσύνην (10:35). With that, the Gentile Pentecost occurs, so that they too speak in tongues and extol God. The new community of faith is then baptized (10:48).

The Noachic Code (Acts 15:1-35)

A more direct set of expectations for new Christians, though considerably more perplexing, can be found at the critical apostolic council. Luke has described a meeting of the first Christians with the express purpose of discussing the validity of the Gentile mission. Paul and Barnabas, back from a successful mission in Asia Minor, attend the meeting as the main protagonists. Some of the more conservative Jerusalem Christians insist that the Gentiles must be treated as proselytes. They must be circumcised and follow the law of Moses (Acts 15:5). That is to say, some Jewish-Christians did not perceive the Way as a movement other than a Jewish deviation. It was Peter, with his Cornelius experience behind him, who insisted that the new faith was a more universal expression of Judaism. Peter won the day. The final compromise reached was the imposition of the so-called Noachic code on all Gentile converts. According to the Talmud, God gave to Adam six laws, and subsequently to Noah a seventh, which were binding on all humankind.[7] There were six prohibitions: against idolatry, blasphemy, murder, adultery, robbery, and eating meat taken from a living animal. The one mandate was to establish courts of justice.

Given Luke's predilection for Septuagintizing and his rather obvious reversal of that historical structure as found in the Priestly document, it is not surprising that he would reach back to Noah and the Noachic code for a minimal set of human standards. The three regulations are abstention from the pollution of idols, from unchastity, and from blood.[8] The

---

7. *Mercer Dictionary of the Bible*, s.v. "Noachic Laws," 618.
8. The fourth regulation — abstention from what is strangled — has a somewhat du-

most apparent way of interpreting these three (or four) abstentions is to retranslate them as abstention from idolatry, immorality, and murder. Translators have indeed felt the necessity to make of these standards something worthy of universal acceptance. Some early copyists even added the negative Golden Rule (notably D and Irenaeus). But perhaps our desire for some Kantian universal has hidden the real meaning from us. The issue was not minimal behavior but acceptable communion. On what basis could Jews and non-Jews exist at a common table and in common worship? If that is the issue (as in Gal. 2:11–21), then the apparent reason for the apostolic council — whether Gentiles should be circumcised — does not refer to faith but to acceptable communion. The council decides against required conversion but asks for sensitivity in matters of religious table fellowship: abstention from serving meat offered to idols, from hierodulic worship (e.g., Dionysiac rites), and from the use of animals with their blood (life) still in them. According to the Acts 15 council, then, commensalism between Christian Jew and Christian non-Jew would be possible.

Jewish Inculturation at the Time of Jesus

Generally speaking it would not seem that Judaism was mission-oriented during the first centuries of the common era. Estimates of a rapid growth of Judaism are questionable as to numbers or as to means of growth. Concomitantly there is little indication of any Jewish cultural takeover (cultural domination). To the contrary, popular Judaism was influenced by the Hellenistic culture as thoroughly as Christianity. A nearly complete list of symbols used by Jews through the sixth century shows ninety-seven decorations and symbols of which only the *etrog, lulab*, menorah, and shofar became consistent signs of Jewish identity.[9] For the most part the remaining ninety-three symbols come from either the general Hellenistic culture (zodiac signs, garlands) or, occasionally, come from Jewish life (the Torah shrine). Although many of these symbols show acculturation from Hellenism, no Jewish symbols became a part of the Hellenistic symbol system.[10]

Judaism at the time of Jesus was not extensively mission-oriented. Not only did Jews eschew conversionary activities, but there is practically no

---

bious textual basis. Mbachu Hilary maintains that the Noachic code was an attempt to implement Christian inculturation (*Inculturation Theology of the Jerusalem Council in Acts 15: An Inspiration for the Igbo Church Today* [Frankfurt: Peter Lang], 1995).

9. Jacob Neusner, *Symbol and Theology in Early Judaism* (Minneapolis: Fortress, 1991), 142–71.

10. Leonard V. Rutgers, "Archaeological Evidence for the Interaction of Jews and Non-Jews in Late Antiquity," *American Journal of Archaeology* 96 (1992): 101–18.

indication that Jewish culture (writings, art, education, language, music, festivals) infiltrated Mediterranean culture (although Roman culture may be deeply indebted to the Jews for a lunar calendar). Although some Gentiles must have worshiped with Jews and contributed financially to the work of the synagogue, basically, Jewish inculturation did not occur.

God-fearers

The identification of the God-fearers is probably one of the most discussed and disputed issues in Lukan studies. It has been assumed that the earliest apostles went first to Jews with the message about Jesus. When the Jews rejected this message, they carried the mission to Gentiles. However, there existed a third group, the God-fearers, who were indeed Gentiles, but were attracted to, if not attached to, Judaism and local synagogues. In other words, the God-fearers served as the bridge whereby the mission shifted to the Gentile world. This thesis has been challenged, perhaps most vigorously by Thomas Kraabel, who doubts that the category "God-fearers" existed historically.[11] First, he argues that although Luke uses the terms φοβούμενος and σεβόμενος to describe such a Gentile category, these terms never appear in inscriptions. The inscriptional term customarily taken as referring to God-fearers is θεοσεβής, a term that refers exclusively to Jews. Secondly, there is no hint from the material evidence that Jews were interested in missionary outreach of any kind. And finally, the literary evidence depends almost entirely on Luke's ahistorical thesis in Acts. On the basis of these observations, Kraabel comes to the following conclusions: (1) The word "synagogue" is used in Acts chiefly to designate the place where Diaspora Christian missionary preaching begins — with one exception (18:26). (2) Paul is the synagogue preacher. After his conversion, Paul's first act is to preach in the synagogue. This is particularly striking in view of the fact that the word "synagogue" is not used once in the letters written by Paul. (3) Luke wishes to show that the missionary path to the Gentiles was through the Jews. Cornelius is the archetypal God-fearer. After him no other God-fearer is described. In fact only two others are named: Lydia in 16:14 and Titius Justus in 18:7. After 18:7 there is a sudden disappearance of the God-fearers, and Kraabel reasons that God-fearers might have served their purpose in the plot of Acts. So, Acts cannot be used as evidence that such groups ever

---

11. Thomas A. Kraabel, "The Disappearance of the Godfearers, *Numen* 28 (1981): 113–26; "The Roman Diaspora: Six Questionable Assumptions," *Journal of Jewish Studies* 33 (1982): 445–64; "Greek, Jews and Lutherans in the Middle Half of Acts," *HTR* 79 (1986): 147–57; "The God-fearers — A Literary and Theological Invention," *Biblical Archaeology Review* 64 (1986): 47–54; "The God-fearers Meet the Beloved Disciple," in *The Future of Early Christianity*, ed. Birger A. Pearson (Minneapolis: Fortress, 1991), 276–84.

existed in the synagogues of the Roman Empire. The God-fearers are a symbol to help Luke show how Christianity had become a Gentile religion legitimately, without losing its roots in Hebrew Scriptures.

Kraabel's thesis has appealed to some.[12] Others find it difficult to accept.[13] Objectors point to the presence of inscriptions and the presupposition that Jews did indeed encourage Gentile participation in the life of the synagogue.

Inscriptions Found in the Region of Asia Minor

Panticapaeum

In 1935 a first-century inscription was published that indicated the presence of God-fearers in the synagogue of this Black Sea community. The inscription mentions that the son of a slave had the protection τῆς συναγωγῆς τῶν Ἰουδαίων καὶ θεὸν σέβων.

Miletus

A second-century inscription from Miletus has been published recently that reads: Τόπος Εἰουδέων τῶν καὶ θεοσεβίον. It was discovered on a seat in the fifth row of the theater and probably reflects the inability of the stone mason to distinguish between Jews and God-fearers. If so, we have a fairly certain indication that a group called God-fearers were associated closely with the Jews (and also attended non-Jewish entertainments).[14]

Sardis Synagogue

Of over eighty Greek inscriptions in the synagogue six make reference to a θεοσεβής (nos. 22, 57, 59, 66, plus two without standardized number). The term must refer either to Jews who considered themselves especially pious or to a class of non-Jews who also participated in the life of the synagogue.[15]

---

12. Thomas H. Finn, "The God-fearers Reconsidered," *CBQ* 47 (1985): 75–84.

13. John G. Gager, "Jews, Gentiles, and Synagogues in the Book of Acts," *HTR* 79 (1986): 91–99; *The Origin of Anti-Semitism: Attitudes toward Judaism in Pagan and Christian Antiquity* (New York: Oxford University Press, 1985).

14. H. Hommel, "Juden und Christen im kaiserzeitlichen Milet," *Mitteilungen des Deutschen Archäologischen Instituts, Istanbuler Abteilung* 25 (1975): 167–95; B. Lifshitz, "Du nouveau sur les 'Sympathisants,'" *Journal for the Study of Judaism* 1 (1970): 77–84; Paul R. Trebilco, *Jewish Communities in Asia Minor* (Cambridge: Cambridge University Press, 1991).

15. Thomas A. Kraabel and Andrew R. Seager, "The Synagogue and the Jewish Community: Impact of the Discovery of the Sardis Synagogue," in *Sardis from Prehistoric to Roman Times: Results of the Archaeological Exploration of Sardis 1958–1975*, ed. G. M. A. Hanfmann (Cambridge: Harvard University Press, 1983), 178–90; Trebilco, *Jewish Communities*, 158–59.

Aphrodisias

The most significant indication of the historicity of God-fearers as a group and their presence in the synagogue comes from the discovery in Aphrodisias of an early third-century Jewish stele having two faces. The stele commemorates persons who have been involved in the construction of a memorial building. Face A of the stele contains many names that are biblical, but also references to three people designated by the term προσήλυτος and two others by the term θεοσεβής. Face B contains two lists. The upper section contains Jewish names, but the second list is introduced by the phrase Καὶ ὅσοι θεοσεβῖς. There are fifty-two persons in this list, with non-Jewish names, who obviously have contributed in some way to the building under construction. At least two appear to participate in Jewish religious activities.[16]

Tralles

A third-century inscription refers to the completion of Capitolina's pledge to contribute a certain building in Tralles, presumably a synagogue. Capitolina speaks of herself as Καπετωλῖνα ἡ ἀξιόλογ(ος) καὶ θεοσεβ(ής). Capitolina was Claudia Capitolina, daughter or sister of Claudius Capitolinus Bassus, proconsul of Asia and member of a highly distinguished family. Obviously she was not born a Jew, but must have participated in the life of the synagogue in order to be known as θεοσεβής.

Deliler

A certain Eustathios contributed a wash basin to the holy synagogue of the Hebrews. In this third-century inscription he identifies himself as Εὐστάθιος, ὁ θεοσεβής. Of course, he could be a pious Jew.

God-fearers are mentioned in a few other inscriptions that have been found outside the Asia Minor region.[17] Admittedly, the epigraphic data is slight, but there is enough to indicate that some non-Jews were known as God-fearers, that they participated in the life of the synagogue, and contributed to Jewish causes and financial campaigns. But the scant evidence does not support those who speak of thousands of God-fearers attached to or converted to Judaism. Martin Goodman has written an important study on the nature of conversion in the time of the Roman Empire.[18] He suggests four types of mission activity: (1) informative —

16. Joyce Maire Reynolds and Robert F. Tannenbaum, *Jews and Godfearers at Aphrodisias: Greek Inscriptions with Commentary*, Cambridge Philological Society Supplementary Volume 12 (Cambridge: Cambridge Philological Society, 1987).

17. Irina Levinskaya, *The Book of Acts in Its Diaspora Setting* (Grand Rapids: Eerdmans, 1996).

18. Martin Goodman, *Mission and Conversion: Proselytizing in the Religious History of the Roman Empire* (Oxford: Clarendon Press, 1994).

the desire to disseminate a message; (2) educational — the desire to promote a better life; (3) apologetic — the desire to seek recognition for the power and nature of a particular divine being; (4) proselytizing — the desire to recruit new members for the religious society. Goodman argues that most religions of the ancient world were not conversionary in the sense of attempting to acquire new members. The epigraphic evidence for massive conversions is nearly nil, and very few Jews speak of concerted missionary activity. Oddly enough, the sense of intense Jewish missionary activity comes from Christians who take very seriously the presence of the God-fearers of Acts, and Jesus' attack in Matt. 23:15:

> Woe to you, scribes and Pharisees, hypocrites! For you cross sea and land to make a single convert, and you make the new convert twice as much a child of hell as yourselves.

As previously stated, this intense attack on the Pharisees reflects more the attitude of a Jew, Jesus, against a specific party of Jews, not the attack of Christians on Judaism as a whole. The data does not support the presupposition that Judaism converted many Gentiles to a class called God-fearers who then wholesale shifted to Christianity. This does not deny the possibility that many Gentiles were attracted to the high level moral and theological presentation by Diaspora Jews. This group, called God-fearers in Acts, was sympathetic to Paul, and indeed may have formed part of the early "Christian" nucleus. Luke includes this group of former Gentiles with the receptive group of Jews.[19]

The Jewish Jesus in a Palestinian Culture

How, then, did Jesus relate to his own social matrix? It has become commonplace to describe Jesus as a wandering charismatic who impacted Palestinian culture. Although other scenarios are possible — Jesus as a teacher,[20] or Jesus as a revolutionary[21] — it is nearly impossible to deny the early tradition that Jesus was seen as a powerful, revelatory

---

19. Ernst Haenchen suspects that the term προσήλυτοι in 13:43 was a gloss. Originally it must have referred to God-fearers (*The Acts of the Apostles: A Commentary*, trans. B. Noble and Gerald Shinn [Philadelphia: Westminster, 1971], 413 n. 5.

20. Vernon Robbins, *Jesus the Teacher: A Socio-Rhetorical Interpretation of Mark* (Philadelphia: Fortress, 1984); Ernest Best, *Disciples and Discipleship: Studies in the Gospel According to Mark* (Edinburgh: T. & T. Clark, 1986); Rainer Riesner, *Jesus als Lehrer: Eine Untersuchung zum Ursprung der Evangelien-Überlieferung*, 3d ed. (Tübingen: J. C. B. Mohr [Paul Siebeck], 1988).

21. R. Horsley and J. Hanson, *Bandits, Prophets, and Messiahs: Popular Movements in the Time of Jesus* (San Francisco: Harper & Row, 1988); S. G. F. Brandon, *Jesus and the Zealots* (Manchester, Manchester University Press, 1967).

person who spoke prophetically to his own culture.[22] Jesus was seen primarily in two ways: as an apocalyptic prophet and as an authoritative teacher. Eventually these two strands or perspectives gave to us two major sources: the Gospel of Mark and the sayings source Q. In New Testament scholarship the question of the primacy of these two strands remains a constant conflict. Ever since Albert Schweitzer's *Quest for the Historical Jesus*, scholars have struggled with the apparent apocalyptic fanaticism of Jesus and his little band of followers. More recently some scholars have insisted on the primacy of a sayings source that became the basis for the *Gospel of Thomas* and its community. Later, more power-oriented followers of Jesus added to Q apocalyptic material derived from intertestamental Judaism.[23]

The solution to this problem does indeed have important implications for this study. Was Jesus a Cynic-like wandering philosopher-teacher or was he a prophetic-apocalyptic visionary? Since the quest will not likely ever lead to Jesus, we can only say that both aspects are present in the followers, so therefore both aspects have impacted the Palestinian social matrix as well as subsequent cultures touched by the Jesus tradition.

Jesus the Teacher

The image of Jesus as a teacher may be a modern problem, but the fact of his teaching belongs to the earliest level of the Jesus tradition.[24] One can see in the Gospels elements of the wandering charismatic, the Cynic-like philosopher, the purveyor of wisdom, or the teacher of righteousness. More critical than the type of teacher is, in this case, the content of the teaching. For the most part the Q sayings of Jesus interpret the revealed intent of the Torah. That is, humans, in their hardness of heart, have created casuistic laws that obfuscate the original intent of the divine covenant.

---

22. Wayne Meeks, *The Prophet-King: Moses Traditions and the Johannine Christology* (Leiden: Brill, 1967); Gerd Theissen, *Sociology of Early Palestinian Christianity* (Philadelphia: Fortress, 1978).

23. Burton L. Mack, *The Lost Gospel: The Book of Q and Christian Origins* (San Francisco: HarperSanFrancisco, 1993); *Who Wrote the New Testament? The Making of the Christian Myth* (San Francisco: HarperSanFrancisco, 1995).

24. Richard A. Edwards, *A Theology of Q: Eschatology, Prophecy, and Wisdom* (Philadelphia: Fortress, 1976); John Kloppenborg, *The Formation of Q: Trajectories in Ancient Wisdom Collections* (Philadelphia: Fortress, 1987); Burton L. Mack, *The Lost Gospel: The Book of Q and Christian Origins* (San Francisco: HarperSanFrancisco, 1993); Ronald A. Piper, *Wisdom in the Q Tradition: The Aphoristic Teaching of Jesus* (Cambridge: Cambridge University Press, 1987); Marvin Meyer, *The Gospel of Thomas: The Hidden Sayings of Jesus* (San Francisco: HarperSanFrancisco, 1992); Stevan Davies, *The Gospel of Thomas and Christian Wisdom* (New York: Seabury, 1983); John Dominic Crossan, *The Historical Jesus: The Life of a Mediterranean Jewish Peasant* (San Francisco: Harper, 1991).

The social fabric called for by Jesus presupposes dyadic relationships that cannot be set aside by contractual laws (e.g., no divorce); it presupposes verbal communication based on truth (e.g., no oath); it presupposes a close relationship between all types of people (e.g., no detrimental type-casting). Jesus taught that the commandments could be summarized by the Great Commandment:

> When the Pharisees heard that he had silenced the Sadducees, they gathered together, and one of them, a lawyer, asked him a question to test him. "Teacher, which commandment in the law is the greatest?" He said to him, " 'You shall love the Lord your God with all your heart, and with all your soul, and with all your mind.' This is the greatest and first commandment. And a second is like it: 'You shall love your neighbor as yourself.' On these two commandments hang all the law and the prophets." (Matt. 22:34–40)

According to the early Jesus traditions, Jesus also acted on the basis of the Sinai revelation. He understood that people were separated from each other by laws regarding diseases. Such divisions caused what society defines as illness. By healing people he restored them to their social context. He sent the ten lepers whom he healed to the priests so that they could return immediately to their villages (Luke 17:11–19; cf. Matt. 8:1–4). The paralytic was healed and restored to his companions and his family (Mark 2:11). At the same time, Jesus broke down social divisions by associating with persons who were unclean or socially inappropriate:

> After this he went out and saw a tax collector named Levi, sitting at the tax booth; and he said to him, "Follow me." And he got up, left everything, and followed him. Then Levi gave a great banquet for him in his house; and there was a large crowd of tax collectors and others sitting at the table with them. The Pharisees and their scribes were complaining to his disciples, saying, "Why do you eat and drink with tax collectors and sinners?" Jesus answered, "Those who are well have no need of a physician, but those who are sick; I have come to call not the righteous but sinners to repentance." (Luke 5:27–32).

In addition to healing and overlooking regulations regarding clean and unclean, Jesus built community by eating with all the people at table fellowship (Mark. 6:30–44 and pars.). So on the one hand, Jesus obliterated social divisions by healing the sick and by overlooking laws of defilement, and on the other hand, Jesus built community by eating and drinking without discriminating.

Jesus the Prophet

Although some recent studies have tried to show that Jesus was primarily a (wisdom) teacher and that the tradition of his prophecy was added,[25] most readers assume the originality of both teacher and prophet.[26] In an early tradition Jesus refers to himself as a prophet without honor in his own country (Matt. 13:57; Mark 6:4; Luke 4:24; John 4:44). Given the above description of Jesus as teacher, it would be difficult to deny the role of Jesus as an apocalyptic prophet. As a teacher Jesus called for a return to the Mosaic covenant. Although his teaching did not call for a violent overthrow of Palestinian society, it certainly did, granted its general acceptance, imply a radical alteration of his particular social matrix. The teaching of Jesus contains a radical reversal. "Blessed are the poor." "The first shall be last." "The one who seeks to save her or his psyche will lose it."[27] The verbal and literary carrier of that radical reversal is apocalypticism.[28]

Although the earliest Jesus tradition may use traditional apocalyptic language sparingly, the structure of apocalypticism lies in the teaching itself. The reversal will require a radical social change. Jesus' parables of the reign of God speak of a quick transformation with a remarkable shift in values, the need for total commitment, and an absolute dependence on divine action. The radical reversal is not an incidental aspect of the Jesus tradition. In order to advance a covenantal understanding of society it will be necessary for society as it is to give way to a value and structure reversal. Just as the teaching of Jesus is universally true, so the reversal is universally true. Or put another way, the teaching of the Jesus tradition has no potentiality unless the old age is constantly passing away. Jesus

---

25. On Jesus as the eschatological prophet see E. P. Sanders, *Jesus and Judaism* (Philadelphia: Fortress, 1985); *The Historical Figure of Jesus* (London: Penguin Press, 1993). If Jesus were crucified because of his attack on the temple, one could hardly think of Jesus simply as a wisdom teacher. On the other hand, Marcus Borg reports that the Jesus Seminar "consistently voted as 'black' all sayings in which Jesus is reported to have spoken of 'the end of the world,' a last judgment, the coming of 'the Son of Man,' or his own second coming. For scholars, this result is news because it constitutes a thorough rejection of the eschatological consensus that had dominated Jesus scholarship for much of this century" ("The Jesus Seminar at Work: The Making of *The Five Gospels*," *The Fourth R* 7, no. 6 [1994]: 7).

26. For the debate see M. Eugene Boring, *The Continuing Voice of Jesus: Christian Prophecy and the Gospel Tradition* (Louisville: Westminster/John Knox, 1991), 56–57. Riesner (*Jesus als Lehrer*, 295) speaks of Jesus as a "prophetischen Lehrer" who spoke in prophetic "Redegattungen."

27. The term "psyche" is a literal rendering of the Greek ψυχή, and by it I mean "personhood."

28. Ernst Käsemann, "The Beginnings of Christian Theology." *JTC* 6 (1969): 17–46; "On the Topic of Primitive Christian Apocalyptic," *JTC* 6 (1969): 99–133; more recently, Dale C. Allison, *Jesus of Nazareth: Millenarian Prophet* (Minneapolis: Fortress, 1998).

taught a permanent eschatology.[29] Without an eschatology the Jesus tradition would rather quickly become the status quo, as indeed, it did and still does.

The Jesus tradition was directed at a specific social matrix, the Palestinian world during the post-Herodian period. Although it may be customary to speak of Christianity as the universalization of a more time-and-space-specific Judaism, that is not true. As we have seen, Judaism at the time of Jesus was neither mission-oriented nor programmed for universality. The Jesus tradition shared the same restriction. Even later forms of the tradition recognized that Jesus did not solicit disciples while among the Gerasenes. To the contrary he even refused the discipleship offer of the demon-exorcised man (Mark 5:18–19). His rejection of the non-Jewish woman, the Syrophoenician, still stands as a story with a remarkable repartee, not a narrative of inclusion (Mark 7:24–30). And however well the case may be made otherwise, it stands that Jesus sent the twelve only to the Jews. These twelve Jesus sent out with the following instructions: "Go nowhere among the Gentiles, and enter no town of the Samaritans, but go rather to the lost sheep of the house of Israel (Matt. 10:5–6). The universal mission of Matt. 28:19 does not come from Jesus but from a deviation group of Jews at Antioch who understood, in contrast to other Jews, that the fulfillment of God's promise would lead to a universal conversion.[30]

Prophetic Catenae

The Jesus tradition combined teaching and eschatology at a very early period. Early Christian miracle lists reflect both the teaching and the eschatology of the Jesus tradition, as well as the experiences of the early churches. Miracle catenae occur in early Christian lists. However, such lists have a longer history than simply the Jesus tradition. In the Hebrew Scriptures they are found primarily in Isaiah's visions of the end time ("that day"). Best known would be Isa. 35:5–6:

> Then the eyes of the blind shall be opened,
> and the ears of the deaf unstopped;
> then the lame shall leap like a deer,
> and the tongue of the speechless sing for joy.
> For waters shall break forth in the wilderness,
> and streams in the desert.

---

29. John Dominic Crossan, *In Parables: The Challenge of the Historical Jesus* (New York: Harper & Row, 1973), 26.

30. Massimo Grilli, *Comunità e Missione: le direttive di Matteo: Indagine esegetica su Mt 9,35–11,1*, Europäische Hochschulschriften, Reihe 23, Band 458 (Frankfurt: Peter Lang, 1992).

According to the Q tradition, in Luke 7:22, Jesus acknowledged the presence of the end time in his response to John the Baptist:

> And he answered them, "Go and tell John what you have seen and heard: the blind receive their sight, the lame walk, the lepers are cleansed, the deaf hear, the dead are raised, the poor have good news brought to them."

The Q adaptation of Isaiah adds the raising of the dead and the healing of lepers, although making the mute to speak has been dropped. Nevertheless, the combined list of Isaiah and Q corresponds closely to the most frequently mentioned miracles in the early Christian catenae. The most striking difference lies in the absence of demon exorcism. Though very popular in the early Christian lists, it does not occur in either the Isaianic texts or Gospel catenae. Apparently, the casting out of demons marks the conflict and oppression preceding the end time, and is not a characteristic of the end time itself.

One suspects that the lists do reflect the needs and experiences of the faith community. That would account in part for the variations. One of the newly published fragments of the Dead Sea Scrolls (4Q521, col. 2) contains a catena that points to an end-time reality. One cannot tell whether the miracles are done by a messianic figure or by God through the community:

> He shall release the captives, make the blind see, raise up the do[wntrodden]. (line 8)

> Then he shall heal the sick, resurrect the dead, and to the meek announce glad tidings. (line 12)[31]

In any case, like the early Christian community, the community of the Dead Sea Scrolls recognizes in the raising of the dead that the end time has already started.

If there is such a "mini-gospel" in the Jesus tradition, how does it appear in the Gospel narratives themselves? Crossan has concluded that in the Markan and Johannine traditions there existed a catena that followed this sequence:[32]

---

31. Taken from Robert H. Eisenman and Michael Wise, *The Dead Sea Scrolls Uncovered* (Rockport, Mass.: Element, 1992), 20–23.
32. Crossan, *The Historical Jesus*, 311.

1. Healing of the Paralytic	Mark 2:1–12	John 5:1–18
2. Multiplication of Loaves and Fishes	Mark 6:33–44	John 6:1–15
3. Walking on the Sea	Mark 6:45–52	John 6:16–21
4. Healing of the Blind Man	Mark 8:22–26	John 9:1–7
5. Raising of the Dead	Secret Mark Fragment 1:5–9	John 11:1–57

The Catena in Mark

The catena of five does not have the same meaning for the Markan redactor as for John. In Mark the five are set in an ecclesiastical framework (as are other miracles). The context for the healing of the paralytic is the preaching of the word (καὶ ἐλάλει αὐτοῖς τὸν λόγον, 2:2), although yet another context, a conflict story stressing forgiveness of sins, was inserted into the healing narrative itself (2:5b–9a). The multiplication of the loaves and fishes was used by Mark as the basis for the early Christian community meal, or even the Eucharist (ἀναβλέψας εἰς τὸν οὐρανὸν εὐλόγησεν καὶ κατέκλασεν τοὺς ἄρτους, 6:41). As for walking on the sea, the faith community context is prayer and its authority or power (ἀπῆλθεν εἰς τὸ ὄρος προσεύξασθαι, 6:46). The healing of the blind man (8:22–26) shows the least ecclesiastical adaption of the five stories. Both it and its twin healing narrative, the healing of the deaf mute (7:31–37) stem directly from Isa. 35:6. The μογιλάλον of 7:32 is found only here and in Isa. 35:6. Although there is no clear ecclesiastical framework for the healing of the blind man, in the healing of the deaf mute the crowd makes a strong christological statement about the power of Jesus over chaos, καλῶς πάντα πεποίηκεν (7:37, an echo of the statement about God in Gen. 1:31). Without any specific contextual adaptation the two narratives based on Isa. 35:6 actually reflect the healing ministry of the church. Since the raising of the dead occurs only in *Secret Mark*, we cannot assign it a *Sitz im Leben* for Mark itself. In the oral tradition it may well have been linked with the man who ran away naked (14:51–52). The excision of the resurrection story could explain why those two dangling verses sit in the Passion narrative without any apparent context. But cause for the excision of the fifth narrative in the catena remains a mystery.

The Catena in John

Though used in the same order as in Mark, the catena in John serves quite another purpose. The healing of the paralytic (5:1–18) emphasizes the powerful presence of Jesus. Without knowing who Jesus is, without making a statement of faith, the paralytic is made to walk. The stories of the multiplication of the loaves and fishes and of the walking on the sea are combined in John to shift attention from the early Christian meal, and the Eucharist, to Jesus himself, who is the real bread of life (the real presence). Walking on the sea serves to take Jesus from the Transjordan (and its manna — the multiplication of the loaves and fishes) to the Promised Land, where this real bread can be received (Passover, Josh. 5:10–12). The healing of the blind man, like the healing of the paralytic, describes the powerful presence of Jesus. Again, the man born blind does not know Jesus and makes no statement of faith. He is made to see by the will of the presence itself. The story then becomes the keystone for describing how the Johannine confession develops once one has "seen." The last narrative in the catena, raising the dead, shows that the eschatological faith of the early church (Martha's confession in 11:24) lacks the power of Jesus as the present resurrection.

The presence of these pre-Gospel miracle catenae in the Jesus tradition indicates that central to the new Way were healings that restored persons to their community, meals (table fellowship) that created new community, and an eschatology that promised new life.

3

Paul and Inculturation

Mission

Paul's approach to culture differs greatly from that of the Jesus tradition. Although a "Hebrew of Hebrews" (Phil. 3:5), Paul, in contrast to the earliest Jesus tradition, has a universal perspective. Given the reluctance of Judaism to seek conversions actively, it is surprising, even incredible, that Paul should mount a massive campaign to take his deviant form of Judaism to the Gentile world. Because the issue of inculturation depends so much on Paul's mission, some further reflection is necessary. Apart from Paul himself, our first account comes from Luke in the book of Acts. Of course Luke wishes to show that the universalism of Adam (Luke 3:38) has been recapitulated in Jesus Christ — a universalism eventually realized when Paul reached Rome.[1] While this may explain the theology of Luke, it does not clarify the role of Paul. In order to explain why Paul the Jew suddenly became a missionary, Luke injects into the narrative the power and authority of the Holy Spirit — a force that directed the church at Antioch to send out Barnabas and Paul (Acts 13:1–3). Indeed it was the Spirit, acting as a divine obstacle, who forced Paul to respond to a vision calling him to Greece (Acts 16:6–10). Although one cannot doubt the critical role of the Spirit as the power of inculturation in the double work Luke-Acts, the Spirit nevertheless appears to be a somewhat nebulous explanation for what had to have been an incredibly complex theological and social shift. That is, in Pauline material, the power of inculturation may well be the "people of God" as empowered and guided by the Spirit rather than the Spirit itself.[2]

---

1. Hans Conzelmann, *The Theology of St. Luke,* trans. Geoffrey Buswell (New York: Harper, 1960).

2. 2. Luke Timothy Johnson has an excellent section on the power of the Spirit in the New Testament. Believers claim to have the "experience of power, whether the term used is 'authority' (*exousia;* see John 1:12; 1 Cor 8:9; 9:1, 4; 2 Cor 10:8; 13:10; 2 Thess 3:9), or 'energy' (*energia;* see Gal 3:5; 5:6; Phil 3:20–21; Col 1:29; 1 Cor 12:6; 1 Thess 2:13; Phlm 6; Heb 4:12), or simply 'power' (*dynamis;* see Rom 1:16; 15:13, 19; 1 Cor 1:18; 6:14; 2 Cor 6:7; 13:4; Gal 3:5; Eph 3:20; Col 1:29; 1 Thess 1:5; 2 Thess 1:11; 2 Tim 1:7; Heb 2:4; 2 Pet 1:16). Such power enabled believers to work 'signs and wonders' (Acts 4:30; 5:12; 14:3; Rom 15:9; 2 Cor 12:12; Heb 2:4) such as healings, prophecies, spiritual

Paul himself does not explain why he shifted from a particularist to a universalist. Like his possible companion Luke, he explains his drive as a divine compulsion. In 1 Cor. 9, in the midst of a debate with the Corinthian Christians about financial support, he argues that preaching the Gospel is not a choice he can make:

> But I have made no use of any of these rights, nor am I writing this so that they may be applied in my case. Indeed, I would rather die than that — no one will deprive me of my ground for boasting! If I proclaim the gospel, this gives me no ground for boasting, for an obligation is laid on me, and woe to me if I do not proclaim the gospel! For if I do this of my own will, I have a reward; but if not of my own will, I am entrusted with a commission. What then is my reward? Just this: that in my proclamation I may make the gospel free of charge, so as not to make full use of my rights in the gospel.
> (1 Cor. 9:15–18)

He defines the compulsion more as a commission (οἰκονομία) than as an energy of the Holy Spirit. As a matter of fact, Paul would appear to base his commission on his own apostleship (1 Cor. 4:9; 9:1; 15:9; Gal. 1:1), though he does not directly make that claim.

Although it is popular to speak of Paul as the first Christian, it may be more accurate to understand Paul as a Jew with a distinct agenda. Understanding some of the earliest Jesus communities as deviations of Judaism permits us to understand the Gentile mission as something other than a failure of Judaism (Rom. 11:7), or a desire to win universal assent to the Jewish God (though note 1 Thess. 1:9), or even as a great compassion for the ignorant pagans (Acts 17:30). The drive to include Gentiles apparently came primarily from the recognition that only by evangelizing the pagans could Judaism itself become revived and complete. In Rom. 9–11 Paul puts it several ways: a divine demonstration of mercy to the Gentiles will enable the Jews to see the meaning of God's wrath (9:14–29); if the Gentiles are justified by faith then the Jews will forego justification by the law (9:30–32); if the Gentiles are included it will make the Jews jealous and therefore more open (11:11–16); Israel can only be saved when a full number of Gentiles have "come in" (11:25). While it may not be the single causative factor for the universalizing of Judaism, Paul's conviction that the future of the Jewish people depended on the mission to the Gen-

---

utterances, and the proclamation of the good news (Rom 1:16; 1 Cor 1:18; 2:5; 2 Cor 4:7; 1 Thess 1:5; 2 Tim 1:8). The power also worked for the transformation of those receiving it (Gal 3:5; 1 Cor 2:16; 2 Cor 3:18; Eph 4:23; Col 3:10; 1 Pet 1:22)" (*Reading Romans: A Literary and Theological Commentary* [New York: Crossroad, 1997], 116–17).

tiles cannot be underestimated. It was Paul's great zeal for his own people (Phil. 3:4–6), his particularity, that led him to a universalizing mission.

If this is true, then we could expect, indeed, that Paul's mission program would contain elements of the contemporary Jewish culture. Or even more likely, the mission program would contain elements of what Jews anticipated as an end-time culture. This is surely true, as we shall see. How did Paul intend to insert this visionary Jewish culture into the Gentile world? Unlike the Jesus tradition, which calls for radical reversal, Paul's method of inculturation does not entail a severe attack on pagan culture. Instead he tends, for the most part, to suspend or relativize the cultures of the Mediterranean basin. Several texts point specifically to Paul's call for cultural suspension.

The ὡς μή Passage (1 Corinthians 7:29–31)

In the midst of his discussion about marriage (1 Cor. 7:25–38), Paul advocates an end-time suspension of marriage practices, even though, in regard to the issue of remarriage (7:1–16) he had asked widows and widowers in the Corinthian church to consider strongly another marriage. As a part of the argument regarding first marriages he penned the highly significant ὡς μή passage:

> I mean, brothers and sisters, the appointed time has grown short; from now on, let even those who have wives be as though (ὡς μή) they had none, and those who mourn as though (ὡς μή) they were not mourning, and those who rejoice as though (ὡς μή) they were not rejoicing, and those who buy as though (ὡς μή) they had no possessions, and those who deal with the world as though (ὡς μή) they had no dealings with it. For the present form of this world is passing away.

Paul does not suggest that first, believers should withdraw from their present culture, but that they should participate as if their society were of relative value. So they should/could continue their married state, but not put ultimate value in their family; they should/could honor the dead and previous generations, but not put ultimate value in it; they should/could celebrate marriages, but not make of marriage an ultimate value; they should/could own and manage businesses, but not make economic stability an ultimate value. In short, they should/could relate to their culture, but ought not accept the values of that culture.[3]

---

3. One could argue, as do David Balch (*Let Wives Be Submissive: The Domestic Code in 1 Peter* [Chico, Calif.: Scholars Press, 1981]) and Bruce Winter (*Seek the Welfare of the*

All Things to All People (1 Corinthians 9:19–23)

While the ὡς μή passage depicts a deliberate attempt by Paul to suspend the present culture, the passage in 1 Cor. 9:19–23, perhaps written with less deliberateness, shows how Paul himself acts in a world of suspended cultures:

> For though I am free with respect to all, I have made myself a slave to all, so that I might win more of them. To the Jews I became as a Jew, in order to win Jews. To those under the law I became as one under the law (though I myself am not under the law) so that I might win those under the law. To those outside the law I became as one outside the law (though I am not free from God's law but am under Christ's law) so that I might win those outside the law. To the weak I became weak, so that I might win the weak. I have become all things to all people, that I might by all means save some. I do it all for the sake of the gospel, so that I may share in its blessings.

Paul identifies freedom with the suspension of present cultural values. In the context of this particular passage he states that although he has a right to the support of the Corinthian house churches, he does not take it. He does not wish to be obligated to them because of any financial outlay on his behalf. By not accepting their support, he argues, he is free to be a slave.[4] In this case slavery means accepting and living by cultural standards without giving them any final significance. It is a peculiar twist of meanings; normally he uses his own slavery as an apostolic metaphor (e.g., Rom. 1:1). But here he means he can enslave himself to cultural norms precisely because he is free of them, and, no doubt, because cultural norms have been eschatologically suspended in any case.

Paul does not act out of apocalyptic radicalness. In order to "infect" the world with the Jesus tradition he is willing to submit to the norms of society.[5] So he is willing to conform to Jewish law when among Jews

---

City: Christians as Benefactors and Citizens [Grand Rapids: Eerdmans, 1994], that in an honor / shame society Paul advises new Christians not to act in such a way as to bring upon them and their faith community the stigma of dishonor. The social sense of honor allows them then to act in a visionary way inside the community (no longer be treated as persons of shame — slaves, women, children).

4. Graydon F. Snyder, *First Corinthians: A Faith Community Commentary* (Macon, Ga.: Mercer University Press, 1992), 134. See also Henry Chadwick, "All Things to All Men, 1 Cor. 9:22," *NTS* 1 (1954–55): 261–75, and a more recent summary by Barbara Hall, "All Things to All People: A Study of 1 Corinthians 9:19–23," in *The Conversation Continues: Studies in Paul and John in Honour of J. Louis Martyn*, ed. Robert T. Fortna and Beverly R. Gaventa (Nashville: Abingdon, 1990), 261–75.

5. Ernst Troeltsch argues that Paul presents a social conservatism beside a radical personal love ethic (*The Social Teaching of the Christian Churches*, trans. Olive Wyon

(note Acts 21:23–24; Phil. 3:6). At the same time he is willing to live among non-Jews as if he were not under the (Jewish) law. In his letter to the Galatians he recounted the decisive encounter with Peter over that very issue (Gal. 2:11–21). Clearly, he ate with non-Jews who were not following dietary laws (1 Cor. 10:31–11:1), and stayed in homes that were "unclean" (note Philem. 22; Acts 16:15; 18:7). Furthermore, he submitted to Roman law by respecting the emperor and paying taxes (Rom. 13:1–7). According to Luke he even insisted that Roman law be utilized (Acts 16:35–40; 25:10–12). Perhaps even more striking, he was willing to sacrifice his freedom for the weak. Assuming that the weak of the Corinthian and Roman communities were people with rigid perceptions of culture (i.e., eating meat offered to idols meant you were worshiping those idols), Paul agreed that he would honor their inflexibility and legalism by also protecting their consciences (1 Cor. 8:12–13; Rom. 14:1–23).

Paul's method of inculturation respects any culture, but does not give it any ultimate value. Put another way, he does not see any culture as the historically designated carrier of the Jesus "virus"; therefore he has no need to attack any culture. Eventually the status quo culture will be altered by the Jesus tradition, perhaps even destroyed in part. So Paul respected, even was proud of, contemporary Jewish culture, but gave it no ultimate value; he respected Roman law and imperial authority, even called on it, but gave it no ultimate value (the "rubbish" of Phil. 3:8); he respected those in the congregations who did not share his sense of freedom and could not, because of their weak conscience, grasp the end-time suspension of culture, but he gave their position no ultimate meaning.

Be Not Conformed to This Age (Romans 12:1–2)

Paul spoke of the "people of God" as a community that always lived suspended in their culture. They themselves did not present a concretized culture, but neither did they give the present age or culture any final value. Paul understands the election of Israel as just such a divine choice. While the firstborn of Pharaoh and Egypt were being "sacrificed," God chose Israel, as the first born, to be a "living sacrifice" (θυσίαν ζῶσαν, 12:1). Israel, as the firstborn, would never develop a permanent culture, but always call for the suspension of ossified cultural values. That

---

[New York: Macmillan, 1931]). Perhaps the conservatism is better understood as a mission strategy (see Balch, *Let Wives Be Submissive*, on the Haustafeln).

state of parabolic suspension was the living sacrifice. Paul saw the new community of faith as an extension of that first election:

> So, by the mercies of God, I beseech you who are members of the Christian family (αδελφοί), be willing in your relationship to each other (τὰ σώματα) to place yourself on the altar as a living sacrifice, which is a life set apart for God and well-pleasing to him. That would be worship in the truest sense of the word. And do not be conformed to this age, but be transformed by a mindset that anticipates renewal, so that you can try out those things that are God's will — that which is good, that which is pleasing to God, and that which is ultimate. (Rom. 12:1–2, my translation)

Paul asks the Roman believers to place their community (τὰ σώματα) on the altar as a continual sacrifice so that the world will always be renewed by their sacrifice and by a lifestyle pleasing to God.

Historically some have misunderstood the admonition μὴ συσχηματί-ζεσθε ("do not be conformed") as a call to set up a culture in conflict with the present age (church versus state; two kingdoms). Paul rather is asking the Christian family to live (as a form of worship!) in such a way that they do not give ultimate value to their present culture, but *always* make possible new forms and new ways.

Given Paul's eschatological attitude toward the present age, one would suspect that his method of inculturation would be to suspend the receiving culture, inject the values of the Jesus tradition with its Jewish derivation, and show how that affects the culture of the present age. We can indeed see that very procedure in the several categories of cultural life to which we now turn.

Family

Although Paul must have been a widower (1 Cor. 7:8; 9:5), he never mentions his own marital experience, and, so far as we can tell, he does not derive from that marriage any advice for the new faith community.[6] Instead, he primarily depends on the Jesus tradition. In 1 Cor. 7:10–11 he utilizes the oral Jesus tradition to speak against divorce:

> To the married I give this command — not I but the Lord — that the wife should not separate from her husband (but if she does separate, let her remain unmarried or else be reconciled to her husband), and that the husband should not divorce his wife.

---

6. E. Arens, "Was St. Paul Married?" *Bible Today* 66 (1973): 1188–91; Joachim Jeremias, "War Paulus Witwer?" *ZNW* 25 (1926): 310–12; Snyder, *First Corinthians*, 95–96.

Later, the Gospel of Mark (ca. 65), followed by Matthew and Luke (ca. 85), utilized the same tradition in a slightly different form (Mark 10:11–12; Matt. 5:32; 19:9 Luke 16:18; note also Rom. 7:2–3).[7] In discussions of marriage Paul maintains the same covenantal reality found in the Jesus tradition. In a remarkable passage, Paul says that a man's identity is determined by a woman, and a woman's identity determined by a man (1 Cor. 7:4). He uses the same sense of dyadic relationship to argue that a believing husband or wife ought to remain married to a nonbelieving spouse because the power of the dyadic relationship should not be underestimated (1 Cor. 7:14). In fact, the same effect spreads to the children. Because identity has been formed by the intimate relationship of marriage, Paul, like the Jesus tradition, would discourage remarriage (1 Cor. 7:8), but he also recognizes the power of the sexual drive and its potential to be a source of community strife. So, unlike the Jesus tradition (except for the later Matt. 19:10–11, which makes a remarriage an option), Paul does concede (1 Cor. 7:6) that the demarried might do well to remarry.

Paul stresses the importance of family and its unity, but at the same time he undercuts the family as found in the Mediterranean social matrix. In fact, he suggests that the eschatological suspension of the present culture makes marriage a dubious choice, especially if it means being anxious about the concerns of this age (1 Cor. 7:32–35). It is in this same context that he suggests marriages may take place, but only if not taken absolutely (1 Cor. 7:29). In 1 Cor. 7:36–38 Paul gives an example, suggesting that a believing father might do well to postpone his daughter's [arranged?] marriage so that she can make her own choices and establish her own identity in the marriage relationship:

> If anyone thinks he is dealing inappropriately with his unmarried daughter, since she is already past the age for marrying, and therefore he ought to do something, let him do as he wishes. He doesn't sin; let the couple marry. But the one who stands firm in his heart, without any distress, having the power to do as he wishes, and has already made up his mind not to pledge his unmarried daughter, he does well. So the one who gives his daughter in marriage does well, but the one who does not give in marriage does even better (my translation).

In contrast to his society, Paul encouraged professional women like Chloe (1 Cor. 1:11) and promoted their leadership. He urged the church

---

7. In large part, the Gospels were created to give believers, who no longer lived according to the present age (culture), some guidance for living in the new, coming age.

in Rome to accept the leadership of Phoebe, even as it had been granted her in Cenchreae:

> I commend to you Phoebe our sister, who is the pastor of the church in Cenchreae, so that you will receive her in the Lord [faith community] as one worthy of the saints, and arrange for whatever she needs from you just as she has made arrangements for many others, even me. (Rom. 16:1–2, my translation)

He spoke in grateful terms about a female relative who was also an apostle:

> Greet Andronicus and Junia, members of my family and prisoners with me, who are eminent apostles, and were believers in Christ before I was (Rom. 16:7, my translation).

In contrast to those of other religious collegia, Paul encouraged married women to lead worship in the house churches.[8] And although he was setting up a different order in family relationships, nevertheless, he asked women leaders to maintain honor in the old age (e.g., keep their heads covered, 1 Cor. 11:5). So although the Pauline vision was not realized, nevertheless, as society was suspended the new culture began to take shape:

> There is no longer Jew or Greek, there is no longer slave or free, there is no longer male and female; for all of you are one in Christ Jesus. (Gal. 3:28)

Community

Paul had no intention of creating communities of shame.[9] Although his eschatological vision did suspend the culture of the present age, he did very little to bring about the demise of the present age. When appropriate (for his purposes?), he advised the new community to follow the laws of the empire. In regard to the man living with his own stepmother, Paul noted that even the pagan law was being broken (1 Cor. 5:1). To the surprise of many later readers, and perhaps the grief of many citizens of totalitarian regimes, Paul insisted that the first believ-

---

8. Antoinette Wire, *The Corinthian Women Prophets: A Reconstruction through Paul's Rhetoric* (Minneapolis: Fortress, 1990).

9. Daniel L. Nighswander, *Paul's Use of Shame as a Sanction in 1 Corinthians* (Th.D. diss., University of Toronto, 1994); Bruce Malina, "Honor and Shame: Pivotal Values of the First-Century Mediterranean World," in *The New Testament World: Insights from Cultural Anthropology* (Atlanta: John Knox, 1981); Jerome Neyrey, *Paul, In Other Words: A Cultural Reading of His Letters* (Louisville: Westminster/John Knox, 1990).

ers should submit to the emperor. Again, it was a question of end-time strategy. Paul did not present a theology of the suffering righteous, but he did insist that the first Christians not be found in conflict with the Roman social matrix (Rom. 13:1–7). Indeed, Paul also calls for all Christians to follow the Jewish social law (Rom. 13:8–10), although, as with the Jesus tradition, he made love of neighbor the core of the social Decalogue.

Paul does not vary from this social perspective. Whatever else one may say about his radical end-time vision, it must be said that he does not call for any open conflict with the status quo. This is most obvious when one examines specific issues. For example, even though many of Paul's converts must have been slaves or freed, Paul never suggests that slavery should be abolished. In fact, he barely suggests that a slave should become free. In the famous, or infamous, slavery passage of 1 Cor. 7:17–24, Paul writes that seeking freedom does not really serve any redemptive purpose. A slave ought not turn down the opportunity to be free (7:21), but achievement of freedom does not affect one's relationship to God or to the faith community. The slavery issue stands at the center of Paul's social-theological program. No social change commends a person to God. Nationality (Jew or Greek) does not make a difference; gender (male or female) does not make a difference; marriage does not make a difference; wealth does not make a difference; class (slave or master) does not make a difference. Nothing in the passing old age makes a difference. So, although Paul seems to have no social program, and he does not encourage social revolution, he holds that stance because the present age has no effective value. *The present age is not worth liberating.* Thus the letter to Philemon is a classic Pauline document.[10] Paul speaks of the slave Onesimus as his brother, and commends Onesimus as a brother to the slave master, Philemon. Clearly, Paul expects Philemon to forego any legal right he may have to punish the absent Onesimus. But he never suggests that the brother Philemon should free his brother Onesimus. And at no point does Paul suggest ethical lethargy because the end is at hand. What we see in the slavery issue is the result of the Pauline worldview.

The same is true of sexual equality. Although in the faith community Paul includes women on an equal basis, he does not countenance an apparent public break with cultural norms. In 1 Cor. 11 he insists that women in leadership roles ought not violate public dress codes (nor men either, for that matter; 11:4, 14). It is not that the Corinthians have been

---

10. Norman Petersen, *Rediscovering Paul: Philemon and the Sociology of Paul's Narrative World* (Philadelphia: Fortress, 1985).

particularly at fault in public matters; such decorum is required in all the churches of God (11:16). If the admonition for women to keep silent is genuine (1 Cor. 14:33–36), and it probably is not,[11] the issue is the same: some women are disrupting the public decorum of one of the Corinthian house churches. Paul does not want the first faith community to be one of dishonor. His concern for decorum goes so far as even to encourage the Holy Spirit to "remain silent in the church" (see 14:27, 34) So one of the house churches in Corinth, presumably the "Christ" house church (see 1 Cor. 1:12), is asked to cut back on ecstatic outbursts lest outsiders be repulsed by what they have seen and heard (1 Cor. 14:23). And rather than allow everyone, as apparently guided by the Spirit, to speak as they wish, Paul insists that the house church limit contributions to just two or three in each category of worship. Otherwise confusion will prevail (1 Cor. 14:26–33).

The church was to attract persons of all types and backgrounds. Indeed, most of the new Christians had come from lower classes of society (1 Cor. 1:26), even from a criminal element (1 Cor. 6:9–11). But the church was not to be seen by the public as a haven, a support system, for unsavory citizens. So Paul urges the Corinthians to cast from their midst such unrepentant persons.

Not every early Christian could handle Paul's perspective. He assumed that the first believers would participate in public life without ghettoizing the new community. For example, he assumed that new Christians would eat in public places with their former friends. But some converts could not handle a relativity that denied the value of meat offered to nonexistent idols, yet at the same time allowed a brother or sister to eat meals in which the meat had been dedicated to a pagan god. Eventually, Paul gave up and asked that new Christians not risk forming their primary identity with nonbelievers (1 Cor. 10:21). Like the Jesus tradition, he too recognized that community was formed through table fellowship. Besides criticizing some divisive meals (1 Cor. 11:17–22; Rom. 14:1–4), he pulled from the oral Jesus tradition the account of the Last Supper and its powerful potential for building a loving and perceptive community (1 Cor. 11:23–34). The new age depended on the dissolution of food distinctions, of clean and unclean, so that the new community could be formed by table fellowship (Rom. 14:1–23). Little wonder that Paul's doctrine of justification by faith was hammered out in the midst of a real conflict over table fellowship (Gal. 2:11–21).

---

11. Snyder, *First Corinthians*, 184–86; Gordon Fee, *The First Epistle to the Corinthians* (Grand Rapids: Eerdmans, 1987), 669–710.

Authority

As indicated above, Paul did not anticipate or direct a revolution against the authority and power of the Roman Empire. In his one major discussion of the issue, he advocated submission to the authority of the emperor (Rom. 13:1–7). As in other cultural values, Paul does not challenge the authority of the political system. But there can be little doubt that Paul included the state among those things passing away. In 1 Cor. 2:8 he says that none of the rulers of this world (οὐδεὶς τῶν ἀρχόντων τοῦ αἰῶνος) knew what they were doing when they crucified the Lord of glory. Because they were anchored in the old age, the truth of history was hidden from them, a truth that had been foreordained from the beginning. Basically, the rulers of this age cannot fathom the μυστήριον of God (1 Cor. 2:7). In biblical apocalyptic terms, the rulers of this world — the state — cannot possibly understand the μυστήριον, because their authority is based on the wisdom of this age rather than on the σοφία θεοῦ. The Greek term μυστήριον translates the Hebrew רז, found in Jewish apocalyptic as a term to describe the course of history, a course hidden from rulers like Nebuchadnezzar (Dan. 2:28–29). The essence of the apocalyptic sense of history lies in the difference between the old age, ruled by human self-concern, and the new age, ruled by the will of God. To the old age the ways of the new age seem like foolishness, a mystery, which only the apocalyptic visionary can discern. However much we are to obey the present state, still the state does not know the μυστήριον, or why the Lord of glory was crucified. Just as a parent takes on dishonor by falsely punishing a child, so the rulers of this world accrued dishonor by crucifying the Lord of glory. Indeed, according to Paul, by their ignorance they created their own end-time cultural suspension. They showed themselves to be unaware of the σοφία θεοῦ.

In the one legal case mentioned in the primary Pauline letters, Paul chastises the first Christians for utilizing the court system of the old age. One cannot tell what the case was, but one should surmise that it was not of great significance (κριτηρίων ἐλαχίστων, 1 Cor. 6:2).[12] Regardless of the substance of the case, the courts of the Roman Empire generally served a political purpose rather than the administration of justice or reconciliation. Paul expressed shock that the first Christians would use a system that could not possibly advance the reign of God. It is not quite clear what he proposed instead. One supposes that he urged the Corinthian Christians to form their own reconciliation committee, much like that described in Matt. 18:16–17. The point is important. Do we find here the beginning of a Christian culture, a system that will take on a

---

12. Winter, *Seek the Welfare*, 106–21.

more concrete form in the Gospel of Matthew? Or do we have Paul the Jew asking the first believers to utilize an already existent Jewish (religious) court or to develop one like it?[13] As is so often the case, has conflict in the community caused the leader to develop regulations and mechanisms that parallel the very system being criticized? On the other hand, the early church did not continue the jury of peers, but developed manuals and codes, like the *Didache* or the *Apostolic Constitutions*, which must have been used by administrators to adjudicate in difficult issues.[14]

Calendar and Celebrations

It is true that the Jewish culture did not make an impact on the Greco-Roman world to the same extent as that of the later Christian culture, but there is at least one area of Western culture that must be considered Jewish in origin. Paul's calendar is Jewish. While he may not always celebrate the Jewish feast days, he does calculate according to the Jewish system. So in 1 Cor. 16:2 he would have the collection set aside κατὰ μίαν σαββάτου ("on the first day of the week"), the day that later Christians would have met for worship (note Acts 20:7).[15] Although the first day of the week is not a Jewish day of celebration, the Christian day is based on the Jewish timekeeping system.

Paul's conflict with the Galatian Christians has resisted a satisfactory explanation, but a simple, apparent solution would be to suppose that a group of Jewish Christians has pressured the Gentile Christians to become, at least in part, Jewish. A key issue would have been the acceptance of the Jewish mark of belonging — circumcision (Gal. 5:2–12). Staying with the simple approach, it would also appear that some Galatian Christians had been persuaded by the Jewish Christians (3:1–5). At the same time, some Galatians must have rejected the demands of the Jewish Christians and decided to abandon the whole enterprise. These would be the Gentiles mentioned in 4:8–11. Paul marvels that they could return to their prior life, enslaved by the solar πτωχὰ στοιχεῖα, divine powers honored by the Greco-Roman world, or observing lunar ἡμέρας…μῆνας καὶ καιροὺς καὶ ἐνιαυτούς. The immediate implication is that some Galatians might be using a Roman religious calendar and some a Jewish religious calendar. Paul is caught between the two with no new Christian calendar to suggest.

---

13. Fee, *Corinthians*, 230–34; Winter, *Seek the Welfare*.

14. *EEC*, s.v. "Canon Law."

15. Fee, *Corinthians*, 813–14; W. Rordorf, *Sunday, The History of the Day of Rest and Worship in the Earliest Centuries of the Christian Church* (Philadelphia: Westminster, 1968); S. Bacchiocchi, *From Sabbath to Sunday, A Historical Investigation of the Rise of Sunday Observance in Early Christianity* (Rome: Pontifical Gregorian University Press, 1977).

In another complex passage, a secondary Pauline text, the Christian author advises the readers not to be upset about criticisms regarding ἑορτῆς ἢ νεομηνίας ἢ σαββάτων (Col. 2:16). The believers at Colossae are criticized either for not holding to the Jewish calendar or for holding to it; there is no hint here of a Christian pagan calendar. One would conclude that the Gentile Christians of Colossae had adopted a Jewish timekeeping system, yet did not keep the accompanying Jewish festivals. The author was defending their freedom to do that. If so, we have an example of what eventually occurred. The Christian Roman world adopted a calendar based on the Jewish Sabbath system, but did not celebrate Jewish festivals. Rather, as we shall see, later Christians inserted into the Jewish system various Roman festivals. In this one particular case, then, we do not see a process of inculturating the Roman timekeeping system, but rather an acculturation or adaptation, through the first Christians, of the Jewish one.

Nature

Considering the emphasis on creation and nature in the Hebrew Scriptures and contemporary Judaism, we are surprised to find, in both the Jesus and Pauline traditions, so few cultural values based on nature. In the Jesus tradition and in Paul there are natural parables and analogies, especially those dealing with fields and vineyards. In the Jesus tradition there are no cultural practices or values based on nature. In genuine Paul there is very little. The most obvious references are to sexual matters. Paul never argues that marriage or family matters are natural, but he does argue, against some Greek philosophers, that homosexuality is not natural, or, more accurately, that homosexuals have given up φυσικός relationships (Rom. 1:26–27). Presumably, Paul says the same thing when he speaks of male and female hairstyles in 1 Cor. 11:14–15. Even though there is very little about nature in the letters of Paul, still, one sees the same apocalyptic suspension of nature as of the rest of culture. In one significant passage κτίσις is held in bondage by the old age and longs for the new age of freedom. Likewise, humanity, or human nature, shares the corruptibility of the old age and is wasting away, to make way for a new humanity (2 Cor. 4:16). It is in this context that we can best understand Paul's understanding of the resurrection:

> Listen, I will tell you a mystery! We will not all die, but we will all be changed, in a moment, in the twinkling of an eye, at the last trumpet. For the trumpet will sound, and the dead will be raised imperishable, and we will be changed. For this perishable body must put on imperishability, and this mortal body must put on

immortality. When this perishable body puts on imperishability, and this mortal body puts on immortality, then the saying that is written will be fulfilled: "Death has been swallowed up in victory." (1 Cor. 15:51–54)

Summary

Using primarily an apocalyptic worldview and often its language, Paul suspends the Greco-Roman culture that has formed the persons he addresses. He does not pretend to alter any social matrix in which he finds himself, and he certainly does not advocate an attack on either Jewish or Roman social institutions. But he does radically devalue culture in its most basic structures: sex, marriage, and family; economics and community; authority; calendar and celebrations; and even the natural order of things. In the place of that suspended culture Paul offers a community based on covenant relationships — relationships of equality, freedom, permanence, and love. At heart that new community was based on Jewish values, though, with the possible exception of a timekeeping system, not in the form of contemporary Judaism. To the contrary, the new form often was based on the oral Jesus tradition.

The problem for Paul was how to commend to new Christians a lifestyle that was neither Jewish nor Greco-Roman, yet could survive in a suspended form.

Chapter 4

The Gospel of John
and Deculturization

The Fourth Gospel's author developed a program of inculturation that stands in stark contrast to that of Paul. Indeed, John's vision is one of the more incredible achievements in Christian history. The author of the Gospel of John [henceforth: John] nearly reversed the tradition of Jesus and the gospel of Paul. Instead of relativizing the old age and seeking a new, John presents to the old age a Jesus who is both compelling, as a reality, yet unhampered by cultural accessories. The Jesus of the Gospel of John is a true "virus," capable of entering any culture without destroying it. The Fourth Gospel has been called a maverick because it does not fit the Gospel pattern and because it will not yield to scholarly analysis. It remains to this day a mystery. Its mysteriousness, however, is the key to its author's intent.

Provenance

The evidence offered for location of writing comes from external sources. The arguments for one locale over against another need not detain us here. Most of us have accepted the statements found in Eusebius, quoted from Papias, regarding a John the presbyter, who was the last living eye-witness. John the presbyter lived in Ephesus and therefore would have been the Beloved Disciple, a younger man during the ministry of Jesus. Except for the fact that this notice appears in Eusebius, there is no reason to suppose that Ephesus was actually the provenance of the Fourth Gospel. Over the years some have suggested Alexandria, because of the Hellenistic style of argument, while others insist on a location where synagogue and church could have been involved in severe conflict (John 9:22, 34).[1] Actually, internal evidence is practically nonexistent. We have the possible conflict with the synagogue. John's friendly treatment of

---

1. Meeks, *The Prophet-King;* David Rensberger, *Johannine Faith and Liberating Community* (Philadelphia: Westminster, 1988).

the Samaritans, who believed when others did not (4:39), might suggest a north Palestinian origin.[2] I have suggested that the conflict of the
Beloved Disciple with Peter (13:8, 16, 23–24; 18:10–11, 15–16; 20:4, 8;
21:15–19) indicates the author came from some locale other than Rome
and those communities that depended on an apostolic eyewitness (i.e.,
Peter).[3] Nevertheless, we cannot establish an origin for the Gospel based
on these meager hints. Although I do believe the argument of the Gospel
does eliminate Rome, nothing else can be determined. John deliberately
eliminated any internal evidence that could link his Gospel to any locale.
John's Jesus simply does not carry with him the cultural characteristics
of *any* city or region. Such severe geographical desocialization marks
the beginning point of John's attempt to present a universally acceptable
Jesus.[4]

Author

Unlike the redactors of the Synoptic Gospels, the final redactor of the
Fourth Gospel identifies his source (21:20–24). The Beloved Disciple was
the first to recognize Jesus and to respond to his invitation to "come and
see" (1:37–39). Although the "first disciple" is never identified, we are
informed that the second was Andrew, who then sought out Peter — the
same Peter, of course, who was the first disciple in the Synoptic Gospels
(1:40–42; Mark 1:16–20). The Beloved Disciple is never identified. Some
traditions make him the apostle John. The final redactor, however, makes
it clear that the unknown disciple is not identical with one of the sons of
Zebedee (21:2). Failing to find the author among the Twelve, many lean
toward John the presbyter of Ephesus as the Beloved Disciple. Lacking
any real reason to place the Fourth Gospel in Ephesus, other than the
quote from Papias, others have sought a location closer to Jerusalem, a
place where there is a strong conflict between church and synagogue.

The term "Beloved Disciple" likely refers to a follower of Jesus who
was indeed the source for some elements of the Fourth Gospel, but the
term signifies more a quality of relationship than a specific person. The
quality of relationship with Jesus is love (17:26). This disciple is the one
Jesus loves (ὃν ἠγάπα ὁ Ἰησοῦς, 13:23); that is, he[5] receives the love

---

2. Meeks, *The Prophet-King.*
3. Graydon F. Snyder, "John 3:16 and the Anti-Petrinism of the Johannine Tradition,"
BR 16 (1971): 5–15.
4. We must not be carried away, however. Based on internal evidence it would not be
easy to establish the provenance of *any* Gospel. Matthew might well reflect Antioch, but
the Jesus of Mark hardly appears to be a Roman, and Luke's Jesus is nearly as enigmatic
as John's.
5. We use the masculine pronoun to refer to the name John. On the other hand, if

of Jesus which is the love of the Father. The Beloved Disciple stands with Mary, Martha, and Lazarus as persons loved by Jesus. The beloved Martha admittedly does not figure positively in the Johannine narrative. She, rather than Mary, first meets Jesus as he comes to Bethany for the resurrection of Lazarus. She receives the critical statement about reconstructed life that does not die (11:25–26), but her response reflects the eschatology of the early church rather than the incarnational faith of the Gospel of John. We know nothing more about Lazarus except that he, as a beloved person, received new life.[6] Mary, on the other hand, receives the love of Jesus and returns it. In an intimate moment she washes the feet of Jesus with ointment and then dries his feet with her hair (12:3), while Peter refuses to engage in the footwashing (13:8). If Mary Magdalene is the same as Mary of Bethany,[7] again the redactor strongly stresses the love connection between Jesus and this woman, who not only stood with the Beloved Disciple at the foot of the cross (19:25), but also first saw the empty tomb (20:2) and first spoke with the resurrected Lord (20:11–18).[8] In other words, Mary plays a role in the Gospel no less than that of the Beloved Disciple. The Beloved Disciple and beloved Mary stand, then, as the two persons most clearly impacted by the incarnation.[9] They are the first to be inculturated by the desocialized Jesus.

Eschatology

The Fourth Gospel is nearly devoid of eschatological statements. The primary references to a future time are the several statements about the coming "hour" (2:4; 4:21–23; 5:25–28; 7:30; 8:20; 12:23, 27; 13:1; 16:2; 16:25; 17:1). Actually, these are not eschatological statements in the traditional sense of the word. They point to a time of revelation, or, better perhaps, a time of public revelation. That time is the crucifixion

---

there is any part of the New Testament written by a female disciple, it would be the Fourth Gospel.

6. As the only man mentioned as loved by Jesus, Lazarus has been identified as the Beloved Disciple. See Floyd Filson, "Who Was the Beloved Disciple?" *JBL* 68 (1949): 83–88; Oscar Cullmann, *The Johannine Circle*, trans. John Bowden (London: SCM, 1976).

7. Sandra M. Schneiders, "Women in the Fourth Gospel and the Role of Women in the Contemporary Church," *Biblical Theology Bulletin* 12 (1982): 35–45.

8. In the Gospel of John the resurrection makes Jesus available to all by freeing Jesus from Jewish culture. When Mary wishes to touch Jesus, she is asked not to draw him back into her present and his former milieu.

9. Jesus passes on his love to the Beloved Disciple, and the Beloved Disciple loves Jesus (his head in the bosom of Jesus, 13:23, 25). The author stresses Mary's love for Jesus; it may be that his love for her has been suppressed (Elisabeth Schüssler Fiorenza, *In Memory of Her: A Feminist Theological Reconstruction of Christian Origins* [New York: Crossroad, 1983], xiii–xiv). On the other hand, Sjef van Tilborg believes that Jesus' love for Mary has been stated clearly (*Imaginative Love in John* [Leiden: Brill, 1993]).

and death of Jesus. As Jesus expires he exclaims, τετέλεσται; the redactor adds that Jesus, bowing his head, παρέδωκεν τὸ πνεῦμα (19:30). The coming hour in John refers, then, to the completion of the revelation and the passing on of the Spirit. It is the moment that God's love is known on the cross (15:12–14). For the Fourth Gospel the cross completes the revelation of divine reality (16:21) and passing on the Spirit (or παράκλητος). Jesus is the deculturized revelation; the Spirit is the universal inculturator.

There can hardly be any debate about John's lack of eschatology. With a remarkable analogy, the Jesus of John says that the beginning of a process and its end are the same thing:

> Do you not say, "Four months more, then comes the harvest"? But I tell you, look around you, and see how the fields are ripe for harvesting. The reaper is already receiving wages and is gathering fruit for eternal life, so that sower and reaper may rejoice together. For here the saying holds true, "One sows and another reaps." (John 4:35–37)

Without an apocalyptic worldview there is no attempt in John to suspend the present age, or contemporary culture. But the divine revelation is nearly devoid of cultural attachments. John's Jesus makes it clear that he is not of this world, i.e., has no cultural attachments (17:14); nor does he wish his disciples to be of this world (17:16), though he recognizes that they cannot be completely devoid of cultural involvement (17:15). Jesus prays only that they not be trapped by this dialectical existence: "I am not asking you to take them out of the world, but I ask you to protect them from the evil one" (17:15). In fact, Jesus cannot ask for them to be taken out of the world — they are the agents of inculturation:

> "Sanctify them in the truth; your word is truth. As you have sent me into the world, so I have sent them into the world. And for their sakes I sanctify myself, so that they also may be sanctified in truth." (John 17:17–19).

The Birth Narrative

Even though John shows little or no reliance on Matthew and Luke, we would assume that he knew a tradition of the birth narrative. If he did, and some texts (6:42; 7:27) might indicate he did not, why was the virgin birth not a keystone in his program to deculturize Jesus? Matthew and Luke had already stated that Jesus was not the product of Israel. However, their model was based on the Jewish apocalyptic model of an end to the old and a new beginning (end time, death and resurrection; transfiguration, baptism and birth). Like Paul, they had adapted the apocalyptic model to signify the death and resurrection of Jesus as the end of the old age and the beginning of the new. Since John has no such model, the death of Jesus signifies the revelation of God's love and the passing on of the Spirit as the effective agent of universal inculturation. In John the lack of an apocalyptic model alters all of the key change moments. In the Synoptics another apocalyptic moment occurs when John baptizes Jesus. The old — ties to the family and race origin — is buried; Jesus comes out of the water (of death, not purification) as the Son of God (Mark 1:11), an agent of the new age (Mark 1:8, 14–15). Jesus does not die to family and race in the Gospel of John. Granted that the words of Mark[10] are used in John's baptismal narrative, there is no indication that Jesus ever entered the water and died to the old age (1:29–34). Instead, like the cross, the baptismal narrative has become a moment of public manifestation to the Jews (ἀλλ᾽ ἵνα φανερωθῇ τῷ Ἰσραήλ, 1:31). The identification of Jesus with the Lamb of God points to the hour when Jesus will reveal God's love to all people.

Although the virgin birth tradition could, and likely did, serve, in an apocalyptic model, to separate Jesus from his primary culture, the author of the Fourth Gospel again did not utilize the apocalyptic worldview. There is no birth narrative. Jesus did not die to his culture — he was never born into it. The prologue makes it clear that the λόγος was effective from the beginning, that it was made known through various means, especially to Israel (1:11), but that the Word had never been incorporated, even in Israel (1:11). The Word never had a cultural home! So the coming of Jesus is the Word finally becoming cultural (σάρξ, 1:14). The "birth" is not described in terms of an apocalyptic break with history, as in the Synoptics, but as the decisive cultural appearance-inculturation of the divine reality.

The redactor makes it clear that σάρξ cannot be a means of achieving reality. Persons born of αἷμα (race), or ἐκ θελήματος σαρκός (culture), or ἐκ θελήματος ἀνδρός (human self-interest), cannot also be born of God, that is, live according to divine reality (1:13). While this statement very likely was added by the redactor to the prologue, it expresses well the evangelist's intent for the Fourth Gospel. The true child of God must be born ἄνωθεν (again from above, a primary word for inculturation); the

---

10. The author of the Fourth Gospel likely knew Mark, but not the other Gospels. However, Mark does not likely go back to the Signs Source. See Urban C. von Wahlde, *The Earliest Version of John's Gospel: Recovering the Gospel of Signs* (Wilmington, Del.: Michael Glazier, 1989); Robert T. Fortna, *The Gospel of Signs: A Reconstruction of the Narrative Source Underlying the Fourth Gospel* (London: Cambridge University Press, 1970).

true child eschews cultural determinism and therefore has no need to go back into the womb (3:3–4).

The Signs Source

The basis for John 1–12 derives from what Johannine scholars have called the Signs Source (from σημεῖον, hence *Semeia-Quelle,* or SQ). SQ has some similarities with the Synoptics, especially Mark, but not enough to assign any formal connection with them. A primary difference has led to the designation SQ: the use of σημεῖον to signify what in the Synoptics appear as acts of power. There are seven such signs, all of which have taken on a meaning other than the miraculous power itself: (1) changing water into wine (2:1–11); (2) healing of the official's son (4:46–54); (3) healing of the paralytic (5:1–9); (4) feeding the five thousand (6:1–14); (5) walking on the water (6:15–21); (6) healing of the man born blind (9:1–41); (7) the raising of Lazarus (11:1–44). The first two are numbered as signs one and two (2:11; 4:54). One might well assume that there were other numbered signs or that the remaining five were once numbered, but, in any case, the numbers and the awkward seams, or *aporias,* point certainly to a pre-Johannine source.

Changing Water into Wine

Water in the Fourth Gospel invariably stands for what in an apocalyptic language would be the old age. John baptizes in water while Jesus baptizes in the Spirit. In the conversation with Nicodemus John's Jesus says that the primary birth is of water while the second birth is of the Spirit (3:5). And with the woman at the well (4:1–26) Judaism is characterized by the rather stationary well water, while what Jesus brings is a living, vibrant water that does not rely on space or time (another agent of inculturation). At the wedding of Cana Jesus took an object of culture — specifically Judaism — the water, and turned it into Spirit, which was free of cultural norms. The sign marks the purpose of the incarnation, though that purpose is not realized until the crucifixion (the hour is not yet). The narrative ends with a remarkable realization. The caterer, who either did not know Judaism or did not know of the change, tasted the wine and recognized its infinite value (2:9–10). The Spirit satisfied.

Healing of the Official's Son

This story serves to make it known that life does not depend on prophetic signs or on wonders. The official believes the word of Jesus and his son lived — lived at the hour Jesus said the word. The reason for the formation of the SQ becomes clear: real life depends on appropriation of the λόγος become flesh.

Healing of the Paralytic

Following the second sign, SQ shifts to the catena of miracles that we have already noted. However, the miracles now serve to explicate the meaning of real life rather than to create the new community. The healing of the paralytic (5:1–9) emphasizes the powerful presence of Jesus. Without knowing who Jesus is, that is, without any cultural network, and without making a statement of faith, the paralytic is made to walk.

Feeding of the Five Thousand

In the Synoptics the multiplication of the loaves and fishes serves to establish the early Eucharist, which consisted of bread, fish, and wine. Jesus breaks the bread and gives thanks; the recipients sit in orderly groups; they save the remainder for distribution to the needy, as did the earliest church.[11] In John a strange thing occurs with this narrative (6:1–14). It remains as the source of the early Christian Eucharist (there is no Passover meal or Last Supper), but the stories of the multiplication of the loaves and fishes and the walking on the water are combined in John to shift attention from the early Christian meal, and the Eucharist, to Jesus himself, who is the real bread of life (the real presence).[12]

Walking on the Water

Walking on the water serves to take Jesus from the Transjordan (and its manna [the multiplication of the loaves and fishes]) to the Promised Land, where this real bread can received (Passover, Josh. 5:10–12). In this way the early Christian Eucharist is lumped with Judaism as religion that has been culturized. It too, like the manna, must be left behind in order to make way for the real Passover, Jesus the bread. This narrative is our first hint that the author considers early Christian faith and practices a hindrance to passing on the universal presence of Jesus. The same thing will occur in the dialogue with Martha (11:17–27).

The Healing of the Man Born Blind

The healing of the man born blind (9:1–41), like the healing of the paralytic, describes the powerful presence of Jesus.[13] Again, the man born blind does not know Jesus, has no cultural interchange, and makes no

---

11. Bo Reicke, *Diakonie, Festfreude, und Zelos* (Uppsala: Lundequistska, 1951).
12. Peder Borgen, *Bread From Heaven: An Exegetical Study of the Concept of Manna in the Gospel of John and the Writings of Philo* (Leiden: Brill, 1965).
13. Judith M. Lieu, "Blindness in the Johannine Tradition," *NTS* 34 (1988): 83–95.

statement of faith. He is made to see by the will of the presence itself, and by his own desire to see. The story then becomes the keystone for describing how inculturation occurs once one has "seen." At first the person impacted by the presence recognizes the actuality and desirability of the change: "Then I went and washed and received my sight"; "Though I was blind, now I see." In the Gospel of John seeing is perception and, rather automatically, if one can see, appropriation of the divine reality. Jesus invites people to "come and see" (1:39, cf. 1:46; 4:29) the reality he embodies. Certain that he now can see, the man born blind refuses to accept theological arguments and institutional threats that might negate what has happened. As a result he becomes disassociated from his cultural past (the famous ἀποσυνάγωγος of 9:22; cf. 9:34). Johannine Christianity does not make a new culture available; Jesus does not go and make disciples. The man born blind swims in a faith limbo. Jesus later comes to him and asks him if he believes in the Son of Man,[14] a strictly Jewish title.[15] Only the presence of Jesus can give new significance to a prior cultural symbol.[16] Inculturation or infusion has occurred.

The Raising of Lazarus

The last sign narrative, also the last in the catena, the raising of the dead, shows that resurrection in the Fourth Gospel refers to a person who has lasting congruity based on divine reality. Death then does not exist (11:25–26), and an end-time resurrection has no place here. It is faith in Jesus (perception and assimilation) that makes this "resurrection and life" possible.[17] The more apocalyptic faith of the early church (Martha's confession in 11:24) lacks the power to create a present resurrection.

As we will see, six of these seven signs comprise the vast majority of early Christian artistic references to the New Testament,[18] and are the most frequently mentioned stories in the miracle catenae.

Religious Practices and Faith Statements

Probably the most remarkable thing about the Fourth Gospel is the incredible variety of mutually exclusive interpretations that it generates. It is the source of high Christology and high liturgical formulations. At the

---

14. With Sinaiticus and Vaticanus.

15. Delbert Royce Burkett, *The Son of Man in the Gospel of John* (Sheffield: JSOT Press, 1991).

16. Paul Diel, *Symbolism in the Gospel of John* (San Francisco: Harper & Row, 1988).

17. It is interesting that the Jews use Jesus' own call to discipleship, "come and see," as an invitation to join with death rather than life (11:34). John's Jesus is so frustrated by this destructive invitation that he weeps (11:35).

18. The healing of the official's son has never been identified as a pictorial representation.

same time, it has been used as the source of religionless Christianity. The argument here is that the author of the Fourth Gospel did indeed intend to present a Jesus not bound by any particular religion, but available to inculturate any social system. We have already seen that John used the feeding of the five thousand and the walking on the water as a means of relegating the early Christian Eucharist to a self-serving meal (6:26) — a meal that did not actually appropriate the divine reality offered by Jesus. Likewise, when Jesus proclaims himself to be the resurrection and the life, we must understand that John has rejected the more end-time-oriented faith statement made by Martha.[19]

The Temple

Following the wedding at Cana, — the proleptic changing of Judaism into a religion of the Spirit — Jesus immediately attacks the temple. In the Synoptics Jesus cleanses the temple as the first act of the Passion narrative. Why did John make the temple cleansing the first public act of Jesus' ministry?[20] Several reasons have been suggested. Narrative displacement would be possible, since other displacements are also obvious (such as the incongruity of chapter 5). But the cleansing of the temple seems too important to be mislaid. The redactor must have intended to place it in the second chapter.

The author apparently wants us to understand that the Passion narrative actually began when the ministry of Jesus began. Salvation or wholeness does not depend on the death and resurrection of Jesus, but on his presence. Public presence, therefore, begins with the ministry. For the reader to understand this clearly, the cleansing of the temple must come first. This process of extending the elements of the Synoptic Passion narrative forward into the ministry has been called "telescoping the Passion story." This explanation has much to commend it. It certainly corresponds to the theological position of the Fourth Gospel. Yet there is more. The story follows the wedding at Cana, where, as we have seen, Jesus changes the "Jewish" water into the wine of the Spirit. The cleansing of the temple follows that introduction. The cleansing itself is not

---

19. Alan R. Culpepper, *Anatomy of the Fourth Gospel: A Study in Literary Design* (Philadelphia: Fortress, 1983); Paul D. Duke, *Irony in the Fourth Gospel* (Atlanta: John Knox, 1985). I assume that every dialogue in the Gospel of John portrays Jesus as the person who represents the author's position, while the other person always represents either an incorrect position or a position so improbable that the reader *must* side with Jesus.

20. The suggestion that John changed the Synoptics contains an unproven assumption that could easily be mistaken. Lacking any easy solution, we assume that the readers knew a Jesus tradition in addition to the SQ, so any difference between John and the Synoptics could be seen as a change, even though John may be more faithful to an original tradition than what we find in the Synoptics.

so critical as the interpretation given it. After a rather hostile cleansing narrative (2:15 — the whip is mentioned only in John), the Jews ask for a σημεῖον (2:18). In response to their request Jesus observes that if the temple were destroyed he could raise it up in three days (ἐν τρισὶν ἡμέραις ἐγερῶ αὐτόν, 2:19). The readers knew indeed that the Jerusalem temple had been destroyed and, furthermore, that Jesus had, at the resurrection, given to them the Spirit in place of the temple. The cleansing of the temple may well be the beginning of the "passion-embodiment" narrative, but it also marks the separation from the temple. It is a narrative of deculturization.

Jesus confirms the deculturation in several narratives. In the dialogue with Nicodemus Jesus says that the one who would enter the reign of God must be born of the water and of the Spirit (3:5); that is to say, one must belong to a social matrix (water), but also live according to the divine reality (the Spirit). In the next parallel sentence water is replaced with flesh so that the reader will correctly interpret water as historical existence (3:6).

In the dialogue with the Samaritan woman Jesus rejects the water of the Jewish fathers as lacking in ultimate satisfaction (4:13), while the water he has to offer (living water = the Spirit) will never need to be replenished (4:14). The water of Jacob's well may be identified with Jewish religion. What Jesus has to offer does not relate to such spaces as Jacob's well, Jerusalem, or Samaria (4:21). In fact, spaces have been eliminated in favor of a universal reality.[21] God is Spirit:

> "But the hour is coming, and is now here, when the true worshipers will worship the Father in spirit and truth, for the Father seeks such as these to worship him. God is spirit, and those who worship him must worship in spirit and truth." (John 4:23–24)

Such statements are not anti-Judaic, but a powerful narrative designed to develop a deculturized Christ.[22] Far from anti-Judaic, Jesus affirms that "salvation is of the Jews"; that is, the water is essential and, more specifically, without Jewish water the Christian Spirit would not be possible. Perception of the Spirit depends on the Jewish faith in a living God, not the syncretism of the Samaritans (4:17–18) or the polytheism of the Romans. At the feast of chapter 7 Jesus goes up to the temple and makes

---

21. Tod D. Swanson, "To Prepare a Place: Johannine Christianity and the Collapse of Ethnic Territory," *JAAR* 62 (1994): 241–63.

22. See George MacRae, "Theology and Irony in the Fourth Gospel," in *The Word in the World*, ed. R. J. Clifford and George MacRae (Cambridge: Weston College Press, 1973), 83–96. In another article MacRae argues that the author presents a Jesus who fulfills the symbolic expectations of the several Mediterranean cultures, but is "caught up in one of them" ("The Fourth Gospel and *Religionsgeschichte*," *CBQ* 32 [1970]:13–24).

the same contrast of water and Spirit. Quoting Isaiah regarding living water, he offers himself as that drink which satisfies (7:37–38).

In the Farewell Discourses Jesus takes up the same theme of the Spirit as the true power of the new faith. Jesus begins the fourteenth chapter with the important observation that the divine reality can take on many forms. He says that there are many abiding places[23] in his Father's house, that is, the temple (ἐν τῇ οἰκίᾳ τοῦ πατρός μου μοναὶ πολλαί εἰσιν, 14:2). Despite rigid interpretations of 14:6 ("Jesus said to him, 'I am the way, and the truth, and the life. No one comes to the Father except through me.' "), these verses indicate not only the singleness of the divine reality, but also the multiplicity of the cultural forms (μοναὶ πολλαί) that the faith can assume. Far beyond the temple at Jerusalem, the Spirit-Paraclete will lead Johannine believers into all the truth (εἰς τὴν ἀλήθειαν πᾶσαν 16:13 — taking the text of Vaticanus); the Spirit will accomplish greater works (καὶ μείζονα τούτων ποιήσει, 14:12); and the Spirit will abide (take cultural form, μένει, 14:17). Clearly, this will not happen until even the cultural reification of Jesus has been left behind (14:12, 27–28; 15:26). In one of the most remarkable passages in the Fourth Gospel, Mary Magdalene, having come to the empty tomb, and having found the resurrected Jesus, moves to hug him (20:17). Jesus responds to the woman who loves him, μή μου ἅπτου; that is to say, "Do not keep me in this cultural milieu." By going to the Father, Jesus relinquishes the cultural specificity of the incarnation and allows the Spirit to be at work in the world.

Seen this way John makes the Spirit (πνεῦμα; παράκλητος; λόγος) the operational divine reality. The world did not know the Spirit-Word (1:10); the Spirit came to Israel through the prophets but was not received (1:11). The Spirit was only known occasionally through what modern scholars call an "altered state of consciousness." The author of the Fourth Gospel speaks of Jesus as one who actually embodied the Spirit, a Spirit that came from God (1:1) and which was released for further embodiment at the death of Jesus (19:30). Because Jesus was the embodiment of the Spirit rather than its agent (as the Synoptics have it), the narrative changes radically. For example, in John healings occur because of the presence of Jesus rather than through the more charismatic exorcisms found in the Synoptics.

When we speak of the agent of inculturation in the Pauline tradition, we mean the Jesus tradition. When we speak of the agent of inculturation in the Johannine tradition, we mean the Spirit. The actual effectual

---

23. See J. C. Dillow, "Abiding Is Remaining in Fellowship: Another Look at John 15:1–6," *Bibliotheca Sacra* 147 (1990),44–53.

difference between the Jesus tradition and the Spirit may not be great, but the method of operation would be quite different.

Christology

Taken in its simplest form, the development of the Johannine community consists of three stages. First, in the initial years they were a deviant group within Judaism who believed that Jesus was the Messiah. The "Gospel of Signs" would reflect the Christology of the earliest period. Second, about the year 70, conflicts arose between the Johannine group and its synagogues. With the destruction of the temple a separation occurred. The Johannine group apparently was expelled (9:22; 12:42; 16:2). The new community, isolated from Judaism, gathered around a Jesus who was the revelatory agent of God. Third, separated from Judaism, the Johannine community eventually spoke of God in terms of a Jesus who embodied the divine reality. The final redaction of the Gospel of John reflects this high Christology throughout. The opening hymn identifies the λόγος as God, the same λόγος that becomes flesh (1:14). In 20:28 the sceptic Thomas exclaims the confession that we all (as readers) will have affirmed: "My Lord and my God!" Jesus frequently identifies himself with the Father (8:19; 14:7, 9–11). Indeed, Jesus and the Father are one (10:30). The great "I AM" sayings attempt to identify Jesus as the κύριος of the Greco-Roman cults in terms of the tetragrammaton of Exod. 3:14 — a marvelous identity because of the Septuagintal translation ὁ ὤν, Ultimate Being.

The present consensus regarding the development of the Gospel of John assumes a conflict situation with the synagogue. Much care has been exercised in the construction of this thesis. However, the history of Johannine research is loaded with landmines. Very few theories have lasted. The major critical objection to the present-day Jewish conflict thesis comes from literary criticism. The redactor of John uses opponents as a means of evangelizing, not as an object of historical conflict. The dialogues are so constructed as either to designate what we ought not believe (11:25–27) or to create dialogue partners who are so dimwitted or mistaken that their response forces the reader to believe in Jesus (3:4; 4:15).[24] Jews (Nicodemus, Pharisees, Caiaphas), early Christians (Mary, Martha, Peter), and Romans (Pilate) serve as dimwitted dialogue partners. If one is to say that John was developed in conflict with the synagogue, then one should also add the Petrine church to the list of opponents.[25]

---

24. Culpepper, *Anatomy of the Fourth Gospel.*
25. Snyder, "John 3:16."

The high Christology of the Gospel of John serves as a mission Christology. It places divine reality, or the Spirit, in one person. By isolating that person it is not the intent of the final redactor to create an extra-historical plane of reality (spiritualism or Gnosticism), but to grant the new church, now in a non-Palestinian context, the possibility of presenting that divine reality to any culture. The Gospel's literary style exemplifies and effects that intent.

Anti-Judaism[26]

Some Jewish scholars consider the Gospel of John the most anti-Judaic of the New Testament writings. There are five main reasons why the Fourth Gospel has that reputation.

First, the high Christology appears to make Jesus equivalent with the Jewish God. Although it is true that the Gospel speaks of equivalency, we have argued above that the divinity of Jesus results from (1) a theology of divine embodiment that differs from the Synoptics, and (2) the desire of the Johannine community to present a Lord untrammeled by cultural specificity.[27]

Second, conflict with the synagogue, as projected by some readers, leaves the impression that the Johannine community was anti-Judaic.[28] Again, as we have shown above, conflicts in the Gospel of John are literary constructions intended to induce faith in Jesus. Dialogues in this Gospel are not to be taken as actual conflicts. To be sure, some dialogues may represent more than literary constructs involving dimwitted characters (e.g., Mary and Martha, the Greeks, Pilate), but even those involving serious content ought not be taken as actually expressing the position of the opponent. For example, one does not suppose Pilate's search for the truth actually represents a primary concern of Roman administrative officials.

Third, and more critical, are direct attacks by Jesus on Judaism. Several times the Jewish law stands in conflict with Jesus (10:34; 15:25;

---

26. C. K. Barrett, *The Gospel of John and Judaism* (London: SPCK, 1975); Luke T. Johnson, "The New Testament's Anti-Jewish Slander and the Conventions of Ancient Polemic," *JBL* 108 (1989): 419–41; J. T. Townsend, "The Gospel of John and the Jews: The Story of Religious Divorce," in *Anti-Semitism and the Foundations of Christianity*, ed. Alan Davies (New York: Paulist, 1979), 72–97; Urban C. von Wahlde, "The 'Johannine' Jews: A Critical Survey," *NTS* (1982): 33–60.

27. A. C. Sundberg, "Isos to Theos Christology in John 5:17–30" *BR* 15 (1970): 19–31.

28. Robert Kysar, "John's Anti-Jewish Polemic," *Bible Review* 9 (1993): 83–95; J. N. Sanders, *Schismatics, Sectarians, Dissidents, Deviants: The First One Hundred Years of Jewish-Christian Relations* (Valley Forge, Pa.: Trinity Press International, 1993); J. Louis Martyn, *History and Theology in the Fourth Gospel* (New York: Harper & Row, 1968); Hayim Perelmuter, *Siblings: Rabbinic Judaism and Early Christianity at Their Beginnings* (Mahwah, N.J.: Paulist Press, 1989); Raymond Brown, *The Community of the Beloved Disciple* (New York: Paulist Press, 1979).

19:7). References to the law certainly do indicate a separation: "your law," "their law." The several references do not attack the Jews for having Torah, but for interpreting Torah in such a way that blocks their recognition of Jesus. Interpretation of the law as it related to Jesus must have been a difference between Judaism and the Johannine community (and well it should have been), but the Fourth Gospel does not attack or depreciate the law.

Fourth, references to the persecution of Jesus by the Jews (5:16; 10:31; 18:36) do point to antagonism. Such references present a problem for interpretation. Persecution language, taken from the Hebrew Scriptures, tends either to indicate the presence of a deviant-conflictive group or to identify someone as the "suffering righteous." If the redactor intended to deculturize Jesus, it hardly seems congruent to identify him as a suffering righteous in the Jewish context. The Synoptics do make Jesus one of the suffering righteous, but normally, John carefully avoids any such victimization on the part of Jesus (10:17–18; 18:6, 36). Still, John uses that psalm of lament, Psalm 22, which was used by the Synoptics to construct the Passion narrative and to indicate that Jesus was a suffering righteous. Yet the purpose of the cross in John is to lift up the suffering love of God (3:14–16). Although designating Jesus as righteous has little value for John, it supports the theological intent of the Gospel to identify him as divine reality that suffers because that reality has been rejected. Jesus as the Passover lamb makes the same point (1:29, 36; 13:1): if you see the lamb lifted up, you may assimilate the suffering love of God.

Fifth, the Jews are children of the devil (8:44). In the deeply conflictive chapter 8 Jesus claims that the listeners are offspring of their father the devil. In 8:42 he has already said that they cannot be children of God the Father, because if they were, they would love (and know) him. References in John to the devil are not easily understood. John seems to have no interest in the source of evil (3:18; 9:3). The devil is the perversion of divine reality. The devil directed the work of Judas (13:2), yet the "betrayal" itself is very difficult to discern.[29] The devil is not a tempter or a source of evil, but symbolizes that shift in Jewish perspective which makes the Jews miss seeing divine reality in the decultured (non-Jewish) Jesus.

Summary

The Jesus tradition recaptures the Mosaic tradition and describes that intended corporate life as the reign of God. The kingdom is close at hand; therefore the present age has severe limits. Indeed, it cannot deliver God's

---

29. William Klassen, *Judas: Betrayer or Friend of Jesus?* (Minneapolis: Fortress, 1996).

will as originally revealed. The tradition left by Jesus became a "virus" that first impacted Palestinian society, and then the Roman. That virus declassified society by obliterating distinctions (e.g., in clean and unclean) and reconstructed the new age through sharing life together, especially as seen in commensalism.

Paul keeps the same perception of the coming age, even using, from time to time, the Jesus tradition to buttress his arguments. His eschatology, however, goes in a different direction. He may support the present age (governmental authorities, family and sexual values, even class distinctions), but he devalues any such elements of the status quo. As a result, one can see in the Pauline letters an emerging social structure that eventually undermines the present age. He asks the congregation to make its own legal decisions; he seeks order in congregational meetings; he opts for stronger family ties; he insists on gender and ethnic evenness. In Paul we can see the inculturation of the Jesus tradition at work in Mediterranean society.

The redactor of the Gospel of John goes yet another direction. Faced with separation from Judaism and an audience that did not know the Jewish culture, John deculturized Jesus. In what might appear as antagonism to some readers, John, with consummate literary skill, took Jesus out of his specific culture and made him available to any culture. The Jesus reality was passed on through the action of the Spirit and the love of the faith community. They "passed on their psyche" (μείζονα ταύτης ἀγάπην οὐδεὶς ἔχει, ἵνα τις τὴν ψυχὴν αὐτοῦ θῇ ὑπὲρ τῶν φίλων αὐτοῦ, John 15:13), which was the act of inculturation.[30] The Gospel of John has become many things to many people over the course of history. These many things were not, and are not, in the Fourth Gospel, but are the result of the inculturation affecting a variety of cultural media.

---

30. As noted in chap. 2, "psyche" means "personhood."

Part 2

Theories of
Transformation

Chapter 5

The Second Generation

The second generation of Christianity reflects the invasion of the Mediterranean culture by the Jesus tradition. Before moving to the specific invasion that led to the Roman-Western form of Christianity, we must consider what other explanations have been proffered to account for the second generation.

For the most part Protestant New Testament scholars speak of the demise of that nascent Christianity found in Jesus, Paul, and John, a demise that they earlier discussed under the rubric of early Catholicism. We consider the term "early Catholicism" a seriously misleading one for this discussion, and it will appear only when historical accuracy demands it. Yet the term indicates the nature of the debate. Something happened to the Christian movement that Protestant scholars, in particular, have found alien to the original impulse.[1] Prior to the "early Catholic" debate, it was generally assumed that the later church was continuous with the early church. Before dealing with theories of change it would be appropriate to mention briefly those who do not assume any inappropriate changes.

Change Has Not Occurred

Faced with the Protestant use of Scripture against the Roman Catholic church, James Benign Bossuet, bishop of Meaux and strong defender of the received faith, insisted that the Catholic church, from its dominical inception, had not changed in either doctrine or practice. As seen in his major work, *The History of the Variations of the Protestant Churches*, variation comes with heresy, not the church itself, "because the Church, who professes to speak and teach nothing but what she hath received, does never vary; whereas Heresy, which began by innovating, daily innovates, and changes not its nature."[2] Bossuet was willing to

---

1. Robert L. Wilken, *The Myth of Christian Beginnings: History's Impact on Belief* (Garden City, N.Y.: Doubleday, 1971).
2. James Benign Bossuet, *The History of the Variations of the Protestant Churches* (Antwerp: n.p., 1742), vol. 1, sec. 5.

grant that there had been changes of words and descriptions, but not of principles.[3]

Disciplina Arcanum

Some Catholic theologians argued for the continuity of the later church with the early church by asserting that later doctrines and practices had been kept secret by the first Christians. Such secrecy was necessary in part because of the private nature of certain practices and in part because of threats from exterior enemies. Despite its use by Catholic theologians the term *disciplina arcanum* was first coined by a Protestant controversialist, John Daillé,[4] in his attempt to discredit examples in the then supposed first-century witness of Pseudo-Dionysius (*De ecclesiastica heirarchia*, par. 7).[5] In the controversy that ensued, primarily between the Protestant Ernest Tentzel and the Catholic Emanuel Schelstrate, the latter insisted that later ecclesiastical developments, such as the doctrine of the Trinity and the practice of the sacraments, had been handed down secretly through initiates.[6] The arguments for a *disciplina arcanum* were sharply rejected by Cardinal Newman, who described later Catholicism as the logical extension and development of the first church.[7] However, Yves Congar's use of unwritten apostolic traditions does not differ in kind from the older argument of a *disciplina arcanum*, i.e., that later developments existed earlier in an unwritten form.

Logical Extension of the Apostolic Tradition

At first, as in the case of Francesco Suarez or Luis Molina, logical inference meant just what it says: doctrinal development could be tested syllogistically.[8] Dhanis, on the other hand, proposed three principles for determining whether a legitimate extension had occurred.[9]

1. The principle of faithful exposition. Those truths that become the explicit items of faith during the development of dogma must have

---

3. Owen Chadwick, *From Bossuet to Newman: The Idea of Doctrinal Development* (Cambridge: Cambridge University Press, 1957), 20.

4. John Daillé, *De scriptis quae sub Dionysius Areopagite et Ignatii Antiocheni nominibus circumferunter* (Geneva: de Tournes, 1666), 140.

5. On the history and text see Paul Rorem, *Pseudo-Dionysius: A Commentary on the Texts and an Introduction to Their Influence* (New York: Oxford University Press, 1993).

6. Emanuel Schelstrate, *De disciplina arcani contra disputationem Ernesti Tentzelli* (Rome: Sac. Congregat. de Propaganda Fide, 1685).

7. John Henry Newman, *An Essay on the Development of Christian Doctrine* (London: Pickering, 1878), 27.

8. Cited in Chadwick, *From Bossuet to Newman*, 21–48.

9. Yves M.-J. Congar, *Tradition and Traditions*, trans. Michael Naseby and Thomas Rainborough (London: Burns and Oates, 1966), 50–64. Congar denies that these teachings were esoteric.

been implicit, by means of faithful exposition, in the teachings of the apostles.

2. The principle of the exclusion of a new revelation. Those truths that become the explicit objects of faith during the development of dogma should have been implicit in the revealed deposit in such a way that the Fathers were able to discover them, as truths of faith without the assistance of a new revelation.

3. The principle of an original and formal witness for all dogmas. Those truths that become the explicit items of faith during the development of dogma should have been implicit, in the apostolic deposit, as the object of a formal witness of God.

Appropriate Development of the Original

Whatever the Catholic antecedents of John Henry Newman,[10] it was he who took the historical evidence seriously, admitted the changes in doctrine, and persuasively propounded an analogy of organic development to show that the true church would be that which, according to principles of development, blossomed forth from the original seed. His famous criteria were: preservation of type, continuity of principles, power of assimilation, logical sequence, anticipation of its future, conservative action upon its past, and chronic vigor.[11]

Despite the power of these arguments in previous historical debate, and even though one may occasionally find a contemporary adherent for one of these positions, actually, in the course of recent Catholic-Protestant debate regarding "early Catholicism" the lines of discussion have changed so radically as to render them useless.[12] The three arguments of Dhanis assume the unity of an apostolic witness on which continuity or logical development could depend. Nearly all historians of the early church would now agree that the divisions that plague us are inherent in the New Testament itself.

Many historians, admittedly primarily Protestant, have assumed that some transformations occurred in the first centuries of the church — transformations that resulted in a second- and third-century church quite different from the "original." While many of these historians also improperly assume a "purity" (and unity) for the New Testament church from which the fatal transformation could occur, still it will be necessary

---

10. Chadwick, *From Bossuet to Newman*, 118–19, and Vittorio Subilia, *The Problem of Catholicism*, trans. R. Kissack (London: SCM, 1964), 103.
11. Newman, *Development of Christian Doctrine*, 169–206.
12. Ernst Käsemann, "The Canon of the New Testament and the Unity of the Church," *Essays on New Testament Themes*, trans. W. J. Montague (London: SCM, 1964), 103.

to catalogue these transformations in order to understand the present discussion.

The Incursion of Heresy

That the church in some way "fell" or lost its primary vision cannot be considered a recent invention of Reformation propaganda. The early historian Hegesippus, as reported by Eusebius (*Hist. eccl.* 4.22), spoke of the first-century church at Jerusalem as a virgin that later was ravished by seven heresies. In a style that prefigured Harnack, the iconoclastic Tertullian claimed that the church's use of pagan philosophy caused its postapostolic woes (*Praescr. haer.* 7).[13] Nevertheless, for our purposes, historiography of early church transformations begins early in the nineteenth century with the work of F. C. Baur. It would be instructive to trace the history of early church transformations from Baur to the present day, but because of the complexity involved in distinguishing between a transformation and its alleged cause or causes, it seems appropriate to catalogue all the transformations proposed, since Baur, by historians of the early church.

The Eschatological Transformation

According to current historiography, the foremost transformation of the church came with the collapse of intense eschatology or apocalypticism. The eschatological nature of the message of Jesus was not fully recognized until 1892. It was the monumental work of Johannes Weiss, which portrayed Jesus as so bound to Jewish apocalypticism that, to utilize the "Jesus story," some transformation was necessary in the early church — to say nothing of the twentieth century.[14] Jesus expected the end immediately;[15] he expected the coming kingdom to be given into his hands;[16] and he taught an ethic of preparation for that kingdom, a kingdom that stood "in diametric opposition to this world."[17] Jesus and those who shared his expectation were mistaken. Consequently it became necessary to transform that eschatological nature of earliest Christianity. Unfortunately scholars cannot agree about the nature of this modification. In a cynical moment one could say that the failure of eschatology resulted in

---

13. See also Wilken, *Myth of Christian Beginnings*, 52–76.
14. Proposed in his *Die Predigt Jesus vom Reiche Gottes*. Quotations here are taken from the English translation, *Jesus' Proclamation of the Kingdom of God*, trans. R. H. Hiers and D. L. Holland (London: SCM, 1971).
15. Weiss, *Jesus' Proclamation*, 85.
16. Ibid., 126.
17. Ibid., 114.

the development of whatever aspect of church and theology the historian disliked. But even this suspicion has one certain exception, to which we now turn.

The Felix Culpa *of Eschatology*

Weiss himself was pleased by the later transformation of the original "imminent eschatology." An ethic of the heavenly kingdom would be more beneficial to our day than that radical, even political, apocalypticism of Jesus.[18] So we must, without regret, give up the notion that today's Christian teaching can be a "simple application of the teaching of Jesus."[19] Christianity could not have existed with radical apocalypticism and is well rid of it. However controversial it may be, in light of subsequent developments, it seems quite clear that Weiss's contemporary, Albert Schweitzer, in the first instance also was happy to see an end to imminent eschatology in early Christianity. Schweitzer had been a convinced Kantian in search of a religious a priori.[20] For him a valid ethic must be world-affirming. An ethic based on the expectation of the coming kingdom of God would be world-denying.[21] The failure of Jesus' apocalypticism left his spiritual heirs, i.e., the early and medieval church, with a world-denying ethic (asceticism) until Renaissance Christians shifted to a world-affirming ethic.[22] That world-affirming categorical imperative sought by Schweitzer was, of course, "reverence for life."[23] Only after disposing of the apocalyptic Jesus[24] and relegating his world-denying, apocalyptic-bound teachings to an ill-fated interim,[25] did Schweitzer realize that the failure of the end to materialize, i.e., the transformation of eschatology, could be used to explain the development of the postapostolic church.

As the latter thesis was developed, the point at which eschatology failed became identified with the beginning of Hellenization, a much repeated "transformation" charge, or the loss of Jewish eschatological

---

18. Ibid., 135–36.

19. Ibid., 113.

20. Albert Schweitzer, *Die Religionsphilosophie Kants von der Kritik der reinen Vernunft bis zur Religion innerhalb der Grenzen der bloßen Vernunft* (Tübingen: Mohr, 1899).

21. Albert Schweitzer, *The Teaching of Reverence for Life* (London: Owen, 1966), 12.

22. Ibid., 16. See also his essay, "The Conception of the Kingdom of God in the Transformation of Eschatology," in E. N. Mozley, *The Theology of Albert Schweitzer for Christian Inquirers* (London: Black, 1950), 99.

23. Schweitzer, *Teaching of Reverence for Life*, 27.

24. Albert Schweitzer, *The Quest of the Historical Jesus*, trans. W. Montgomery (London: Black, 1954), 396–97.

25. Ibid., 364, 358.

vitality.[26] Strangely enough, now Schweitzer looks with sadness on what he previously applauded:

> The abandonment of eager expectation meant that Christianity lost the joy which characterized it in the days of Paul and the early Church. It started in bright sunshine, but had to continue its journey in the chilly gloom of a vague and uncertain hope.[27]

Although the impetus for both Weiss and Schweitzer may have derived from the desire to free Christianity (ethics, particularly) from a fanatic Jesus, their net effect was to trigger a basic discussion of how the failure of the Parousia affected the life and doctrine of the early church.

From Eschatology to Incarnation

Johannes Weiss never defined the point at which eschatology was transformed, but for Schweitzer, and after him, Martin Werner, incarnational theology as expounded by Ignatius of Antioch and the author of the Gospel of John marked the first and foremost attempt of the early church to transform a hopeless and useless theology.[28] Other texts can be cited to show disappointment in and rationalization of the failure of the Parousia (Heb. 10:35–39; 2 Pet. 3:8–9; 2 Thess. 2:1–12), but only in incarnational theology do we find the attempt so to revise eschatology that Christians now have a totally different raison d'être. Schweitzer finds this primarily in the confessional shift from a more eschatological dying and rising with Christ to a more Hellenistic union of flesh and spirit (ἕνωσις σαρκική τε καὶ πνευματική, Ign. *Magn.* 13:2).[29] In this way the divine was united with the human in Jesus so as to bring redemption by means of the incarnation itself as mediated by participation in the sacraments. Such, then, was the major transformation of the early church, perpetuated by the Logos theology of John and Justin Martyr.[30] Martin Werner tried to show how other transformations, e.g., regarding baptism and ecclesiology, as

---

26. Albert Schweitzer, *Christianity and the Religions of the World* (London: Allen and Unwin, 1923), 25–26.

27. Schweitzer, "Conception of the Kingdom of God," 83.

28. Schweitzer placed Ignatius before John chronologically in *The Mysticism of Paul the Apostle* (London: Black, 1931), 339. For Werner, more appropriately, the author of the Gospel of John was the first Christian incarnationalist; see his *Formation of Christian Dogma* (London: Black, 1957), 62–64.

29. Schweitzer, *Mysticism of Paul the Apostle*, 343. Schweitzer failed to note the context of such sayings. They are never metaphysical, but always ethical or hierarchical. See C. C. Richardson, *The Christianity of Ignatius of Antioch* (New York: Columbia University Press, 1935), 33–39; Édouard Bruston, *Ignace d'Antioche: ses épîtres, sa vie, sa théologie* (Paris: Fischbacher, 1897), 222.

30. Schweitzer, *Mysticism of Paul the Apostle*, 348.

well as the eucharist, could be explained by this primary theological shift from eschatology to incarnation.[31]

The thesis of Schweitzer and Werner has been rejected out-of-hand except, perhaps, for a more extended debate in post-World War II Switzerland.[32] Nevertheless, as will be seen, their basic thesis has had a profound effect on New Testament scholarship. Few would say that early Catholicism, i.e., sacramentalism, ecclesiasticism, hierarchicalism, and moralism, resulted from an incarnational theology. However, most would say that these "changes" were due to the delay of the Parousia. As Cullmann has noted, one wonders if those who rejected Schweitzer and Werner have not indeed utilized precisely the same thesis dressed in less inflammatory language.[33] For example, does Käsemann actually differ radically from Schweitzer when he finds in John a nascent early Catholicism that has transformed eschatology into protology, and presents Jesus as God walking on earth?[34] Or could not Helmut Koester be quoting Schweitzer when he says that Ignatius made of Jesus a metaphysical reality, the purpose of which was "to bring about the unification of flesh and spirit in order to give to those who are flesh the possibility of partaking of the spirit though the sacrament?"[35]

At the same time, it should be noted that the shift from Jesus and Paul to John has not always been lamented. At least Rudolf Bultmann denies that John has transformed the Parousia; rather, John wrote to show that the "parousia has already occurred."[36] So the struggle between those who lament the early Catholicism of John and those who applaud his realized eschatology has yet to be resolved.

From Eschatology to Historicization

Interest in Johannine incarnationalism has waned, largely because in recent times the historicizing tendency of Luke has become the locus of the transformation debate. Once the eschatology of Jesus had been positively interpreted through existential categories — the "noch nicht aber doch schon" of Bultmann[37] — it became possible to see the basic transformation of eschatology in the normative use of tradition or history. That this

---

31. Werner, *Formation of Christian Dogma*, 165–92, 269–82.

32. Oscar Cullmann, "Parusieverzögerung und Urchristentum," *TLZ* 3 (1958): 2.

33. Ibid., 5–6.

34. Ernst Käsemann, *The Testament of Jesus*, trans. G. Krodel (London: SCM, 1968), 73.

35. Helmut Koester, "History and Cult in the Gospel of John and in Ignatius of Antioch," *JTC* 1 (1965): 111–23.

36. Rudolf Bultmann, "The Eschatology of the Gospel of John," in *Faith and Understanding*, trans. L. P. Smith (London: SCM, 1960), 175.

37. Rudolf Bultmann, *Theology of the New Testament*, trans. K. Grobel (London: SCM,1952), 1:7.

occurred in the patently historical work of Luke-Acts (Luke 1:1–4) had long been noted.[38] But just where the present controversy started cannot be ascertained. Most likely it was Philipp Vielhauer, in his article, "On the Paulinism of Acts,"[39] who first pinpointed the way in which the transformation occurred. He suggested that Paul had no quantitative understanding of the "noch nicht aber doch schon";[40] i.e., there was no redemptive history between Easter and the Parousia (1 Cor. 15:20–24). However, according to Vielhauer, Luke keeps both Easter and the Parousia, but gives the "in between" a quantitative value — *Heilsgeschichte*. In Acts 13:16–41, through the mouth of Paul, Luke no longer presents a rupture of the old age by a breaking in of the new, but a series of actions whereby God increasingly fulfills ancient promises. The stages of this history are: (1) the period of Israel, (2) the period of Jesus, and (3) the time of the Spirit.[41] At about the same time, H. Conzelmann wrote his study of Luke's theology along the lines suggested by Vielhauer.[42] And Käsemann gave considerable weight to the position with several approbative remarks.[43]

Like the advent of incarnational theology for Schweitzer, the historicization of the eschatological interval by Luke has become for present-day scholars the causative factor in the development of dogma and the growth of an ecclesiastical hierarchy.[44] Whether or not this analysis of Luke-Acts can be sustained,[45] it remains that somewhere, sometime, historicization did occur. Therefore just as incarnationalization was the key to the postapostolic church for Schweitzer, so now historical consciousness has become the pivotal point. Conzelmann writes:

38. Franz Overbeck had spoken of the "Degeneration des Paulinismus" in his "Über das Verhältnis Justins des Märtyrers zur Apostelgeschichte," *ZWT* 15 (1872): 349. Philipp Vielhauer credits Overbeck with breaking from the Tübingen view of Acts and setting the stage for the present position. See Vielhauer's "Franz Overbeck und die neutestamentliche Wissenschaft," *EvT* 10 (1950–51): 200.

39. P. Vielhauer, "On the Paulinism of Acts," in *Studies in Luke-Acts,* ed. L. E. Keck and J. L. Martyn (Philadelphia: Fortress, 1966), 33–50.

40. Ibid., 46.

41. Ibid., 46–47

42. Hans Conzelmann, *The Theology of St. Luke,* trans. G. Buswell (New York: Harper, 1960); see p. 14.

43. Ernst Käsemann, "The Problem of the Historical Jesus," in *Essays on New Testament Themes,* trans. W. J. Montague (London: SCM, 1964), 28–29; "New Testament Questions of Today," in *New Testament Questions of Today,* trans. W. J. Montague (Philadelphia: Fortress, 1969), 21–22.

44. Ernst Käsemann, "Ministry and Community in the New Testament," in *Essays on New Testament Themes,* 89–93.

45. See Haenchen, *Acts of the Apostles,* 48–49; W. C. van Unnik, "Luke-Acts, A Storm Center in Contemporary Scholarship," in *Studies in Luke-Acts,* ed. L. E. Keck and J. L. Martyn (Philadelphia: Fortress, 1966), 22–28.

The key for the understanding of this period is the altered self-consciousness of the church. Its founder has been pushed into a more distant past. The church which originally consciously faced the end of the world and understood itself as a sign of the end time, now has taken on a historical dimension and can look back on its own development [*Geschichte*].[46]

For some scholars the importance of this transformation lies not so much in historicization as in the developing self-consciousness of the church as the locus of that historicization, i.e., ecclesiasticism.

From Eschatology to Ecclesiasticism

As we shall see later, the development of an ecclesiastical hierarchy would be one of the major marks of early Catholicism. Ordinarily the origin of church organization, as far as Protestant scholars are concerned, has been understood as a failure of the Spirit. However, some have understood so-called ecclesiasticism as a failure of the Parousia to materialize. Needless to say, historicization would have to engender organization. For Käsemann, the church had to protect its now historical *depositum fidei* by the development of authorized officials. No longer was every baptized person an office holder (1 Pet. 2:5–10),[47] but only certain ones were ordained and given the charisma (1 Tim. 4:14; 2 Tim. l:6).[48] Bultmann regards church organization as the necessary result of a de-eschatologized sacramentalism.[49] But even if church organization is not taken simply as a necessary evil, without which early Catholicism could not have functioned, then it could be seen as a direct transformation of eschatological thought. We have already seen that eschatology was historicized in the early church, but very likely it also was spatialized.[50]

So while the "orthodox" church may have created a *Heilsgeschichte* between Easter and the Parousia, the spiritual, or "gnostic," church used eschatological literature in part to describe heavenly realities.[51] Whether or not it can be shown that fragments of apocalypticism contributed

---

46. H. Conzelmann, *History of Primitive Christianity*, trans. John E. Steely (Nashville: Abingdon, 1973), 122–23; German original, *Geschichte des Urchristentums*, Das Neue Testament Deutsch, Ergänzungsreihe 5 (Göttingen: Vandenhoeck & Ruprecht, 1969), 104.

47. Käsemann, "Ministry and Community," 80.

48. Ibid., 86–87.

49. Rudolf Bultmann, *History and Eschatology* (Edinburgh: Edinburgh University Press, 1957), 53.

50. Graydon F. Snyder, "The Literalization of the Apocalyptic Form in the New Testament Church," *BR* 14 (1969): 5–18.

51. R. M. Grant, *Gnosticism and Early Christianity* (New York: Columbia University Press, 1959), 40–42; Graydon F. Snyder, *The Shepherd of Hermas*, vol. 6 of *The Apostolic Fathers* (Camden, N.J.: Nelson, 1968), 8–10.

to the gnostic mythology, still, if in eschatological thought the church was the sign of the end, standing, as it were, between the "already" but "not yet," now, in the later church, it stands between the earthly and the heavenly. Since the tension had shifted from chronology to space, the function of the church was altered accordingly.

The nature of this change was first noted by Heinrich Schlier.[52] On the basis of appropriate texts in Ephesians, Colossians, and Ignatius,[53] Schlier showed that the Pauline body of Christ, an eschatological entity, had, in deuteropauline literature, become a gnostic entity in which the earthly σῶμα participated in the heavenly nature of the κεφαλή. For Schlier, and subsequently also Käsemann, who considerably expanded the thesis,[54] this transformation was due to the incursion of Gnosticism. However, it would be quite possible to maintain that it was the spatial inversion of eschatology (frustrated by the failure of the Parousia) that made it possible for the church to become the visible manifestation of the heavenly body. This has been said no more clearly perhaps than by Franz-Heinrich Kettler, who found especially in Ignatius a church that had become an interim (!) on the way to heavenly existence: "The accent of the concept of the church shifted more and more from the end of history to heaven present in the church."[55] For Kettler the hierarchy was no functional accident (as with most nineteenth-century Protestant critics), but a deliberate attempt of Christians to pattern the earthly church after the heavenly hierarchy that it represented. For Ignatius the heavenly hierarchy of Father (God), Christ (head), church (body) was manifest in the church with the bishop replacing God or Christ (Ign. *Smyrn.* 8:2; Ign. *Trall.* 3:1; Ign. *Magn.* 6:1).

In the early church the union of the heavenly with the earthly was symbolized not only by the κεφαλή-σῶμα image, but also by the marriage of Christ and the church (Eph. 5:32; 2 *Clem.* 14) and by the image of the church as a heavenly structure (Eph. 2:20–22; Ign. *Eph.* 9; *Herm. Vis.* 9–16).[56] The visibility of the church was in the sacrament and in authorized charismatic leadership, both of which have been named as

---

52. First in *Religionsgeschichtliche Untersuchungen zu den Ignatiusbriefen* (Beihefte zur Zeitschrift für die neutestamentliche Wissenschaft, no. 8 (Giessen: Töpelmann, 1929); then in *Christus und die Kirche im Epheserbrief*, Beiträge zur historischen Theologie, no. 6 (Tübingen: Mohr [Siebeck], 1930), 37–48.

53. Eph. 1:22–23; 2:15; 3:6; 4:12, 15, 25; 5:23, 29–30; Col. 1:18, 24b; 2:10, 19; 3:15; Ign. *Smyrn.* 1:2; 11:2; Ign. *Trall.* 11:2; Ign. *Eph.* 4:2.

54. Ernst Käsemann, *Leib und Leib Christi*, Beiträge zur historischen Theologie, no. 9 (Tübingen: Mohr [Siebeck], 1933), 156–59.

55. Franz-Heinrich Kettler, "Enderwartung und himmlischen Stufenbau in Kirchenbegriff des nachapostolischen Zeitalters," *TLZ* 79 (1954): 388.

56. Likewise Schlier, *Christus und die Kirche*, 49–60. See my critique in *Shepherd of Hermas*, 42–43.

signs of nascent Catholicism. And for some scholars sacramentalism, too, resulted from the transformation of eschatology.

From Eschatology to Sacramentalism

None of the so-called transformations are easy to document and clarify, but the rise of sacramentalism ranks high among the complicated issues of New Testament research. At this point we will simply outline the thesis without demonstrating the difficulties.

It was Hans Lietzmann who first delineated the two forms of Eucharist in the early church. On the one hand, the Jerusalem type (Serapion) consisted of the breaking of bread (1 Cor. 10:14–17), a prayer of thanksgiving (Acts 2:42–47), and a statement of expectation: *maranatha* (*Did.* 9–10; cf. 1 Cor. 16:22). On the other hand, there is the Pauline type (Hippolytus) as found in 1 Cor. 11:23–27, which obviously is joined to the Last Supper (Mark 14:22–25 and pars.), contains a statement of institution, and reenacts or recalls the death of Jesus, his resurrection, and his coming again.[57]

According to Lietzmann both forms, equally early, had an end-time expectation. It would be tempting to suppose that the breaking of bread was primarily an eschatological meal that was eventually replaced by the Pauline memorial meal, but Lietzmann cannot find any developmental bridge between the two types.[58] And both do have eschatological sentences (*Did.* 10:6; 1 Cor. 11:26). Nevertheless, it was the simple Jerusalem meal that did tend to disappear, while the Pauline Eucharist became the dominant type.

As time passed, eschatological sayings in the Eucharist liturgy waned in importance so that eventually the elements of the memorial meal became the means of salvation for the believer. In the sacraments, especially the Eucharist, the heavenly Christ was made available. According to Bultmann this shift can be seen most clearly in the famous "medicine of immortality" passage (Ign. *Eph.* 20:2),[59] though John 6:51–58 may have the same intent.[60] So the net effect of the eschatological failure was to shift the interest of the believer from the "destiny of the world" to the "salvation of the person" as mediated through a sacramental system.[61] It

---

57. Hans Lietzmann, *Mass and Lord's Supper: A Study in the History of the Liturgy,* trans. Dorothea H. G. Reeve (Leiden: Brill, 1979), 204–5.

58. Ibid., 206.

59. Bultmann, *History and Eschatology*, 53. See my critique in "The Text and Syntax of Ignatius PROS EPHESIOUS 20:2c," *VC* 22 (1968): 8–13.

60. Rudolf Bultmann, *The Gospel of John*, trans. G. R. Beasley-Murray (Oxford: Blackwell, 1971), 234–37.

61. Bultmann, *History and Eschatology*, 51

was this shift from eschatology to sacramentalism that gave rise to that church order and hierarchy so characteristic of early Catholicism.[62]

From Simplicity to Complexity

Although the debate over early Christian transformation centers primarily on the fate of eschatology, this was neither the first nor foremost concern of past New Testament scholarship. As mentioned above, it was F. C. Baur who first articulated a theology (or philosophy) of early Christian transformation. Dissatisfied with Catholic and Protestant historians both, he condemned their separation of the history of dogma from the history of the church itself.[63] Catholic historians falsely insisted that dogma did not change and Protestant historians unrealistically yearned for pre-Constantinian purity. By means of a complex, but dynamic, mixture of Kantian and Hegelian categories Baur demonstrated the unity of dogma with history (for Baur that meant church order).[64] As Jesus was at once divine and human so did he at the same time embody the idea of the Absolute in historical structures. The Spirit of Jesus — involving both absolute and history — was also articulated by Paul, but encroached upon by Judaism, or Jewish Christianity, a religion of law and ceremony. Increasingly the Absolute became determined by circumstances; that is, autonomous Christianity was gradually replaced by heteronomous Jewish Christianity. In reaction some Christians fled into an ahistorical spiritual purity called Gnosticism, to which others reacted by making of dogma a tradition, and changing the self-determining congregation into a universal hierarchy headed by Rome. This latter reaction he called early Catholicism.[65] As we have seen, Baur did not himself scorn dogma and church order. He understood them to be the twin expressions of the Spirit of a religion.[66] So the transformation of which Baur spoke was not the loss of the Spirit, but a shift in the intellectual and historical embodiment of the Spirit. Taken that way, Baur does see church history much like the non-transformationists do: historical changes are merely the working out of an interior dialectical dynamic. In the end, Protestantism best expresses the position of Jesus and Paul because it exists

---

62. Ibid., 53.

63. Ferdinand C. Baur, *Die Epochen der kirchlichen Geschichtschreibung* (Tübingen: Fues, 1852), 70–71; Peter C. Hodgson, ed., *Ferdinand Christian Baur on the Writing of Church History* (New York: Oxford University Press, 1968), 104–5.

64. Hodgson, *Baur on the Writing of Church History*, 57–59; F. C. Baur, *Die Epochen*, 12–17.

65. F. C. Baur, *The Church History of the First Three Centuries*, trans. A. Menzies (London: Williams and Norgate, 1878), 1:112–14, 184–87, and passim.

66. Hodgson, *Baur on the Writing of Church History*, 244.

autonomously (apart from the state!).[67] However difficult it may be precisely to place Baur in the history of New Testament interpretation, there can be no question about his pivotal importance. Many of his perceptions became the dogmas (usually greatly altered) of later transformationists. And to this day the transformation of Christianity, i.e., the rise of early Catholicism, usually is conceived in terms of growing dogmatization and increasing hierarchicalism.

The Transformation of Spirit to Law

In 1831 Baur published his famous study of the conflict between Peter and Paul at Corinth.[68] He showed that the Christ and Peter parties, on the one hand, representing Jewish Christianity, had attacked, on the other hand, the Paul and Apollos parties, representing the absolute religion of Jesus and Paul. The history of early Christianity is the gradual reconciliation of these two parties to the extent that the late work Acts can present a reconciling parallel account of both Peter and Paul.[69] Having determined this inner dynamic of early Christian history, Baur could place and understand other literature according to its function in the transformational continuum. *First Clement*, 1 Peter, and Ephesians represented, in the name of Paul, the reintroduction of the Old Testament (now however without Judaism) as a new law; the Pastoral Epistles, on the other hand, introduced, in the name of Paul, a church structure that could maintain "sound doctrine."[70] Even though the literary reconstruction of the Baur school has been totally rejected, still the thesis persists that the Pauline tradition, and therefore early Christianity, was altered by its struggle with Jewish Christianity.[71] This alteration resulted in the loss of autonomy (Spirit) and the return to heteronomy (law) in the guise of dogmas that reintroduced Judaism (e.g., the preexistence of Christ) and a hierarchy based on the Old Testament priesthood (*1 Clem.* 40).

Even though one must return to F. C. Baur for the origin of liberal-Protestant transformation theories, it was not his system of thought that prevailed. Baur did indeed set the problem, but it was Albrecht Ritschl

---

67. Ibid., 249.

68. F. C. Baur, "Die Christus Partie in der korinthischen Gemeinde, der Gegensatz des petrinischen und paulinischen Christentum in der ältesten Kirche, der Apostel Petrus in Rom," *Tübinger Zeitschrift für Theologie* 5 (1831): 61–206. Available also in Baur's *Ausgewählte Werke in Einzelangaben* (Stuttgart: Fromann, 1963), 1–146.

69. F. C. Baur, *Church History of the First Three Centuries*, 1:131–34. Baur's thesis was expanded by Otto Pfleiderer. On Acts as the last document of the reconciliation see his *History of Paulinism in the Primitive Church* (London: Williams and Norgate, 1877), 2:228–53.

70. Ibid., 134–214.

71. Johannes Munck, *Paul and the Salvation of Mankind,* trans. Frank Clarke (London: SCM, 1959), 69–86.

and the Ritschlians who provided the method. In the second edition of his *Die Entstehung der altkatholischen Kirche*,[72] Ritschl broke radically with Baur. As it pertains specifically to the problem of transformation, the following variations on Baur's theme resulted:

1. It was no longer Judaism that created the transformation, but Hellenism. Jewish Christianity had little influence on the early church, but early Catholicism arose from the anti-gnostic teaching of Irenaeus, Tertullian, Clement, and Origen. In fact a major cause of early Catholicism was the inability of Hellenistic (Gentile) Christianity to understand the Old Testament basis for the teaching of Jesus and Paul.[73]

2. Influenced by Schleiermacher more than Hegel or Kant, Ritschl no longer spoke of the "essence" of Christianity as the manifestation of the Idea in Jesus Christ, but more as the relationship (*Verhältnis*), on the one hand, of humanity with God, as determined by God and mediated through Jesus Christ, and, on the other hand, the concomitant behavior (*Verhalten*).[74] In early Catholicism this relationship was replaced by the particularity of Mosaic ceremonial laws.[75]

3. Earliest Christianity had officials of a Jewish type (presbyters and deacons, Acts 15) who were not distinguished in kind from the Jewish community as a whole. The monarchical episcopacy, which so characterizes early Catholicism, did not appear before Ignatius and itself derives from the Hellenistic world, not Judaism.[76]

In summary, Christianity consisted of two foci: the divine relationship and the human social counterpart (still keeping the unity of dogma and history sought by Baur), both of which were expressed with great clarity by Jesus and Paul. These relationships, Jewish in origin, were obfuscated on the one hand by Hellenistic dogma in the place of faith, and on the other hand by Roman organization in the place of a redeemed community — all held together by certain ceremonial practices reintroduced from Judaism. Though derived from Baur, it was Ritschl's perception of early Catholicism that became, and largely still is, the liberal Protestant approach to early Christian transformation. Needless to say, in

---

72. Albrecht Ritschl, *Die Entstehung der altkatholischen Kirche*, 2d ed. (Bonn: Marcus, 1857).

73. Ibid., 331, 338

74. Ibid., 331. Regarding philosophical changes see David L. Mueller, *An Introduction to the Theology of Albrecht Ritschl* (Philadelphia: Westminster, 1969), 24–25.

75. Ritschl, *Entstehung der altkatholischen Kirche*, 331–32.

76. Ibid., 419.

subsequent history there were many variations of the Ritschlian theme. Despite the complications caused by variations, we will try to deal with all types under the three categories set by Ritschl himself: from faith to dogma, from brotherhood to church, and from worship to sacrament.

From Faith to Dogma

For the followers of Ritschl, the faith of Jesus, though simple, was profound. Jesus called for a trust in God,[77] voluntary singleness of moral purpose,[78] and communion with the brethren[79] — or in the well-known words of Harnack, "the idea of God as Father...and...the message of the communion of brethren realising itself in love."[80]

This simple teaching gave rise to a community of believers in Christ. But when these believers, being Gentile, were cut off from the Jewish foundation of the faith, that original piety, that inner experience, was objectified in a Hellenistic philosophical structure that we call dogma. Or, in his famous dictum,[81] Harnack claims that the development of dogma was due to the transfer of the simple Jesus of Galilee to the complex soil of Greece.[82] Harnack did not try to locate precisely that transformation of the simple Gospel. Like Ritschl, he thought it was Irenaeus who, because of his struggle with Gnosticism (the acute secularization of Christianity), first expressed thoroughgoing Catholicism.[83] But others, such as Clement of Rome and Ignatius, had paved the way. For Harnack the primary theological shift occurred in the confession "Christ is Lord," where Jesus, at first the mediator, replaced God as redeemer.[84] Harnack's British counterpart, Edwin Hatch, was far more explicit. For him faith, in the Old Testament sense of the word, was "trust in a person" whereas in Greek philosophy it was "intellectual conviction."[85] Theologically speaking, Christianity was transformed when "faith passed beyond the moral stage, or simple trust in a person, to the metaphysical stage, or belief in certain propositions or technical definitions concerning Him, His nature, relations and actions."[86] Although allusions to some such

---

77. Adolf von Harnack, *History of Dogma*, trans. N. Buchanan (New York: Russell and Russell, 1958), 1:40–41, 63–64.

78. Ibid., 62–63. Also Adolf von Harnack and Wilhelm Herrmann, *Essays on the Social Gospel*, trans. G. M. Craik (New York: Putman's, 1907), 188–91.

79. Harnack, *History of Dogma*, 1:43–44, 67–68.

80. Ibid., 70.

81. Ibid., 71–72.

82. Ibid., 17, 21–22.

83. Ibid., 226–27.

84. Ibid., 183–203.

85. Edwin Hatch, *The Influence of Greek Ideas and Usages upon the Christian Church* (London: Williams and Norgate, 1890), 310–11.

86. Ibid., 312–13.

creedal statements might be found in the New Testament itself (Rom. 6:17; 1 Tim. 6:12; 2 Tim. 1:13; 2 John 9; Jude 3), by and large it was the Greek Apologists, such as Justin Martyr, who made the fatal transition.[87] We need to be aware, however, that the Harnack-Hatch critique means much more than simply a comparison of the "faith of Jesus" with "faith about Jesus." The ramifications of this position for later New Testament scholarship have been enormous and widespread. From this school has emanated a veritable onslaught against second-century Christianity. Harnack himself led the attack:

> How and by what influence was the living faith transformed into the creed to be believed, the surrender to Christ into a philosophic Christology, the Holy Church into the *corpus permixtum*, the glowing hope of the Kingdom of heaven into a doctrine of immortality and deification, prophecy into a learned exegesis and theological science, the bearers of the spirit into clerics, the brethren into laity held in tutelage, miracles and healings into nothing, or into priestcraft, the fervent prayers into a solemn ritual, renunciation of the world into a jealous dominion over the world, the "spirit" into constraint and law?[88]

We shall attempt to enumerate briefly the results of the Ritschl-Harnack-Hatch bridgehead.

From Hebrew to Greek

The Hellenization of the faith has been documented primarily by the "word study" method in New Testament scholarship. It would be rash to suggest that the entire impetus for the Greek-Hebrew debate is lodged in the Ritschlian system, yet its popularity and power would be difficult to explain otherwise. However appropriate to nineteenth century liberalism, its roots can be traced elsewhere. To discover in Hebrew language (and translation Greek) a more primitive pattern of thought derives from the interest in primitivism generated by the anthropologist Lévy-Bruhl at the turn of the century.[89] For biblical scholarship, that force was felt primarily through the seminal work of Johannes Pedersen,[90] and by a host of others who made the "biblical mentality" normative for interpreting the New Testament.[91] At the same time, "covenant theology" came into

---

87. Ibid., 314–15
88. Harnack, *History of Dogma*, 1:45–46.
89. Lucien Lévy-Bruhl, *The Primitive Mentality*, trans. L. Clare (London: Allen and Unwin, 1923), 442–43.
90. Johannes Pedersen, *Israel* (Copenhagen: Branner og Korch, 1926), 1/2:132.
91. Thorlief Boman, *Hebrew Thought Compared with Greek*, trans. J. Moreau (London: SCM, 1960), 17–26; Brevard Childs, *Biblical Theology in Crisis* (Philadelphia:

its own, stressing, from a more conservative perspective than Harnack's, of course, the unity of the Bible and the uniqueness of its message.[92] From this combination of interests came the theological wordbook movement that has engaged a high percentage of the labor of New Testament scholars this century.[93]

The collaboration of all these forces resulted in the following "Biblical theology" consensus: (1) the faith of the New Testament should be understood from the Old Testament forward, not the Fathers backward; (2) New Testament faith was a simple, primitive trust relationship and a straightforward moral code that had no philosophical value, indeed, was destroyed by the postapostolic Greek Apologists. The philosopher Emile Bréhier states the consensus well:

> While in Rome the philosopher was preaching rationalism, in Galilee Jesus was instructing uneducated people who knew nothing at all about the Greek sciences or the Greek conception of the world, and who could grasp parables and images more readily than the intricacies of dialectical argumentation.... The development of philosophical thought was not strongly influenced by the advent of Christianity and ... there is no Christian philosophy.[94]

The "Hebraic mentality" approach to the New Testament created a new canon within the canon out of those writings presumably untouched by Hellenism, or at least by Greek philosophy. In this way nontransformationists were deprived of their favorite historical bridge: second-century Christian literature. In light of this division it is surprising that not more New Testament scholars have responded in the manner of Claude Trésmontant: the so-called Hebraic mentality has a metaphysic in its own right.[95] However, for our purposes the point at which New Testament Christianity became Hellenized will be an issue to which we must return again and again.

From Agape to Eros

At first glance Anders Nygren's famous transformationist slogan — from *agape* to *eros* — will appear to be a maverick. To be sure, he does in-

Westminster, 1970), 32–50; James Barr, *The Semantics of Biblical Language* (Oxford: Oxford University Press, 1961), 8–10.

92. Gerhard Friedrich, "Die Problematik eines Theologischen Wörterbuchs zum Neuen Testament," *Studia Evangelica* (*Texte und Untersuchungen* 73) (1959): 481–86.

93. Childs, *Biblical Theology in Crisis*, 47; Hermann Cremer, *Biblisch-theologisches Wörterbuch der neutestamentlichen Grazität* (Gotha: Perthes, 1911), xvi–xvii.

94. Emile Bréhier, *The History of Philosophy: The Hellenistic and Roman Age*, trans. W. Baskin (Chicago: University Press, 1965), 219, 225.

95. C. Trésmontant, *La métaphysique du christianisme* (Paris: Editions du Seuil, 1961), 13; *A Study of Hebrew Thought*, trans. M. F. Gibson (New York: Desclee, 1960), 175–78.

sist that Christianity changed,[96] but that "fall" has nothing to do with increasing philosophy or growing ecclesiasticism. His understanding of early Catholicism — a synthesis of *agape* with *eros* and *nomos* — reminds us simultaneously of Baur's Judaizing and Harnack's Hellenizing. Nevertheless, Nygren's *Agape and Eros* does belong in the Harnackian camp. Nygren, like Ritschl, started with the search for a religious a priori in Kantian-Schleiermacherian categories.[97] Instead of Schleiermacher's "feeling of absolute dependence," Nygren spoke of "communion with God" as the essence of a religion, especially Christianity.[98]

Communion with God in early Christianity was designated by the Greek word *agape*, "unmotivated" love. It was "indifferent to value," "creative," and initiated "fellowship with God."[99] In contrast, Jewish fellowship with God was determined by *nomos*, law; while in the Hellenistic world it was designated by the word *eros*, acquisitive love, or humanity's way to the divine (in contrast to God's way to humanity).

Nygren finds *agape* defined in such parables as the prodigal son (Luke 15:11–32) or the laborers in the vineyard (Matt. 20:1–16). In Paul's *agape* of the cross, early Christian theology reached its apex, expressed not only in God's action in Jesus Christ (2 Cor. 5:18–19), but also as Paul's basic love motif (1 Cor. 13). After the apostolic period all three motifs could be found in Christianity: the *nomos* type in the Apostolic Fathers (especially the "two ways" [see *Did.* 1:1]) and the Apologists; *eros* in Gnosticism; and *agape* in Marcion.[100] Eventually all three were synthesized by Augustine. Theologically speaking, *agape*, being "voluntary" and "unmotivated" corresponds to the divine autonomy in more Tübingenian terms, while *nomos*, which requires performance prior to acceptance, and *eros*, which requires reciprocation prior to acceptance, correspond to heteronomy. In Nygren's *Agape and Eros* we find yet another way of saying that the pure, simple, untrammeled relationship with God found among the first Christians was later adulterated during the postapostolic period.

---

96. Anders Nygren, *Essence of Christianity*, trans. P. Watson (London: Epworth, 1960), 11–12.

97. Nygren, *Dogmatikens vetenskapliga grundläggning med särskild hönsyn till den Kant-Schleiermacherska problemställningen*, Lunds Universitets Årsskrift N.F. Avd. 1, Bd. 17, Nr. 8 (Lund: Gleerup, 1922), 161–65.

98. Nygren, *Essence of Christianity*, 46–47, 56–57; *Agape and Eros*, trans. P. Watson (London: SPCK, 1953), 45, 68, 206–7; see also Bernhard Erling, "Motif Research as a General Historical Method," in *The Philosophy and Theology of Anders Nygren*, ed. C. W. Kegley (Carbondale, Ill.: Southern Illinois University Press, 1970), 101–19; William A. Johnson, *On Religion: A Study of Theological Method in Schleiermacher and Nygren* (Leiden: Brill, 1964), 91–92.

99. Nygren, *Agape and Eros*, 75–81.

100. Ibid., 253.

From the Human Jesus to the Divine Christ

It would be unkind to lay the quest for the historical Jesus also at Schleiermacher's feet, but his considerable influence in the argument must not be overlooked. For the problem had been set by Rationalism well before Baur or Ritschl. It was Hermann Samuel Reimarus who first distinguished in an irreconcilable manner between the religion of Jesus and the faith of the disciples.[101] He found in Jesus' teaching a natural (rational) religion, while in the disciples he found an unscrupulous crew that, after Jesus failed to return,[102] fabricated the story about his resurrection, his supernatural nature, and his miraculous powers.[103] Reimarus intended his anonymous work to be an attack on orthodox Christian doctrine. But his posthumous publisher, G. E. Lessing, in making them public as the *Wolfenbüttel Fragments* (1774–78), intended to show that Christian dogma need not depend on historical antecedent; that is, the Christian faith does not need a historical origin in order to be grounded in reason, or, as he said in his famous dictum: the religion is not true because the evangelists and apostles taught it, but they taught it because it was true. Written traditions must be explained according to their inner truth, and no writing down of tradition can give it inner truth if it has none.[104]

But Schleiermacher, in crossing Lessing's "ditch" between faith and history, insisted on the unity of Jesus with his disciples. Religion was for Schleiermacher an inner consciousness of God perfectly manifested in Jesus of Nazareth, who redeemed persons by calling forth that consciousness in them also. Schleiermacher did distinguish between Jesus and his redemptive act (*Urbildlichkeit*) and later communication and assimilation of that God-consciousness (*Vorbildlichkeit*), but he made it quite clear that the disciples did not misunderstand or alter Jesus' consciousness.

Significantly enough, Schleiermacher took the Jesus of the Fourth Gospel and of Hebrews to construct his *Urbild*.[105] So although the perfect God-consciousness of Jesus aroused a similar consciousness in his disciples, still, by distinguishing between *Urbildlichkeit* and *Vorbildlich-*

---

101. Schweitzer, *Quest of the Historical Jesus*, 20–21; A. C. Lundsteen, *Hermann Samuel Reimarus und die Anfänge der Leben-Jesu Forschung* (Copenhagen: Olsen, 1939); C. H. Talbert, ed., *Reimarus: Fragments* (Philadelphia: Fortress, 1970), 26.
102. Therefore Reimarus anticipated Weiss and Schweitzer. See Hermann Samuel Reimarus, *The Goal of Jesus and His Disciples*, ed. G. W. Buchanan (Leiden: Brill, 1970), 1.
103. Reimarus, *Goal of Jesus*, part 1, 7; part 2, 53.
104. Gottfried Ephraim Lessing, *Werke*, ed. H. G. Göpfert (Munich: Hauser, 1973), 7:813.
105. Friedrich Schleiermacher, *The Christian Faith*, trans. H. R. Mackintosh and J. S. Stewart (Edinburgh: T. & T. Clark, 1928), 377–80; Richard R. Niebuhr, *Schleiermacher on Christ and Religion* (New York: Scribner's, 1964), 219–24.

keit, between proclaimer and proclaimed, between *Chronik* (historical chronicle, or *Historie*) and *Geschichte* (biography),[106] and in placing God-consciousness over against dogma as the essence of Christianity, Schleiermacher made it possible for at least two things to occur. First, the Ritschlians (Harnack, Hatch, and countless others) could speak of an increasingly earlier shift from the essence of Christianity, the Fatherhood of God,[107] to sterile objective dogma. Furthermore, because Jesus' relationship to God was a valid object of historical research, it was possible to move behind the documents of the New Testament to the historical Jesus himself. From this came not only the "liberal lives of Jesus" that so aggravated Schweitzer,[108] but eventually studies, such as Wrede's, that questioned also the historicity of Jesus' consciousness.[109] Second, Schleiermacher also set up the reaction of Strauss. David Friedrich Strauss, writing in the stream of German Rationalism, expanded Lessing's thesis with considerable critical skill. He showed that most of the Gospel stories, meaning primarily narrative material, were "historical myths" (theology in the form of historical narrative) that were produced as a matter of course by the early Christian community.

The nonmythical Jesus was not the historical Jesus sought by the Ritschlians, but one on whom no theology could be based. A Christian faith (rational, of course) would have to be constructed without being historically based on the man from Nazareth. Strauss "destroyed" the historical Jesus in order to set free the formation of rational faith in the human soul: "If Schleiermacher claims a miracle for the origination of his real Christ, we have an equal right to claim one for the origination of the ideal of a Christ in the human soul."[110] Granting many intervening distinctions, it is not difficult to see in Strauss's Jesus an antecedent for the role of Jesus in Bultmann's New Testament theology, while post-Bultmannians, with their "new quest," take up once more the argument of Schleiermacher regarding the unity of Jesus and his disciples — except this time that unity occurs in the words rather than the redemptive act or narrative of his God-consciousness. Our final example of this quest will be the Jesus Seminar.

---

106. Friedrich Schleiermacher, *Life of Jesus*, trans. S. Maclean Gilmour (Philadelphia: Fortress, 1974), 1.

107. Adolf von Harnack, *The Essence of Christianity*, trans. T. B. Saunders (London: Benn, 1958), 54–59.

108. Schweitzer, *Quest of the Historical Jesus*, 307.

109. William Wrede, *The Messianic Secret*, trans. J. C. G. Greig (London: Clarke, 1971), 6–7, 230.

110. David Friedrich Strauss, *The Life of Jesus Critically Examined*, trans. George Eliot and Mary Hennell (London: Sonnenschein, 1898), 772. On how Strauss saw himself in this debate see his entire concluding dissertation (pp. 757–84).

In any case, the major theological transformation of the New Testament must have been the shift from "Jesus" to "Lord"[111] — whether or not such a change builds on a sympathetic or mute Jesus. For sooner or later either the philosophical divinization of Jesus or the church's defensive response to Gnosticism destroyed the gospel of the earliest Christians.[112]

Strangely enough, little attention was given to the Hellenization of God-consciousness itself. Because nineteenth-century Protestantism was so concerned with the anthropological nature of religion or with communion with God, little study was made regarding changing understandings of the nature of God. For the most part, though, these scholars saw a change in *theo*logy late in the second century.[113] This Hellenization of God, i.e., the cosmologizing of divine love, was perpetrated, from Harnack's point of view, by Marcion's separation of the Old Testament creator God from the New Testament redeemer God.[114] The church responded to Marcion with the canonization of both Testaments as well as a metaphysically grounded doctrine of God.[115] By and large, transformationists have not been interested in how the understanding of God changed, so Harnack's observations have remained a side issue.

From Psychosomatic Unity to Hellenistic Dualism

Just as radical changes occurred in the understanding of Jesus (and God), so also that positive view of humanity found in the Old Testament was transformed into a negative, dualistic anthropology. This transformation gave rise to the asceticism of the early church.[116] Probably it was the Ritschlian-Lüdemann complex that first distinguished between Jewish and Hellenistic understandings of σάρξ,[117] which, to the misfortune of later Christianity, lay side by side in the letters of the apostle Paul.[118]

---

111. Wilhelm Bousset, *Kyrios Christos,* trans. J. E. Steely (Nashville: Abingdon, 1970), 116–17.

112. Eduard Schweizer, *Jesus,* trans. David E. Green (London: SCM, 1971), 169–71; R. Bultmann, "The Christological Confession of the World Council of Churches," in *Essays Philosophical and Theological,* trans. J. C. G. Greig (London: SCM, 1955), 276–80.

113. J. K. Mozley, *The Impassibility of God* (Cambridge: Cambridge University Press, 1926), 28.

114. Adolf von Harnack, *Marcion: Das Evangelium vom fremden Gott* (Leipzig: Hinrichs, 1921), 246–47.

115. Harnack, *History of Dogma,* 2:202–6; James Mackinnon, *From Christ to Constantine* (London: Longmans Green, 1936), 364, 366.

116. Bultmann, *Theology of the New Testament,* 2:207–8; see also Samuel Laeuchli, *The Language of Faith* (Nashville: Abingdon, 1962), 153.

117. Hermann Lüdemann, *Biblical Christianity,* trans. M. A. Canney (London: Owen, 1905), 80–81.

118. At least H. J. Holtzmann, writing on the same subject, remarks that anything prior to Lüdemann would be out of date. See his *Lehrbuch der neutestamentlichen Theologie* (Freiburg i.B.: Mohr, 1897), 2:10 n. 3.

Lüdemann claimed, for example, in an exegesis of Rom. 1–8, that in chapters 1–4 σάρξ was used by Paul in the Jewish sense of family and human solidarity (4:1), while in chapters 7 and 8 it could be used as the seat or locus of evil (8:3).[119] Lüdemann further identified the σάρξ ἁμαρτίας with the outer person (2 Cor. 4:16; cf. Rom. 7:22–25), thereby making apparent a dualistic view of the human being (a soul entrapped in a body) already in the teaching of Paul.[120] Holtzmann, who now has placed Paul among the early Catholics (!), follows Lüdemann in his Hellenistic reading of flesh and spirit, and inner and outer person in Paul.[121] Not all scholars agreed with this anthropological analysis,[122] but nevertheless it became standard exegesis for those who found in Paul the beginnings of Hellenistic Christianity.[123]

The idea of an anthropological transformation in the early church received both confirmation and revision in 1955 from Oscar Cullmann's Ingersoll Lectures on immortality.[124] He insisted that a psychosomatic view of humanity supporting a belief in death and resurrection could not also support an anthropological dualism that led to immortality of the soul.[125] The New Testament clearly maintained a doctrine of pyschosomatic resurrection throughout and so did the church, even through the apologists (Justin Martyr, *Dial.* 80).[126]

From Brotherhood to Hierarchy

The twin anchors of those arguing for the continuity of the "Catholic" church[127] have been the appropriate development of doctrine and the historical succession of the priesthood. Baur himself insisted on the congruity of faith and organization as the church moved from autonomy to heteronomy. Once the Ritschlian arguments took away any notion of an interior development of Christianity, there was no need to yoke together

---

119. H. Lüdemann, *Die Anthropologie des Apostels Paulus* (Kiel: Universitäts Buchhandlung, 1872), 198–217.

120. Ibid., 27–31, 48.

121. Holtzmann, *Lehrbuch*, 2:9–22.

122. W. David Stacey, *The Pauline View of Man* (London: Macmillan, 1956), 40–55.

123. Wilfred L. Knox, *St Paul and the Church of the Gentiles* (Cambridge: Cambridge University Press, 1939), 136–40.

124. Oscar Cullmann, *Immortality of the Soul or Resurrection of the Dead? The Witness of the New Testament* (London: Epworth, 1958).

125. Ibid., 25

126. Ibid., 59–60.

127. Though the arguments presented in this chapter tend to be a nineteenth- and twentieth-century debate between Roman Catholic and Protestant scholars, it would be a serious error to suppose that this is the actual dividing line. For example, arguments defending the church organization here called Catholic could be found in almost any Anglican or conservative Protestant study. Furthermore, almost any of the arguments here labeled "non-Catholic" could be found proposed in studies written by Roman Catholics.

"faith and order." Yet these two aspects of Christianity remained the two primary loci of the debate. So nineteenth-century liberals attacked not only the Hellenization of faith, but they also tried to document the increased Hellenization of church life, though in contrast to Baur they did not see any particular unity in the development, i.e., the elevation of the bishop did not correspond inherently with the divinization of Jesus.

While the distinction between clergy and laity, as well as the threefold ministry itself may be found even in the New Testament (1 Tim. 3–5), it probably was Irenaeus who first articulated the doctrine of an ordained succession of bishops reaching back to the apostles themselves, a succession that taught only what had been delivered to them.[128] Regardless of whether such an assertion is demonstrable, liberal Protestants did claim that it was Irenaeus who solidified the hierarchical principle of early Catholicism.[129] The problem of a dominically ordained threefold ministry was first stated, in defense of the episcopacy (!), by Richard Rothe in 1837.[130] He argued that "in the...so-called apostolic period (up to A.D. 70) there was no Christian church, but at first only isolated Christian communities."[131] These communities were held together by the authority of the apostles, who at death were replaced locally by apostolic delegates (bishops) in each community.[132] Ritschl shifted Rothe's argument for his own purposes. He saw a development of two entirely different episcopal systems. One was the Jewish Christian or Jerusalem organization, which copied Jesus and the Twelve with an analogous bishop and twelve presbyters. The Jerusalem-style organization died out with the Bar Kochba rebellion, although as a system it was transplanted to Alexandria. However, among the Gentile churches such a distinction between members (laity) and leaders (clergy) was not to be found. The local churches were administered by presbyters who acted as "presidents." It was only with Irenaeus that the bishopric as an office was to be found.[133]

Although Rothe and Ritschl broke the ice, it remained for British scholars, struggling with definitions of ministry offered by the Oxford movement,[134] to state the historical case for a postapostolic origin of the threefold ministry. In 1868 J. B. Lightfoot included in his commentary

---

128. See the famous passage in *Haer.* 3.3.
129. Heinrich Ziegler, *Irenaeus der Bischof von Lyon: Ein Beitrag zur Entstehungsgeschichte der altkatholischen Kirche* (Berlin: Reimer, 1871), 143–47.
130. R. Rothe, *Die Anfänge der Christlichen Kirche und ihrer Verfassung* (Wittenberg: Zimmermann, 1837), 1:141–310.
131. Ibid., 310.
132. Ibid., 309.
133. Ritschl, *Entstehung der altkatholischen Kirche*, 434–41.
134. See the summary in A. T. Hanson's introduction to R. C. Moberly's *Ministerial Priesthood* (reprint, London: SPCK, 1969), vii–xi.

on Philippians a pioneering essay, "The 'Christian Ministry."[135] Though obviously dependent on his two predecessors,[136] he argued in quite a different way that the first church had no priesthood, or perhaps, all were priests. Administrative functions were gifts of the spirit — both the permanent (bishop, presbyter and deacon) and the temporary (apostle, prophet, and evangelist). The development of ecclesiastical organization was simply the emergence of a permanent ministry "as the Church assumed a more settled form and the higher but temporary offices, such as the apostolate, fell away."[137] As for the permanent offices, the diaconate was created de novo, the presbytery was borrowed from contemporary Judaism, while the episcopate developed later from the presbytery when the church was under attack and dissensions were widespread.[138]

Continuing in the same debate, the British scholar Edwin Hatch delivered in 1880 his famous Bampton lectures, "The Organization of the Early Christian Churches." He argued that even the presbytery, i.e., rule by senior heads of member families, was common to many cultures. Consequently its use among Hellenistic church circles could be due to Greco-Roman patterns rather than Jewish. The development of the episcopal office was simply the gradual supremacy of a "president" of the presbytery — a style not different from other Hellenistic associations.[139] Harnack was so impressed by this argument that he translated it for the German-speaking audience in 1883.[140] The publication of the newly discovered *Didache* that same year gave him just the proof he needed for Hatch's thesis. In his study of that document Harnack found the decay — by death or loss of significance — of the universal leadership of the church (apostles, prophets, and teachers) accompanied by the takeover of their organizational functions (spiritual, patriarchal, and administrative) by coequal local leaders (bishops, presbyters, and deacons).[141] A fourth order of leadership, the aristocratic, came into being when the previously collegial bishop took over all three functions.[142]

---

135. J. B. Lightfoot, *St Paul's Epistle to the Philippians* (London: Macmillan, 1868), 179–267.

136. Ibid., 185 n. 1.

137. Ibid., 184.

138. Ibid., 194.

139. Edwin Hatch, *The Organization of the Early Christian Churches* (London: Rivingtons, 1888), 62–66, 84–85.

140. Edwin Hatch, *Die Gesellschaftsverfassung der christlichen Kirchen im Altertum*, trans. Adolf von Harnack (Giessen: Ricker, 1883).

141. 141. Adolf von Harnack, *Die Lehre der Zwölf Apostel* (Leipzig: Hinrichs, 1884), 145–46.

142. Ibid., 153–55. Regarding the influence of the *Didache* on Harnack see especially Olaf Linton, *Das Problem der Urkirche in der neueren Forschung*, Uppsala Universitets Årsskrift, Teologi 2 (Leipzig: A. Lorentz, 1932), 31–48

The Hatch-Harnack thesis was so widely accepted by New Testament scholars that Olaf Linton could speak of it as a consensus.[143] Of course the consensus had its able opponents,[144] but as a matter of fact the future belonged to an even more radical train of thought, rather than the conservative. For Rudolf Sohm's debate with Harnack served not only to sharpen the issues, but also to change the nature of the issue. Sohm argued that the earliest church was a charismatic entity that corresponded to any meeting of two or three gathering in Jesus' name.[145] That community had no inherently correct structure, no priesthood, no fixed body of doctrine, and above all, no church law.[146] The church assembled primarily for the purpose of celebrating the Eucharist.[147] At this house church meeting it was necessary for someone to preside and for other elected representatives to assist. Here, then, is the origin of the bishop and elders. However, such an organization arose from the community itself as directed by the Spirit.[148] Even in Acts and the Pastoral Epistles the presence of bishops and elders only reflects this flexible charismatic leadership that developed around the Eucharist.[149] It was when the offices (especially that of the bishop) became inflexible and "successive" that the essence of Christianity was lost and Catholicism began. The essence of Catholicism is that it cannot distinguish between the church in a religious sense and the church in its legal sense.[150]

For, as goes the famous dictum of Sohm, "Das Kirchenrecht steht mit dem Wesen der Kirche in Widerspruch."[151] The fatal change occurred with Clement of Rome who, in response to a Corinthian attempt to change its presbyter, insisted that apostolic ordination should determine legitimate leadership (*1 Clem.* 44:2).[152] It was Ignatius then who insisted that no meeting of the community could be held without the bishop (Ign.

---

143. Linton, *Problem der Urkirche,* 29.

144. For example, R. C. Moberly, *Ministerial Priesthood* (London: Murray, 1897); Charles Gore, *The Church and the Ministry* (London: Rivingtons, 1882).

145. Rudolph Sohm, *Outlines of Church History,* trans. M. Sinclair (London: Macmillan, 1895), 32; *Kirchenrecht* (Leipzig: Duncker & Humboldt, 1892), 1:20.

146. Sohm, *Outlines of Church History,* 32; *Kirchenrecht,* 1:22–38.

147. Sohm, *Outlines of Church History,* 36; *Kirchenrecht,* 1:67–68. In his debate with Harnack, Sohm did agree that the congregation also met around the Word, but this meeting was not "led." It was a spiritual "free-for-all" (cf. 1 Cor. 14:26) or "pneumatische Anarchie." See Sohm's *Wesen und Ursprung des Katholizismus,* Abhandlungen der philologisch-historischen Klasse der königlich sächsischen Gesellschaft der Wissenschaft, Bd. 27 (Leipzig: Teubner, 1909), 384.

148. Sohm, *Kirchenrecht,* 1:68, 84; *Wesen und Ursprung,* 377.

149. Sohm, *Kirchenrecht,* 1:69.

150. Sohm, *Wesen und Ursprung,* 345.

151. Sohm, *Kirchenrecht,* 1:1.

152. Ibid., 69.

Magn. 4; Ign. *Trall.* 7).[153] At this point "nicht die Gemeinde hat den Episkopat, sondern der Episkopat hat die Gemeinde hervorgebracht."[154]

At first glance it would appear Sohm only carried the Harnack-Hatch argument to its logical conclusion. But far more is involved. For Sohm the rise of Catholicism is *not* due to Hellenistic intellectualizing and moralizing, but the shift from a charismatic community to a legal community based on divine law.[155] For Sohm the development of church organization was no longer a concomitant aspect of rising dogmatic speculation (Baur, Ritschl, Harnack, and Hatch), but an institutionalization of the worship structure. In this sense Sohm was not just a radical Harnackian but the first of another breed, the *Religionsgeschichte* school that saw the transformation of early Christianity primarily in terms of changes in the confessional and liturgical life.

From Charisma to Cultic Society

It would be foolhardy to categorize under this rubric all those who perceive the fall of early Christianity as the loss of the Spirit. While that would be the trademark of the Sohm position, one cannot easily distinguish between his original community and Harnack's universal or "spiritual" ministry.[156] A list of those who see the loss of the Spirit as the basic transformation of early Christianity would include nearly every New Testament scholar in the nineteenth and twentieth centuries. Gunkel ended his work on the Holy Spirit with precisely that conclusion.[157] Early Catholicism has substituted the office for the Spirit. In the worship of the early church, says Alexander Macdonald, at first the Spirit was manifest, but the fatal flaw came with the "waning" of the "first Enthusiasm."[158] In more recent times Eduard Schweizer can say that the development of an official church, or, conversely, special groups of ecstatics would be a sign that the *Gemeinde* "therefore could no longer suppose that the Spirit had been given to all its members."[159] Or Campenhausen can conclude that Paul based all on the Spirit with no authority figures. So the

---

153. Ibid., 193–94.

154. Ibid., 195.

155. Sohm, *Wesen und Ursprung*, 338.

156. A. von Harnack, *The Mission and Expansion of Christianity,* trans. James Moffatt (New York: Harper, 1962), 341.

157. Hermann Gunkel, *Die Wirkungen des heiligen Geistes* (Göttingen: Vandenhoeck & Ruprecht, 1888), 110.

158. Alexander B. Macdonald, *Christian Worship in the Primitive Church* (Edinburgh: T. & T. Clark, 1934), 68. Macdonald likely owed his structure to Ernest F. Scott's study *The Spirit in the New Testament* (London: Hodder and Stoughton, 1923), 244–45.

159. Eduard Schweizer, *Geist und Gemeinde im Neuen Testament und Heute,* Theologisch Existenz Heute, N.F. 32 (Munich: Kaiser Verlag, 1952), 27.

first Christian elders were "obedient to the Spirit," even in *1 Clement*, but in Ignatius and the Pastorals we begin to see office for the sake of office.[160] All in all, such opinions do not differ radically from previous categories of nineteenth-century German theology. Christianity was transformed from a voluntary autonomous expression to a religion of authority and heteronomy. In this way Protestantism and Catholicism can be distinguished.[161]

Whether Sohm consciously broke from his predecessors cannot be easily determined. Certainly he realized his argument was different in kind from that of Harnack.[162] In any case the *religionsgeschichtlich* perception of early Christian transformation differed from the Ritschlian. In *religionsgeschichtlich* analysis the arena of concern no longer was dogma, church organization or ethics, but the nature of the Christian cult and the function of its cultic center — Jesus the Lord. Perhaps Wilhelm Bousset best presented the new thesis. For him the church was not gradually Hellenized. From its inception it had been Hellenistic. The greatest historical moment of the church was its nearly immediate shift to that Hellenistic Christian community from which came Paul and the most of what we know as early Christianity.[163] That primitive Hellenistic community, like other Hellenistic communities of the East, organized itself as a close fellowship around its cultic Lord.[164] Paul came from such a community, and his writings reflect a corporate mysticism with Jesus (Christ as Lord).[165] It was the cultic Lord or Spirit who guided the community and gave the members gifts of the Spirit (charisma).[166] At the center was the sacramental identification with the Lord by dying and rising with him. In time this primitive community developed into a cultic society, a mystery religion, in which the Lord no longer reigned, but the community dispensed its gifts through the sacraments (Ignatius).[167] This was the second great moment of the church — the shift to Catholicism. Now, for the first time, the Christian community was open to intellectual dogmatization (the Apologists) and authoritative leadership.

---

160. Hans von Campenhausen, *Ecclesiastical Authority and Spiritual Power in the Church of the First Three Centuries*, trans. J. A. Baker (London: Black, 1969), 79–80, 84, 97–123

161. Auguste Sabatier, *The Religions of Authority and the Religions of the Spirit*, trans. Louise Seymour Houghton (London: Williams and Norgate, 1904), xxiv. For his relationship to Schleiermacher see Thomas Sillistone, *Religion, Symbolism and Meaning* (Oxford: Cassirer, 1968), 17.

162. Sohm, *Wesen und Ursprung*, 338.

163. Bousset, *Kyrios Christos*, 12.

164. Ibid., 146.

165. Ibid., 167

166. Ibid., 160–72.

167. Ibid., 83.

Increasingly scholarship has moved from a formal to an experiential understanding of early Christianity. That is, Sohm and Bousset would argue that the earliest Christians experienced a Lordship of Christ and a fellowship with its concomitant spiritual gifts (charisma) that the second-century Christians did not enjoy. From this perspective came the sociological analyses of the early church. For example, Ernst Troeltsch described early Christianity as a cult formed around the Pneuma-Christ, which consisted of two sacraments: baptism and the Eucharist. For various reasons — growth of hysterical enthusiasm, syncretism, lack of a secure sociological point of reference — there arose a sacerdotal and sacramental society that we call early Catholicism.[168] However, the original impulse was not lost. It appeared again and again in the medieval monastic movement and later in the sect-type church.[169] And as for Sohm and Bousset, few have accepted their picture of early Christianity, yet the power of their thesis continues in various guises. T. F. Torrance, arguing from a theological survey of the period, shows that grace, which lies at the heart of the work of Christ, became, starting with Ignatius, a depository of the church, dispensed in the form of sacraments.[170] Or Vincent Taylor can argue that in Hebrews the eucharistic sacrifice of Jesus lost its meaning when separated from the mystical suffering with Christ as found in Paul.[171] Though differently stated by a variety of authors, the net result would be the same: the church lost its original nature when it lost its charisma.[172]

From Gospel to Law

In categorizing transformationist theories under these four rubrics — incursion of heresy, failure of eschatology, increasing complexity, and loss of charisma — we have touched the major historical perspectives. Nevertheless, there are variations on these themes that are worthy of mention even though they ought not be understood as yet another category. For example, Reformation scholars in general and Lutherans in particular speak axiomatically of the transformation of the Pauline *gospel* to an early Catholic *law*. It would be futile to attempt to trace the history

---

168. Ernst Troeltsch, *The Social Teaching of the Christian Church*, trans. Olive Wyon (New York: Macmillan, 1931), 89–92.

169. Ibid., 161–64.

170. T. F. Torrance, *The Doctrine of Grace in the Apostolic Fathers* (London: Oliver and Boyd, 1948), 141.

171. Vincent Taylor, *The Atonement in New Testament Teaching* (London: Epworth, 1940), 187.

172. E. Käsemann, "Geist und Geistesgaben im NT," in *Die Religion in Geschichte und Gegenwart: Handwörterbuch für Theologie und Religionswissenschaft*, 7 vols., 3d ed. (Tübingen: Mohr [Siebeck], 1957–65), 2:1271–79.

of this "transformation" theory, and it would be repetitive. The very first Protestant scientific historian of the New Testament, F. C. Baur, utilized the distinction even though his use of law and gospel fit better in Hegelian categories than the New Testament.[173] But whether gospel was understood as the coming of the Lord, the Spirit, freedom, the Absolute, redemption, simple faith, charisma, or whatever, it was the gospel that was lost and the law that prevailed. Whatever law may be, it will be important for our study to note from whence comes the law. For example, some scholars consider the early Christian faith a unique point in history, when people rose above their normal way of life. So Sohm considers the rise of early Catholicism as the return to "natural man." "The natural person is a born Catholic."[174] Others might agree for various reasons. Dibelius supposed that even Paul introduced law and ethics because his eschatological teachings were too impractical for the average person.[175] Goppelt, representing a more classic Protestant position, is not so kind. For him there were two ways in which second-century Christians adapted to their historical existence.

The first was to stress the proclamation of the Word concretized in the sacrament. This part came from the New Testament. The second was to relax the discipline of the church by means of a system of penance. This part came from the Apostolic Fathers. "The early Catholic alignment originated with the Apostolic Fathers because the apostolic traditions were watered down during the post-apostolic age and were enervated by Hellenistic and Jewish influences."[176]

In sharp contrast others see the new law as a heightening of the "imperative" at the expense of the "indicative."[177] For Bultmann this means primarily an emphasis on sanctification and renunciation of the world, as far even as encrateia and asceticism (*Shepherd of Hermas*),[178] though he admits that some tendencies led to the adoption of ethical demands familiar and available to all (Pastoral Epistles).[179] But the latter observation seems to have been overlooked by others. Eva Aleith carried the thesis to an extreme by claiming that the Pauline gospel was replaced almost

---

173. Baur, *Church History of the First Three Centuries*, 82–83. See also the Tübingen historian Albert Schwegler, *Das nachapostolische Zeitalter* (Tübingen: Fues, 1846), 34–35.

174. Sohm, *Outlines of Church History*, 35.

175. Martin Dibelius, *A Fresh Approach to the New Testament and Early Christian Literature* (New York: Scribner's, 1936), 142–50, 219–21.

176. Leonhard Goppelt, "The Existence of the Church in History According to Apostolic and Early Catholic Thought," in *Current Issues in New Testament Interpretation*, ed. W. Klassen and G. F. Snyder (New York: Harper & Brothers, 1962), 204, 207.

177. Bultmann, *Theology of the New Testament*, 2:201–18.

178. Ibid., 220–24.

179. Ibid., 225.

immediately by a Catholic works-righteousness.[180] And with Hellenistic dualism came a hatred or fear of the flesh that led inevitably to its denial.[181]

From Wisdom Teaching to Apocalypticism

Since its inception in 1985 another approach to the issue of cultural transformation has received considerable attention, especially in the United States. The Westar Institute and its best-known program, the Jesus Seminar, has added considerable interest to the issue of acculturation. The Seminar, which consists of well-known New Testament scholars meeting twice a year, has discussed thoroughly each passage of the Synoptic Gospels. At the end of the discussion they vote on issues of authenticity.[182] The results of the Jesus study were published in 1993 under the title *The Five Gospels: The Search for the Authentic Words of Jesus.*[183] The stated objective of the Westar Institute is to increase religious literacy. Consequently much of the work of the Jesus Seminar has attracted the attention of the media and popular discussion. The scholarly thesis, however, pushes the debate of assimilation to its utmost limit. Funk, speaking for the Seminar, believes that Jesus is the legitimate center of the Christian faith; the Gospels contain that Jesus; the real Jesus can be recovered by serious scholarly pursuit; and recovery of the real Jesus can enable us to approach the kingdom of God.[184] The confidence of the Seminar lies in continuing investigation of the sayings of Jesus as found in Q, and in the discovery of a full text of the *Gospel of Thomas.*[185] Burton Mack, Seminar member, has proposed a method for combining the Matthean Q and the Lukan Q. His result is one document that he calls the "lost" or "first Gospel."[186] Seminar members find in the *Gospel of Thomas* a very early confirmation of the Q reconstruction. This belief reinforces their method: authenticity can be found when material is found neither in Judaism nor later Christianity, and when there is multiple attestation

---

180. Eva Aleith, *Paulusverständnis in der alten Kirche* (Berlin: Töpelmann, 1937), 3.

181. Laeuchli, *Language of Faith,* 156. See also Georg Kretschmar, "Ein Beitrag zur Frage nach dem Ursprung frühchristlicher Askese," *ZTK* 61 (1964): 29.

182. See Robert W. Funk, *Honest to Jesus: Jesus for a New Millennium* (San Francisco: HarperSanFrancisco, 1996), 8.

183. Robert W. Funk, Roy Hoover, and The Jesus Seminar, *The Five Gospels: The Search for the Authentic Words of Jesus* (New York: Macmillan, 1993).

184. Funk, *Honest to Jesus,* 10–11.

185. Davies, *Gospel of Thomas;* Edwards, *Theology of Q;* Kloppenborg, *Formation of Q.*

186. Burton Mack, *The Lost Gospel: The Book of Q and Christian Origins* (San Francisco: HarperSanFrancisco, 1993).

at early chronological levels.[187] This original gospel of Jesus[188] later was contaminated by the culture of Jewish radical eschatology (or apocalypticism). The impact of radical eschatology has irreparably altered the Synoptic Gospels and Christianity as we know it.[189] In 1998 the intended work of the Jesus Seminar was completed and made public.

Summary

When all the theories of "continuity" and "transformation" are seen vis à vis each other, any reliable historical reconstruction of the period seems impossible. Competent scholars have adduced the same data to produce widely divergent interpretations. Nevertheless, from this survey of opinions and interpretations, we could offer some minimal conclusions:

1. Some changes did occur in early Christianity. The issue is whether these changes are true or alien to the earliest faith.

2. The problem of change has concentrated on the dual foci of dogma and organization. Only to a much lesser extent have liturgy and ethics played a role in the debate.

3. To a large extent Protestants have found the transformation occurring outside the boundaries of the New Testament. Even today we can find those who are reluctant to find early Catholicism in the New Testament (Goppelt, for example). At the same time it must be noted there were from the very beginning those who saw elements of early Catholicism in the canon itself (Baur, Bousset, Schweitzer, and Bultmann, for example).

4. Despite the divergent theories of transformation, the causative factors for such transformations can be reduced to a few basic ones. The major internal factors are "the delay of the parousia" and the "loss of charisma or spirit." External factors have been the "influence of Judaism" and the "assimilation of Hellenism."

---

187. Crossan, *The Historical Jesus*, 427–50.
188. For Crossan's version see *The Historical Jesus*, xiii–xxvi.
189. Marcus Borg, "Jesus — A Sketch," *The Fourth R* 7 (1994), 10–15.

Plate 1. Jewish Inscription, Titulus, Vatican Museum

Plate 2.
Anchor and Fish, Titulus,
Priscilla Catacomb, Rome

Plate 3. Boat with Name Paulus, Sarcophagus, Museo del Palazzo dei Conservatori, Rome

*Plate 4.
Orante, Sarcophagus,
Santa Maria Antiqua,
Rome*

*Plate 5.
Bread and Cup,
Sarcophagus,
Rome*

Plate 6. Bread and Fish, Fresco, St. Callixtus Catacomb, Rome

Plate 7.
Good Shepherd, Sarcophagus,
L'eglise Sainte Quitterie du Mas,
Aire-sur-l'Ardour, France

Plate 8.
Torah Niche,
Dura-Europos Synagogue,
Damascus, Syria

Plate 9. Daniel and the Lions, Sarcophagus, Arles, France

Plate 10. Three Young Men in the Fiery Furnace,
Fresco, Priscilla Catacomb, Rome

Plate 11. Susanna and the Elders, Fresco, Priscilla Catacomb, Rome

Plate 12. Noah in the Ark, Sarcophagus, Arles, France

Plate 13. Baptism of Jesus, Fisherman, Fresco,
St. Callixtus Catacomb, Rome

Plate 14.
Baptism of Jesus,
Sarcophagus,
Santa Maria Antiqua,
Rome

Plate 15. Jonah Cycle, Sarcophagus, Vatican Museum

Plate 16.
Moses Striking
the Rock,
Sarcophagus,
Arles, France

Plate 17. Healing of the Paralytic, Sarcophagus,
L'eglise Sainte Quitterie du Mas, Aire-sur-l'Adour,
France

Plate 18.
Healing the Blind, Sarcophagus,
L'eglise Sainte Quitterie du Mas,
Aire-sur-l'Adour, France

Plate 19. Multiplication of the Loaves and Fishes,
Wooden Door, Sta. Sabina, Rome

Plate 20. The Resurrection of Lazarus,
Sarcophagus, L'eglise Sainte Quitterie du Mas,
Aire-sur-l'Ardour, France

Plate 21. Christian Inscription, Titulus, Catacomb, Rome

*Plate 22. Christ Helios, Mosaic,
St. Peter's Excavations, The Vatican*

Plate 23.
Ascension of Elijah,
Wooden Door,
Sta. Sabina, Rome

Plate 24.
Manger Scene,
Sarcophagus,
Arles, France

Plate 25. Fractio panis, Fresco, Priscilla Catacomb, Rome

Plate 26. Agape Meal, Fresco,
St. Peter and St. Marcellinus Catacomb, Rome

Plate 27. Agape Meal, Fresco,
St. Peter and St. Marcellinus Catacomb, Rome

Plate 28. Agape Meal, Fresco,
St. Peter and St. Marcellinus Catacomb, Rome

Part 3

Trajectories of Inculturation

Chapter 6

Symbols

The impact of the Judeo-Christian worldview, as expressed by the Jesus tradition, changed the nature of the Greco-Roman world. Although Christian theologians and historians have been deeply interested in this encounter of the Jesus tradition with the Greco-Roman world, for the most part, as we have seen, they have concerned themselves with the demise of the original Jesus-Paul-John faith rather than with the extent to which that tradition altered and utilized the Greco-Roman world.

Without necessarily depreciating the importance of studying a culture's metaphysical worldview, we might better understand the changes of the second and third centuries if we also ask how the impact of the Jesus tradition affected some selected social-cultural components of the Greco-Roman world.

Jewish Symbols

According to Jacob Neusner's study of Jewish discourse in iconic form, the four major Jewish symbols found in early synagogues are the *menorah, etrog, lulab*, and *shofar*.[1] Granted the mathematical limitations of a small sample, a chart of extant Jewish symbols used will be helpful in assessing the symbolic interaction.

In the second and third centuries, twenty-eight sites have been identified. In these we find the distribution of symbols as shown in table 6.1 on the following page. While the menorah clearly appears as a definitive mark of a pre-Constantinian Jewish synagogue, other symbols are not so obvious. That is, symbols such as the amphora, birds, the cross, an eagle, genii, lions, rosettes, shells, wreaths, and others are just as prevalent as patently Jewish symbols such as the etrog, lulab, and shofar. Neusner does not include the Torah shrine in his Jewish foursome, though in this list it is the only other definitively *Jewish* symbol. Under the historical criterion of dissimilarity (not used in the non-Jewish world), there are

---

1. Jacob Neusner, *Symbol and Theology in Early Judaism* (Minneapolis: Fortress, 1991). The archaeological tables, based on the remains of early synagogues, were prepared by Andrew G. Vaughn and revised by James F. Strange.

Table 6.1. Distribution of Jewish Symbols in Synagogue Sites

Symbol	Sites	Instances	Symbol	Sites	Instances
Amphora	2	3	Lulab	3	3
Birds	4	7	Meanders	1	1
Cross	3	3	Menorah	13	26
Crown	1	1	Oil jug	1	1
Eagle	7	7	Plant motifs	3	3
Etrog	5	6	Rosette	7	7
Flowers	2	2	Shell	4	4
Genii	3	4	Shofar	5	5
Geometric	1	1	Swastika	1	1
Grapevine	3	3	Torah shrine	3	4
Hercules knot	2	2	Torus	1	1
Incense shovel	2	2	Vine	8	8
Leavers	3	3	Wheel	2	2
Lions	3	4	Wreath	5	5

indeed five Jewish symbols in this list: etrog, lulab, shofar, menorah, and Torah shrine (plate 8). In their synagogues Jews of the first centuries in the Christian era were quite willing to use a large number of Greco-Roman decorations and symbols. Some scholars, like Goodenough, see in such symbols signals of a more mystical Judaism.[2] Others assume that Jewish leaders had no choice but to use ateliers who offered, as a matter of course, pagan decorations and symbols. Or, in terms of interaction, Jews were willing to utilize the decorations and symbols of their non-Jewish neighbors.[3] By so doing they indicated their active participation in the Greco-Roman culture. But *none* of these symbols became a part of the Jewish iconic conversation. In that sense, by the first two centuries of the Christian era Judaism had developed a firm symbolic identity. It could accept and utilize pagan symbolic material, but did not incorporate it. Likewise, Judaism of that time did not contribute any symbols to the Roman world, nor, as far as we can determine, did it infuse Roman symbols with a Jewish meaning.

On their funerary *tituli*, where only a bare minimum of iconic conversation was possible, the Jews of Rome utilized their primary identity symbols: menorah, shofar, etrog, and lulab (plates 1, 8).[4] It could be that

---

2. Erwin R. Goodenough. *Jewish Symbols in the Greco-Roman Period,* 12 vols. (New York: Pantheon, 1953–65); see vols. 2, 3, 4.

3. Leonard V. Rutgers, "Archaeological Evidence for the Interaction of Jews and Non-Jews in Late Antiquity," *American Journal of Archaeology* 96 (1992): 101–18; *The Jews in Late Ancient Rome: Evidence of Cultural Interaction in the Roman Diaspora* (New York: Brill, 1995).

4. Good examples can be found in Adia Konikoff, *Sarcophagi from the Jewish Catacombs of Ancient Rome* (Stuttgart: Franz Steiner Verlag, 1986), plates 11, 12.

the flask (amphora or vase?) also serves as a Jewish ceremonial symbol, but such items are too common to make a firm identification. Leon lists 534 Jewish inscriptions from Rome. Of these, 144 show the menorah, 34 the lulab, 27 the etrog, 27 a flask, 14 the shofar, and 6 (all from Monteverde) show the Torah shrine. Other items such as birds and branches are very occasional.

Early Christian Symbols

In sharp contrast to the Jewish symbolic interaction, the earliest Christian communities came to Rome with no firm identifying symbols. Their earliest examples were taken, albeit with varying degrees of popularity, from the Roman culture.[5] As in any culture the first symbols not only identify the developing faith, but serve as an artistic resolution for what otherwise are significant conflicts or tensions for the community. Symbols are to be read in terms of such temporal conflicts rather than necessarily as dogmatic theological signs.

Prophetic Symbols

The Jesus tradition that relativizes the dominant culture can be found in the numerous symbols, several involving water.

The Anchor

As a simple symbol the anchor appeared frequently on catacomb *tituli* (marble grave markers) of the third century (plate 2). By the fourth century it had almost totally disappeared. In the Greco-Roman world the anchor had no significant prior use as a religious symbol. Since any significance in Hellenistic culture was lacking, it has been suggested that the anchor represents a hidden cross, a disguise no longer needed when Christianity went public. However in third-century popular Christianity there were few, if any, symbols of efficacious suffering and dying. As a popular symbol the cross was not hidden; it simply was not utilized. As a Christian metaphor the anchor occurs only once in the New Testament (Heb. 6:19, as a symbol of hope). Since early Christian symbols or scenes seldom reflect any biblical meaning, there is no reason to assign the sense of hope to the anchor. Along with the other nautical symbols mentioned by Clement, the anchor reflects Christian conflict with the environment (implied by water). In the faith community the believer finds security.

---

5. Patrick Bruun, "Symboles, Signes et Monogrammes," in *Sylloge inscriptionum christianarum veterum musei vaticani*, ed. Henrik Zilliacus, Acta instituti romani finlandiae 1, no. 2 (Helsinki: Tilqmann, 1963), 73–166.

Once that conflict subsided (fourth century), the anchor fell into disuse as a symbol.

The Boat

Like the anchor, the boat expresses security in an alien environment; but unlike the anchor, it had a prior history. In some ancient religions the boat bore the dead to the netherworld, while in the Bible boats normally offered protection from threatening waters, e.g., the ark (Gen 6:19), Jonah's boat (Jon. 1:4), and the stilling of the storm (Mark 6:45–52). The boat of the first two centuries signified a community "floating" on the culture of the Greco-Roman world (plate 3). The highly favored Jonah story portrays the Christian, as the Orante (see below), cast into the alien culture and surviving (plate 15). The boats of early Christianity are not yet the salvific church of the fourth century (Cyprian, *Unit. eccl.* 6 [e.g., the ark at Monreale]).

The Fish

Though one of the most frequently used symbols of the early church, the fish nevertheless defies accurate analysis. Like the other nautical symbols, the fish signifies life in a conflictive cultural situation (plate 2). Sometimes the fish is found with another nautical symbol, the anchor. One famous stele, that of Licinia (Museo Nazionale, Rome), contains a fish on each side of an anchor. An inscription reads "fish of the living" (ΙΧΘΥΣ ΖΩΝ-ΤΩΝ). Some suppose that this inscription, and the fish itself, refers to the use of Greek ἰχθύς ("fish") as an acrostic meaning "Jesus Christ, God's Son, Savior." While no other symbols bear such a dogmatic meaning, and many uses of the fish symbol cannot refer to the Jesus acrostic, still, the identification of the fish with Jesus cannot be denied. Tertullian wrote, "But we little fish, according to our *ichthun* Jesus Christ, are born in the water, nor were we saved in any other manner than by remaining in the water" (*Bapt.* 1).

While Tertullian knew the social context of the fish (the newly baptized Christian remains in the culture/water), he also knew the acrostic reference of "fish" to Jesus. Apart from the acrostic, Jesus can be identified with the fish of the agape meal. Every known representation of the agape meal prior to Constantine shows fish, bread, and wine. While the meal may be based on the New Testament eucharistic passage of the feeding of the five thousand (Mark 6:30–44), other inscriptional material identifies the fish meal with "the Fish from the Fountain, the very great, the pure, which the holy virgin seized" (Epitaph of Abercius). Fourth-century literary material can speak of the Eucharist as the Christ feeding the people with five loaves and two fishes, and of Christ himself being that bread and that fish (Paulinus of Nola, *Epist.* 13, 11). The fish symbol then refers both to the social implication of entering the faith community (baptism into a community of security) and to a major means of maintaining membership in that community (the fish of the Eucharist and/or Agape). By the end of the third century this powerful symbol had also started to take on the literary, dogmatic nature of the famous acrostic.

The Olive Branch

Although the olive branch does not relate primarily to water and has no significant prior use as a Greco-Roman symbol, it should be considered a piece of the prophetic conversation. As a symbol the olive branch occurs primarily with the dove (plate 21), though sometimes alone. In pictorial representations, however, it is found almost always in boat scenes — normally with Noah and the ark, sometimes with Jonah. Occasionally it is found in the beak of a dove, as with the three young men in the fiery furnace. Its consistent placement makes fairly certain its symbolic identification with *pax* — the peace of the community in the face of conflict, as well as the peace of the *refrigerium* (meal with extended family and special religious dead). It did not continue as a significant symbol after the "peace of Constantine."

The Dove

This symbol has a rich and extensive history. In other cultures it can refer to fertility, sexuality, love, and religious sentiments. In early Christianity the dove, as a symbol, appears often with the olive branch, a symbol of security in the face of cultural conflict, and frequently with the inscription, *IN PACE* (see table 6.2).[6]

Table 6.2

	without *IN PACE*	with *IN PACE*
Dove alone	45	37
Dove with olive branch or tree	21	30
Dove with Christogram	17	24
Dove with other symbols	16	15

Prior to Constantine (and the Christogram: ☧) the early Christians used the dove to signify that peace and satisfaction which derived from faith and participation in the faith community (plates 10, 12, 21). At the same time, the dove and its counterpart, the Orante (see below), occurred

6. Ibid., 87.

often in biblical scenes of conflict with the dominant culture. In the use of the dove symbol the non-Christian could see that redefinition infused by the prophetic Jesus tradition. After the "peace of Constantine," when social conflict had lessened, the dove referred more to peace of the soul (Ravenna), while the Orante eventually disappeared altogether.

The Orante

One of the two human symbols consists of a woman with upraised hands (plate 4). Her head is nearly always covered with a veil and a tunic of the third century (*orans tunicata et velata*). She exists as a separate figure, but, more important, through the fourth century she is the main figure of nearly every biblical scene, both fresco and sculpture. She is Noah in the ark, Jonah in the boat, Jonah spewed out of the sea monster, Daniel between the lions, Susanna with the elders, the three young men in the fiery furnace, and sometimes Lazarus. She is the most important symbol in early Christian art. The Orante has a long history in the Greco-Roman social matrix. Since there seems to be no major significance assigned to the biblical contexts in which the Orante is placed, it must be assumed that the Orante has kept something of its traditional meaning, now transferred to a Christian pictorial backdrop. From examples of the Orante in public art (coins) and sepulchral art, it seems to have been associated mainly with familial piety. Given the biblical contexts used by the artists, the scenes must indicate a community (familial) victory in the midst of various social conflicts. Once the conflicts diminished during the reign of Constantine, the Orante essentially disappeared from Christian art.

Community Formation

In the first symbols of the early Christians there are no iconic representations for either the teaching or the healing tradition. Apart from the cultural conflict, the primary symbols reflect community formation either through eating together and/or inclusive acceptance.

The Bread

The symbol of bread refers primarily to the agape meal (plate 5). It always appears in table scenes with fish and wine (note the well-known combination symbol from the crypt of Lucina in St. Callixtus, Rome [plate 6]). Normally the artist portrayed bread as a small round object, often placed in a basket. In the eucharistic meal scenes there are five or seven such baskets (see Mark 6:30–44; 8:1–10). Such loaves or baskets of bread can be found in the symbol systems of many religions.[7] For most

---

7. Goodenough, *Jewish Symbols*, 5:62–95.

unofficial religions of the Mediterranean area, bread symbolized the fellowship of a religious meal or fellowship with the extended family and community through meals for the dead.

The Vase

Although the vase does not appear as a eucharistic calix (or chalice) until the peace of Constantine, it does appear fairly often as a symbol in early Christian art (plate 5). It cannot be the container from which the Eucharist / Agape wine was drunk, since that was uniformly a small glass beaker. The vase occurs often with a dove, the primary symbol of peace for early Christians. Given that meaning and its frequency in both Christian and non-Christian burial areas, we can suppose that it represents the unity of the extended family or faith community. As such, it symbolically held the wine for the nearly universal meal for the dead. After Constantine its meaning and function shifted to the newly formed orthodox Eucharist, where it was then portrayed as a calix.

The Vine and Grapes

The artistically ubiquitous vine brought a rich history of meaning. In Judaism and early Christianity it signified the source of life, especially the life of the faith community (Isa. 5:1–7; John 15:1–11), and was prominent in Hellenistic religions (e.g., the cult of Dionysius). The most prominent surviving use of the vine in early Christianity occurs in Mausoleum M in the necropolis of St. Peter's. A green vine surrounds a gold sky with Christ Helios driving across it (plate 22). Grapes sometimes occur with the vine, though more often a dove. The dove signifies the peace of the faith community, achieved by eating the grapes (drinking the wine) of the community meal. Early Christians hardly needed to inject new meaning into the grape and vine. It only needed to be adapted to the Christian community. As with the fish and bread, eventually the grape was identified with Christ, a grape (wine as blood) that suffered for us (Clem. *Paed.* 2, 2). The grape survived the peace of Constantine because it took on the Christological, cultic meaning.

The Good Shepherd

The second human figure is a male shepherd pictured with a member of the sheep family, normally a ram, on his shoulders (plate 7). The symbol, a *criophorus*, has an ancient history, dating, in Near Eastern circles, as far back as 1000 B.C.E. Several meanings for the symbol have been suggested. While in the Mediterranean world it likely signified sacrifice, the use of the Good Shepherd in baptistries (Dura-Europos, Naples?), as well as catacombs and meeting places, indicates that the shepherd bore the religious actor into the faith community (or family of the dead). For that reason the Good Shepherd has been identified as *humanitas*, in contrast to the Orante as *pietas*. One might think of it as ecclesial hospitality. After Constantine, the Good Shepherd became the most popular symbol for Christ himself.

The Lamb

In most instances the lamb of early Christianity appears in bucolic scenes (plate 21), either with the Good Shepherd or an Orpheus-like figure. Although it would be tempting to identify the lamb with such biblical images as the innocent ewe lamb of Nathan's parable (2 Sam. 12:1–6), it is more probable that pastoral scenes reflect the hospitality of the early church. Like the sheep of John 10:1–8, the lamb symbolizes the religious actor enjoying the presence of (and community associated with) the Good Shepherd (plate 7). That sense of community can be found as late as in the apse of St. Apollinare in Classe, Ravenna, though there restricted to the community of the apostles.

After the peace of Constantine the lamb became a major symbol of the crucified Christ (Gallia Placida, Ravenna). The celebrative Passover lamb, as Jesus (1 Cor. 5:7; John 1:29), has become the sacrificial *agnus dei* (Rev. 5:6).

Chapter 7

Representation Art

Just as a comparison with Jewish symbols has elucidated the Christian interaction with Roman symbols, so a similar comparison in the area of figurative art will show a comparable situation.

Jewish Art

As was seen in the discussion of symbols, Jews did not hesitate to borrow non-Jewish ornamentation, though no such ornamentation became a mark of Judaism. In the earliest synagogues (Second Temple period) there was no figurative art (Masada, Herodium, for instance). Presumably the prohibition against "graven images" (Exod. 20:4–5; Deut. 5:8–9) suppressed nearly all Jewish figurative art. Any relational- or dyadic-based culture would have understood the dangers of substituting an icon or image for the real person/divinity. There are some exceptions. The primary examples of Jewish figurative art come from the synagogue at Dura-Europos. For reasons not yet clear the membership of that synagogue chose to line the walls with fifty-eight biblical scenes (plate 8). The dress, gestures, and style are primarily Hellenistic, but in no instance has the artist utilized a Greco-Roman icon to express a Jewish perspective. The figures can be identified as well-known persons from the Hebrew Scriptures, so one can assume pictorial art at Dura-Europos was primarily illustrative.

Christian Figurative Art

The early Christians were quite willing to use Hellenistic symbols in their iconic conversations.[1] As with the symbols themselves, early Christian art was dominated by the prophetic tradition.

---

1. For references to a more traditional understanding of early Christian art see my *Ante Pacem: Archaeological Evidence of Church Life before Constantine* (Macon, Ga.: Mercer University Press, 1985), 31–65, and the list on p. 43.

The Prophetic Tradition

A Hellenistic figure, the Orante, was the primary icon for security and distance from the dominant culture. She occurred in several biblical scenes, normally from the Hebrew Scriptures, as one trapped in threatening situations, yet not overcome by adverse circumstances.

The Daniel Cycle (Conflict with Political Power)

Daniel in the Lions' Den. A favorite picture portrayed Daniel as an Orante between two lions with, sometimes, a palace as a backdrop (plate 9). Early Christians saw in the well-known Daniel story their own conflict with various plenipotentiaries in the Roman Empire. The presence of the Orante, untouched by the lions, signaled the presence of a power far superior to the state that threatened them with persecution, or even the animals of the coliseum.

The Three Young Men in the Fiery Furnace. In the same way, the story of Shadrach, Meschach, and Abednego portrayed three Orantes in a space filled with fire (plate 10). The three young men had refused to recant their faith even under threat of terrifying death. Early Christians saw the same threat by the state if they failed to recant their new faith. The presence of the Orantes assured them that the power of the Christian God was strong enough to overcome such dangers. In some cases there appeared in the furnace a dove with an olive branch in its beak.

Susanna and the Elders. The third story of the Daniel cycle points to a corrupt judicial system. According to the apocryphal story, Susanna was pressured for sexual favors by two judges who threatened to say, falsely, that she was having an affair with a young man. Susanna refused, and was nearly condemned. But Daniel intervenes just in time. In early Christian art Susanna appears as an Orante in the context of political corruption (plate 11). Although Susanna appears in several portrayals (almost a cycle in itself), invariably she signals legal security in the faith community. The fact that Susanna is female may simply reflect that the Susanna story is the paradigmatic biblical story on judicial blackmail. On the other hand, there were more women in the early church than in the population as a whole. One reason for that larger percentage was the more egalitarian way women were included in the faith community. Some of the new ways, such as the authority of the husband regarding divorce and childbirth, contravened Greco-Roman customs. Surely these changes placed the Christian woman at greater legal risk. This may explain the popularity of the Susanna cycle.

Water Narratives (Conflict with Greco-Roman Culture)

We saw in the basic symbols of early Christianity several iconic references to survival in a dominant culture. These were expressed by symbols that could exist in water: anchor, boat, and fish. When the early Christian artists shifted to pictorial representations, they used these symbols to express the same prophetic critique. As in the Daniel cycle the religious actor appears as the Orante.

Noah in the Ark. The primary water narrative contains an Orante, who is apparently Noah, in a box, which serves as a boat, floating on flood waters. Sometimes the dove and olive branch also appear (plate 12). The Orante, infused with the Christian sense of peace (see the discussion of the dove), lives in the culture but does not actually belong to it. Once the interpreter realizes that the Noah-Orante refers to the Christian in everyday life rather than a departed deceased, then the water scenes take on considerable meaning.

Jesus Walking on Water. On the wall of the baptistery in the house church at Dura-Europos an artist drew a boat on the water with a figure, apparently Jesus, walking toward the boat. The meaning of this singular scene matches Noah in the ark: Jesus, though not an Orante, participates in the culture, but overcomes it.

The Fisher. Other water scenes deal more directly with the interchange between the faith community and culture. The fisher, which significantly occurs in the St. Peter's necropolis in Mausoleum M, pulls a fish from the water (plate 13). While the fisher occurs as a figure in Hellenistic art, there is no particular discernible symbolic meaning. Apparently, early Christians saw in the fisher icon a power (Jesus?) that facilitated their potential release from the dominant culture.

The Baptism of Jesus. The earliest portrayal of the baptism of Jesus happens to be the most instructive. On the sarcophagus of St. Maria Antiqua the nude boy Jesus stands in water, touched on the head by a much larger old man (plates 13, 14). Above the man's head a dove is descending. Of course it looks to us like the Gospel story of the baptism of Jesus. But there were no biblical illustrations until the early fourth century. In 180 C.E. viewers would have seen a heroic youth standing in water blessed by a Neptune-like figure. Viewers accustomed to Christian symbolism would have seen also a dove indicating the peace of the faith community as Jesus began the act of cleansing the water (culture). The line between iconic conversation and illustration is so fine that clear distinctions seem impossible. Surely at an early stage a Jesus tradition that relativizes culture has infected Hellenistic symbols in such a way as to signify a Christian critique of the Greco-Roman world. But sometime afterward, even until today, the same symbols had the baptism of Jesus as the referent. As only an illustration of the baptism of Jesus the scene lost its original prophetic intent.

The Jonah Cycle. The Jonah cycle must be taken with absolute seriousness. Although the number of extant examples of early Christian pictures varies between one and ten for each subject, there are as many as forty Jonah cycles. The cycle consists of three parts: (1) A boat with two men in it (sometimes as Orantes). Jonah is being cast, or is diving, out of the boat (always as an Orante, plate 15). (2) Having swallowed Jonah, a sea animal, or *ketos*, regurgitates him as an Orante (plate 15). (3) Jonah lies under a vine on which lambs are climbing. The reclining figure under the vine is always that of Endymion (plate 15). (Endymion was a human joined with Selene, the moon goddess. After siring forty children he rested on his back with his right arm crooked behind his head.) The Jonah cycle symbolizes the mission of the first Christians, its effort at inculturation.

Leaving the security of the boat and its Orante figures, Jonah enters the chaos of the dominant culture. To be sure, the sea monster swallowed the Christian witness, but could not destroy it. Instead, the Orante was cast up alive on a beach. There the Jonah figure who has survived multiple encounters with the Greco-Roman culture takes a deserved rest, not unlike the famous Endymion seen so often on non-Christian sarcophagi. Popular as it was, the Jonah cycle did not survive the peace of the church, even as an illustration. Once Christianity was dominant that iconic conversation had no more significance.

Moses Striking the Rock. At first glance it would seem that the miracle of Moses securing water from a rock in the desert would belong to a miracle or deliverance series rather than the water theme (plate 16). And that may be. If, however, we take the water as a sign of culture, we could say that the early Christian artist was portraying the flowing water as a new "culture" given by God, sprung from no prior source (not unlike the deculturized Jesus of the Gospel of John). Although this may not seem convincing in itself, the history of the representation gives us pause. By the end of the third century, Moses has shifted to Peter. It is not Moses who facilitates inculturation, but Peter, the rock of the church. To be sure, in the first portrayals of Moses striking the rock, it would appear that the recipients of the water are dressed the same as Moses, but in later examples of Moses/Peter striking the rock the recipients are quite differently dressed (sarcophagus, Arles Museum). Someone other than the Christian community is receiving the "new culture."

The Woman at the Well. If Moses striking the rock eventually refers to the "miraculous" gift of a new culture, the two extant examples of the woman at the well (see the baptistery at Dura-Europos) probably reflected the same meaning. The well would signify a new source of life (culture).

The Healing Tradition

Though missing in the symbols, the healing tradition plays a very important role in early Christian art. Renewed interest in oral transmission of the gospel tradition makes one suspect that such narratives were transmitted in the continuing pool of oral material. It would be reasonable to suppose that early Christian art would reflect the content of that transmission. Of particular interest is whether a healing tradition or even community of the miracle catenae, as found in the Gospels of Mark and John, can be found in early Christian art. In the case of the miracle catenae we have an opportunity to test that hypothesis. There are very few examples of any biblical representation, so the field is small. Apart from the Jonah cycle (thirty to forty times), the largest number of any one narrative would be eight for Noah's ark, and six each for Daniel in the lions' den and the baptism of Jesus. In terms of the miracle catenae there are five of the resurrection of Lazarus, three of the healing of the paralytic (add two for lame and crippled?), two of the multiplication of the loaves and fishes, and one of Jesus and Peter walking on water. The healing of the blind person may occur once. In Crossan's unpublished recount of my list there are seven examples of raising from the dead and five examples of making the paralytic walk. Because he adds the Christian meal to the feeding of the five thousand, he actually has twenty-seven examples of the multiplication of loaves and fishes.

There are not many other New Testament healing stories to be found in early Christian Art. Casting out of demons (or conflict with the powers of the old age) and curing of lepers (or destruction of artificial social barriers) are missing. Although the healing of the blind person is nearly missing from pre-Constantinian art, it became quite popular in the fourth century. Its absence in third-century art probably has little meaning. Or perhaps, by accident, no early examples survived.

The Healing of the Paralytic. This healing miracle is consistently shown as a man walking with a bed on his head — indeed, with his head piercing the rope springs of the bed (plate 17). Jesus is never present. Since the portrayal of this healing narrative has no counterpart in Greco-Roman art, the religious actor must either know the story of the paralytic (Mark 2) or must, in some sense, adhere to the community of the miracle catenae. Without Jesus present, of course, the representation has little if any christological value. Soon after the peace of the church this representation of the healing of the paralytic disappeared. In Ravenna, the narrative is told by the friends lowering the paralytic into a house.

The Healing of the Blind Person. Jesus places his hand on the eyes or head of the blind person (plate 18). Unlike the healing of the paralytic, there is no portrayal of the cure. The early Christians have borrowed the iconography of a thaumaturge who heals by touching or waving a wand. Because of the Greco-Roman iconic predecessor, the early Christian religious actor can see the healing even though none has (yet) occurred. Our primary examples of this representation occur after Constantine, but it disappears by the fifth century.

Walking on Water. Of all the members of the miracle catenae, walking on water appears the least often. Our primary example occurs in the baptistery of the *domus ecclesia* in Dura-Europos. I have stated above that it is an icon in the prophetic series even though it belongs in the miracle catenae. As a miracle it portrays the power of Jesus (and Peter) over the environment. After the peace of the church this representation disappeared.

The Feeding of the Five Thousand. This miracle is portrayed by a figure with a wand, apparently Jesus, standing before a series of baskets (five or seven). I count only two examples prior to Constantine, although the number increases quite demonstrably after 313 c.e. (plate 19). Crossan has argued that the scenes I categorize as the Agape are actually to be included with the feeding of the five thousand. In my opinion, the artisan did intend to portray the early church Agape; however, the connection with the feeding of the five thousand cannot be overlooked. Invariably there are seven baskets of bread, two fish, and wine. Normally there are also seven people sitting at a round table. If one wishes to consider the Agape (plate 25) as a reflection of the feeding of the five thousand, then the miraculous meal becomes second only to Jonah as the most frequent biblical representation. Put another way, the Jonah story reflects the prophetic tradition, with its intent to infuse the Greco-Roman culture with the Jesus tradition, while the feeding of the five thousand reflects the way in which the new community of faith was formed.

The Resurrection of Lazarus. As there is no pre-Constantinian portrayal of the cross, or crucifixion, so there is no portrayal of the resurrection of Jesus. That comes first in Ravenna. The resurrection narrative in the miracle catenae makes Jesus the miracle worker instead of the one resurrected. So for several centuries the resurrection refers to Lazarus. The event is fairly consistently depicted with Lazarus wrapped from head to toe coming out of a mausoleum (plate 20). That can be sufficient, but normally Jesus stands close by, pointing at Lazarus with a wand.

The prophetic and the healing traditions are well represented in early Christian art. These artistic traditions appear side by side, not as two discrete communities. The miracle catenae of the later church, like the art, contain both traditions.

Early Christian Lists

It has been noted in recent times that miracle catenae of later Christian literature bear some clear similarities to each other and to certain miracle patterns in the Gospels. Julian Hills has provided a useful series of such lists from early Christianity.[2] A typical list would be the excerpt from *Acts Pet. Paul* 41:

> And they [or, I] saw him enlightening the blind, cleansing lepers,
> healing paralytics, expelling demons from men,
> raising the dead,
> subduing the winds, walking upon the waves of the sea,
> and doing many other wonders,
> and all the people of the Jews calling him Son of God.

Of the nineteen examples listed by Hills,[3] we find the following miracles and the number of times each is mentioned:

1. raising the dead (17)

2. healing diseases (6)

3. curing lepers (14)

4. making the blind see (18)

5. making the paralytic walk (10)

6. exorcising demons (14)

7. making the lame walk (11)

---

2. Julian Hills, *Tradition and Composition in the Epistula Apostolorum* (Minneapolis: Fortress, 1990), 40–44. A similar list has been compiled by Paul Achtemeier, "The Origin and Function of the Pre-Marcan Miracle Catenae," *JBL* 91 (1972): 199–200. Using the "consensus" texts, David T. M. Frankfurter reflects on the miracle-list tradition in his article, "The Origin of the Miracle-List Tradition and Its Medium of Circulation," in *Society of Biblical Literature Seminar Papers 29* (Atlanta: Scholars Press, 1990), 344–74.

3. Hills's list of nineteen, which we are using, includes Paul's preaching in Rome from the *Acts of Paul*; the speech of Jesus in the *Acts of Paul*; Pseudo-Hippolytus, *Frag. ps.* 2; Hippolytus, *Noet.* 18.7; Tertullian, *Apol.* 21.17; Cyprian, *Quod idola dii non sint* 13; Pseudo-Cyprian, *De rebaptismate* 8; *Acts of Phileas* 6; *Sib. Or.* 1.351–59; *Testim. Truth* 2.22–33.9; *Const. apost.* 5.7.27–28; *The Teaching of Addai*; *Acts of Andr. Mth.* 10; Justin, *1 Apol.* 48.1–2; *Acts Pet. Paul* 41; *Ps.-Clem. Hom.* 1.6; *T. Adam* 3.1; *Anaphora Pilati* A 1–5; *Vindicta Salvatoris* 6.

8. multiplying the loaves and fishes (6)

9. walking on the sea (7)

10. stilling the winds (8)

11. changing water into wine (6)

12. making the deaf hear (6)

13. making the mute speak (5)

14. healing palsy (1)

15. restoring a withered hand (2)

16. plucking a coin from the mouth of a fish (1)

17. straightening a hunched back (2)

18. finding something lost (1)

19. healing the woman with an issue of blood (2)

Raising the dead (sometimes Lazarus) and making the blind to see were almost always listed. Curing leprosy and casting out demons were next in frequency. Healing those who could not walk was next in importance, with a large number of lists mentioning both the healing of the paralytic and the lame person. Finally, a fairly popular motif was controlling the water by either walking on it or commanding the storm to cease.[4]

In these popular lists the predominance of the miracle catenae is clear. The number of miracles has been expanded. Speaking statistically, it is primarily the healing of lepers and the casting out of demons that caused the numerical increase. Still prominent in the catenae lists are the Gospel miracles: healing of the blind, making the lame to walk, feeding the multitudes, walking on water, and resurrecting the dead, items we have identified as singularly prominent in early Christian art. The Jesus tradition continued to construct the life of popular Christianity.

---

4. See Frankfurter's chart in "Miracle List Tradition," 373–74.

Chapter 8

Architecture

Granted that there could be mitigating circumstances such as the size of the plot, the environmental context, or the nature of resources,[1] still, by and large, the theology of a religious community can be seen in the shape of its meeting place.

Symbolism of the Built Form

Circular

The earliest meeting places probably were round. Appropriate worship consisted of moving with the seasons in a circular fashion. The religious actors stressed fertility rites and dancing.[2]

Rectangular/Longitudinal

In this built form the religious actor moved forward to a sacred place (altar), a divine presence (icon), or an authoritative person (priest). I call this a marching, or end-time (goal-oriented) religion as over against the round, dancing type.

Square/Box/Hall

The square building stresses neither dancing nor marching, but perfection of the human community where sacred boundaries exist. The sides of the meeting place are even, and the boundaries of the community are clear. Human considerations (often confused with divine law) determine how one leaves the state of perfection and how one enters it. Meeting places such as the synagogue or the house church tended to be square.

To oversimplify: circular foundations stress a heavenly reality; longitudinal foundations stress an end-time vision; and square foundations stress a present reality or realized eschatology.

---

1. Strzygowski argues with considerable vigor that the dome originated in Iran and Armenia because they had to use sun-dried bricks for roofs rather than timber. See Josef Strzygowski, *The Origin of Christian Church Art* (Oxford: Clarendon, 1923), 59.
2. John Gordon Davies, *The Origin and Development of Early Christian Church Architecture* (London: SCM, 1952), 51–80; Strzygowski, *Origin of Christian Church Art*.

The Synagogue Building

One would reasonably suppose that the first Christians developed meeting places comparable to those that Jewish Christians would have known. One of the major surprises in early Christian archaeology is to discover that the architectural, artistic, and epigraphic continuity between Judaism and Christianity is nearly nil. To be sure, as in early Christianity, many of the extant Diaspora synagogues are in fact rebuilt houses (Dura-Europos, Stobi, Priene, and Delos). In that sense some early synagogues and churches show a parallel development. But other synagogues have hall-like qualities, perhaps were even built into public buildings (Sardis). Early synagogues were halls with a small Torah niche.

Antecedents of the Christian Built Form

As for Christians, the earliest meeting places were homes. To be sure, some halls are mentioned (ἐν τῇ σχολῇ Τυράννου, in a place of leisure and learned discussion [Acts 19:9]; τῷ ὑπερῴῳ, upper chamber, second story, or women's chambers, [Acts 20:8]), and admittedly we have very little archaeological evidence for house churches prior to 300. But what evidence we do have indicates a nearly complete practice of meeting in homes or reconstructed houses.[3] Archaeologically we have a nearly complete house church from Dura-Europos, and a less certain example in SS. Giovanni and Paolo in Rome. In contrast to Diaspora synagogues, there is no known example of a house being rearranged to create a longitudinal pattern. A very few examples of the *aula ecclesia*, which was normally longitudinal, did exist by the beginning of the fourth century (St. Crisogono), but they should not be seen as an architectural step between house and basilica.[4]

According to the older consensus, the house churches developed into fourth-century churches.[5] Indeed the *tituli* churches of Rome often bear the name of the person (normally a wealthy first-century Christian) who

---

3. The comment to the contrary by Eusebius (*Hist. eccl.* 8.1.5) cannot be taken at face value: "They were no longer satisfied with the buildings of olden times, and would erect from the foundations [ἐκ θεμελίων] churches of spacious dimensions throughout all the cities." As with orthodox theology, Eusebius was anxious to show that the church at the time of Constantine had always been there. There is no evidence to support either his theological or architectural contention. Though an occasional Roman may have complained about Christian buildings, third-century Christian writer Minucius Felix declared, "We have no temple and no altars" (*Octavius* 32.1).

4. The early hall in SS. Giovanni and Paolo was built in an apartment over a "shop" church. The earliest known *aula*, St. Crisogono, has no previous *domus* history. The *aula* at Aquileia lies adjacent to a house that might have been a *domus ecclesia*.

5. So Robert Milburn, *Early Christian Art and Architecture* (Berkeley: University of California Press, 1988), 13–16.

supposedly lived in the house below the present edifice (St. Clemente). Careful archaeological work has shown that there is almost no church that was built over a house church (except possibly, for example, SS. Giovanni and Paolo, or the double church at Aquileia).[6]

The Suburban Villa

The earliest known "pure" churches were longitudinal with two rows of columns creating a clerestory (figure 8.1 on the following page). At the entrance were three doors — one for the nave and one each for the side aisles. At the front of the church was an apse in which the liturgical acts occurred. While no one claims that any church was ever built over a suburban house, the architectural comparison is most instructive. A suburban house consisted of an atrium at the entrance, a peristyle (an open courtyard) formed by columns in a longitudinal axis (with rooms on each side of the axis), and a triclinium (dining room) at the front (figure 8.1). The pattern of the suburban house matches almost perfectly the plan of an early church like St. Sabina or St. Crisogono. It is deeply tempting to say that the first Christians met in wealthy suburban homes with longitudinal peristyles. When they first came to build their own buildings dedicated to worship, they designed them to match the houses they had already experienced.

The Roman Basilica

Nevertheless, many scholars assume that the Roman basilica was the antecedent for early church architecture. The Roman basilica was the location for governmental hearings and official actions (figure 8.2). It was built longitudinally, normally with a central nave and two side aisles. At the front was a bema where officials sat during the proceedings. There was no clerestory; the roof was flat or barrel-shaped over the nave. If the first Christians thought hierarchically about the priesthood, and had a positive attitude toward state functions, it stands to reason that the basilica would provide an architectural model. One suspects that those two conditions were not present at the beginning of the fourth century.[7]

6. On the types of homes used by early Christians see Robert Jewett, "Tenement Churches and Communal Meals in the Early Church: The Implications of a Form-Critical Analysis of 2 Thess 3:10," *BR* 38 (1993): 23–43. For the areas in Rome where Christians lived see Peter Lampe, *Die stadtrömischen Christen in den ersten beiden Jahrhunderten* (Tübingen: Mohr [Siebeck], 1987), 30–35.

7. See Ejnar Dyggve, *Dødekult, Kejserkult og Basilika: Bidrag til Spørgsmålet om den oldkristne kultbygnings Genesis* (Copenhagen: Branners Forlag, 1943), 8, 24. The basilica was built because "the emperor is a god, so it follows that his house is a temple" (my translation). See also J. B. Ward-Perkins, "Memoria, Martyr's Tomb, and Martyr's Church," *JTS* 17 (1966): 20–38.

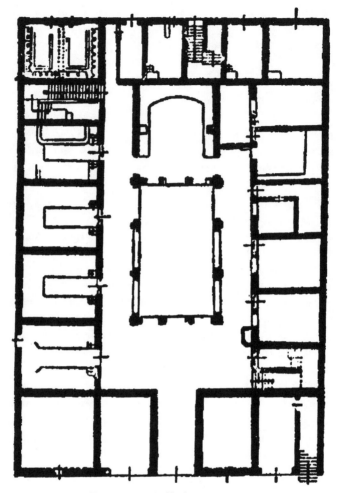

Figure 8.1. Villa house plan

However, like the suburban house, the plan of the basilica does indeed match that of the Romanesque church.

Functional Antecedent: The Family

The issue of antecedents cannot be solved on the basis of formal architectural similarities. We must also consider the function of early Christian buildings.

There can be no doubt that the first church met in homes. In the letters of Paul particularly we have frequent references. In 1 Cor. 16:19 he sends

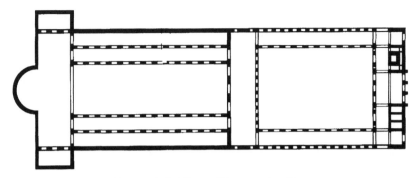

Figure 8.2. Plan of Roman basilica

a greeting from Aquila and Prisca σὺν τῇ κατ' οἶκον αὐτῶν ἐκκλησίᾳ. Paul sends the same greeting to Aquila and Prisca in Rom. 16:5. In Col. 4:15 he greets Nympha and τὴν κατ' οἶκον αὐτῆς ἐκκλησίαν. In fact, it is more of a problem to conceive of a single church at Rome or Corinth. When and where did all these house churches come together? Or perhaps they never did![8] As we have seen, our only examples of early Christian meeting places are indeed relatively small house churches.[9] In any case, the community language of the first church was familial. Women and men addressed each other as sister and brother. The divinity or authority was father or mother. The religious actors were children of God. The meetings were familial. House churches contained areas for worship and meetings, for food preparation, and even for baptisms. It is close to inconceivable that the early church would have dropped this familial community and meetings in the house atmosphere in favor of a hierarchical, liturgical, longitudinal architecture.

The church obviously could have adopted some other form of architecture prior to 313 c.e. The Diaspora Jews did. The Christians intentionally

8. My personal opinion is that every house church had a manager (or minister?) who not only owned the house and made the preparations, but also represented that house church in the larger community. I assume that one house belonged to the city manager (elder or bishop) who on occasion held council with the other house owners (*gerousia*). See John Reumann, "One Lord, One Faith, One God, but Many House Churches," in *Common Life in the Early Church*, ed. Julian V. Hills (Harrisburg, Pa.: Trinity Press International, 1998), 106–17.

9. Eusebius argued that there were formal churches before 300 c.e., but they had been destroyed during the various persecutions. On house churches in early Christianity see Michael L. White, *The Social Origins of Christian Architecture*, vol. 1, *Building God's House in the Roman World: Architectural Adaptation Among Pagans, Jews and Christians* (Baltimore: Johns Hopkins University Press, 1990 [repr. Valley Forge, Pa.: Trinity Press International, 1996], 111–23); Robert Banks, *Paul's Idea of Community: The Early House Churches in Their Historical Setting* (Grand Rapids: Eerdmans, 1980); Snyder, *Ante Pacem*, 67–82. Hans-Josef Klauck, *Hausgemeinde und Hauskirche im frühen Christentum* (Stuttgart: Verlag Katholisches Bibelwerk, 1981).

kept the house church even after they were sufficiently established and wealthy to build edifices to meet their own needs and specifications. When the early Christians did shift to buildings, what were the causative factors?

Martyria

Some of our problems regarding early Christian architecture arise from a lack of understanding the first three centuries. Most cultures of the Mediterranean basin considered the dead as members of the family. Families were buried together in mausolea or private plots. They built mensae, or tables, in the cemeteries so that families could eat with those who had died (*refrigeria*). This occurred on the death date of the deceased. Obviously a large family could spend considerable time eating with their dead (Augustine, *Conf.* 6.2). The dead themselves received their food through a pipe inserted into the grave, though some early art shows the dead person actually sitting and eating at the meal. Special chairs might be present for their use.[10] Early Christians continued this practice of eating with the dead family members.

In addition to *loculi* and *cubiculae* in the catacombs, some people were buried in round mausolea much like the Greco-Roman heroon. Most of these burials afforded opportunity for communion with the special dead. Some of the *martyria* were square (Bonn, Salona [figure 8.3]), but others adapted the round edifice of the Greco-Roman culture. A special example would be the *memoria apostolorum* discovered under St. Sebastiano in Rome earlier this century. It appears to have acted as a mausoleum for all the apostles. Whatever the history of that circular edifice, during the same excavation, archaeologists found nearby a remarkable hall in which early Christians ate with their dead in the presence of Peter and Paul. Their prayers (147 remain) are scratched on the plaster wall of the triclia. This third-century hall may not be the first *martyrium*, but it does point to a significant development. Early Christians ate with their heroes, the martyrs, and built special places so that they could be buried near the martyrs and could eat with them as well as their families. Eventually these special places tended to be round.

Coemeteria Subteglata

As the number of Christians increased dramatically, the burial practices became a problem. More space for burials and for the family meals was needed. As the peace of Constantine approached, churches began to build

---

10. Theodor Klauser, *Die Cathedra im Totenkult der heidnischen und christlichen Antike* (Münster: Aschendorf, 1927), 98–151.

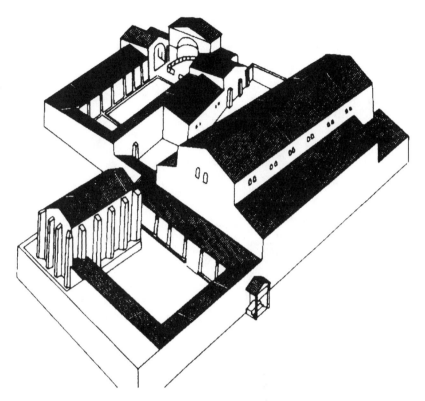

Figure 8.3. Martyrium complex at Salona

extensive cemetery buildings above ground. Most of the cemeteries followed a specific pattern. The significant dead were buried in a round
edifice, like the heroon, which then was elongated along a longitudinal
axis (figure 8.4). The elongated building had three aisles formed by long,
parallel columns. Most had a clerestory. Other than the few instances
of an *aula ecclesia*, these were the first Christian buildings (St. Sebastiano, St. Lorenzo, St. Agnese). What appeared to be an altar in the
apse was actually a mensa for the *martyrium*. The building itself was
not a place of worship. Instead, there were many burials and frequent
meals for the dead. There was no clergy and no liturgy. Covered cemeteries (*coemeteria subteglata*) were very popular. Constantine supported
the cemetery style, so that most of his first churches consisted of a nave
with side aisle, a clerestory supported by columns, all of which led to a
supposed *martyrium* surrounded by burials (St. Lorenzo fuori le mura,
St. Agnese, St. Sebastiano, St. Peter's, SS. Pietro e Marcellino [figure 8.4],
St. Constanza, Church of the Nativity, Church of the Holy Sepulchre).

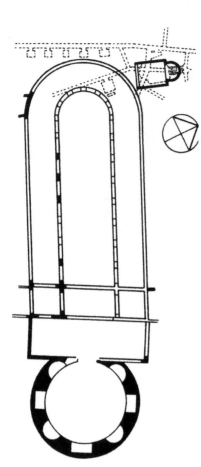

Figure 8.4.
Covered cemetery at
SS. Pietro and Marcellino

Architecturally speaking, eventually the meal for the dead was moved into the traditional hall. Relics of the martyrs were, for the first time, placed under a mensa, now become altar, where the death of Jesus was celebrated alongside the death of the martyrs. The presence of the relics of the martyr(s) under the altar brought the meals for the dead into the traditional church and allowed reverence for church heroes, while the longitudinal axis acknowledged the authority of the church hierarchy.

Shifting the familial architecture of the house church to include the extended family created the need for a more extensive cemeterial building. That building, rather than the suburban house or the basilica, became the architectural prototype of the early Christian basilica. The shift occurred, of course, when Constantine resolved to copy for public use what had previously been more private and familial.

9

Inscriptions

Language and Names

Jewish Inscriptions

According to Leon's study of Roman Jewish inscriptions, 405 (76 percent) are in Greek, 123 (23 percent) in Latin, and only three in Hebrew.[1] There is nothing surprising here. Diaspora Jews spoke primarily Greek, some Latin, and practically no Hebrew or Aramaic.[2] While language could be an issue of interaction of Jews with non-Jews in Rome, there is no reason to suppose that the data for Jews in Rome would be significantly distinctive. It is not clear where and at what point Jews adopted the lingua franca of the Roman world.

The same is true of names, though perhaps more can be learned, because the use of names does not necessarily reflect the absolute need to communicate with the dominant culture. According to Leon, the Jews of Rome did not attempt to maintain identity by means of names. Of his 551 names, only seventy-two (13.1 percent) are Semitic. In fact, Latin has become predominant with 254 examples (46.1 percent), followed by Greek with 175 examples (31.8 percent). The predominance of Latin names found in inscriptions that are primarily Greek indicates that the Jews of Rome spoke the common language of the Mediterranean world, but named their children according to the custom in Rome.[3] In terms of interaction, the Jews did not contribute their symbols to the Western

---

1. At least two of which came from the same Monteverde catacomb, which had the five Torah shrines. See Harry J. Leon, *The Jews of Ancient Rome* (Philadelphia: The Jewish Publication Society of America, 1960), 67–92.

2. Wolfgang Wiefel assumes that the Jewish congregations must have spoken in Greek ("The Jewish Community in Ancient Rome and the Origins of Roman Christianity," in *The Romans Debate,* ed. Karl Donfried [Peabody, Mass.: Hendrickson, 1991], 90). Tessa Rajak notes that the balance between Latin and Greek varies according to the catacomb, so that so-called Romanization may well have differed from synagogue to synagogue ("Inscription and Context: Reading the Jewish Catacombs of Rome," in *Studies in Early Jewish Epigraphy,* ed. Jan Willem van Henten and Pieter Willem van der Horst [Leiden: Brill, 1994], 232–33).

3. In Osiek's revision of Leon's *Jews of Ancient Rome* (Peabody, Mass.: Hendrickson, 1995), twenty of her forty-one additional names are Greek (49 percent), fifteen Latin (37 percent), and three Semitic (7 percent) (see pp. xv–xvi).

world,[4] did not contribute a language, but did contribute many favorite names, such as Esther, Jacob, Jonathan, Isaac, Mary, Martha, Rebecca, Samuel, Sara, and Simon.[5]

Christian Inscriptions

Again, the first Christians of Rome did not bring with them names that would mark their identity. So most of their names are Roman or the virtue-names of slaves (such as Fortunatus, Irene, Agape). When Christians did begin to develop identifying names, they produced four types:[6] (1) biblical names and names of early martyrs; (2) names incorporating names for God; (3) calendar names; and (4) Christian virtues. In the larger collection of Christian inscriptions found in the Vatican (*SICV*) there is only one example of a name taken from the Hebrew Scriptures — Susanna. Two of the New Testament names have Hebrew roots (Johannes and Maria), but in any case, only three other New Testament names are used (Andreas, Paulus, Petrus). It is possible that the name Laurentius refers to the early martyr. God-names appear in such appellations as Theophilus, Timotheus (or is it a New Testament name?), Theonis, and Cyriacus / Cyriace / Cyriacete. Calendar names have Jewish roots. The *SICV* examples are Paschasius and Sabbatius / Sabbatia. As for virtues, it is difficult to tell whether frequent names such as Elpis and Irene are actually Christian. Probably Anastas, Redempta, Renatus / Renata are of Christian origin. Nevertheless, the one certain Christian virtue name was Agape, though one cannot claim uniqueness.

Perhaps it is not the names themselves that are most important. It is somewhat remarkable that the lasting names of the Western world include a large number of names from the Hebrew Scriptures and names of Jews who were primary figures of the New Testament. Even more important, though, is the process of name democratization. The formal male name in the Roman world contained three names, while the formal female name contained two. Of the 541 names listed by Leon, only three are triple and only forty-nine are double. Of the names listed in the *SICV*, 20 percent are proper Roman names. Although chronology is, unfortunately, uncertain for most of these inscriptions, it is clear that Roman names took a sharp drop after the peace of Constantine. By the sixth century only 4 percent of the men had proper Roman names, and

---

4. See chapter 6.

5. Gerard Mussies, "Jewish Personal Names in Some Non-Literary Sources," in *Studies in Early Jewish Epigraphy*, ed. J. W. van Henten and P. W. van der Horst (Leiden: Brill, 1994), 250.

6. According to Iiro Kajanto, "Les Noms," in *Sylloge inscriptionum christianarum veterum musei vaticani*, Acta instituti romani finlandiae, vol. 1, no. 2, ed. Henrik Zilliacus (Helsinki, 1963) 68–71.

only 2 percent of the women. Jews and Christians in Rome participated in (caused?) a sociological shift that obviated the social distinctions between noble, artisan, and even slave.[7]

Burial Vocabulary

In terms of the vocabulary itself, there is much to observe. In the Jewish collection from the Vatican museum nearly every inscription is introduced by the terms ἐνθάδε κεῖτε (plate 1).[8] This simple statement about the presence of the deceased in the tomb contrasts sharply with the nearly universal introduction on Roman inscriptions: *DM* or *dis manibus* ("to the spirits").[9] Christians dropped the *DM*, sometimes in favor of *BM* or *bene merenti*, or *depositus / deposita*, meaning, one assumes, that the deceased is here only temporarily. Both ἐνθάδε κεῖτε and *depositus / deposita* break with the sense that the deceased now exists only with the spirits or daimons.

Jewish and Christian burials are frequently marked by the key word "peace."[10] In the Vatican Jewish inscriptions, nos. 1, 3, 9, 10, 14, 15, 17, 18 end with some form of the acclamation "in peace." The final phrase follows this formula: (1) the acclamation "in peace"; (2) the condition wished, "sleep"; (3) a pronoun reference to the deceased person. A typical example would be no. 15, ἐν ἰρήνη ἡ κοίμησις αὐτῆς," or no. 10, ἐν εἰρήνη ἡ κοίμησις αὐτοῦ. Of the 294 complete inscriptions described by Leon, 239 open with ἐνθάδε κεῖτε, and 167 end with ἐν εἰρήνη. Of the 167 ending with "in peace," 136 contain the complete phrase, in varying forms, ἐν εἰρήνη ἡ κοίμησις αὐτοῦ.[11] In addition, at least ten of the remaining examples mention sleep in some form. Several speak of sleep with the saints, e.g., μετὰ τῶν δικέων ἡ κύμησις αὐτοῦ (no. 110).

---

7. An observation so lamented by Jérôme Carcopino, *Daily Life in Ancient Rome*, trans. E. O. Lorimer (New Haven: Yale University Press, 1963).

8. For the Vatican examples see Snyder, "The Interaction of Jews With Non-Jews In Rome," *Judaism and Christianity in First-Century Rome*, ed. Karl Donfried and Peter Richardson (Grand Rapids: Eerdmans, 1998), 69–90.

9. The very few inscriptions with *DM* must have inexplicably slipped into Jewish and Christian catacombs (Rajak, "Reading the Jewish Catacombs," 239–40). Note *dis manibus* and discussion in no. 16 of Osiek's additions to *The Jews of Ancient Rome* (pp. 383, 20). See also Rutgers, *Jews in Late Ancient Rome*, 269–72.

10. Erich Dinkler, "Shalom-Eirene-Pax: Jüdische Sepulkralinschriften und ihr Verhältnis zum frühen Christentum," *Rivista Archeologia Christiana* 50 (1974): 121–44.

11. Leon, *Jews of Ancient Rome*, 122. Of the forty-one additional inscriptions listed by Osiek in the revised edition of *The Jews of Ancient Rome*, three include the complete set of formulas, four others have the closing formula "in peace, sleep," two include the opening formula "here lies" and the closing formula "in peace." Of the remainder, four close with "in peace," and twelve open with "here lies." Or, put another way, seventeen open with "here lies" and thirteen close with "in peace."

Although one cannot deduce from a few epexegetical phrases that the sleep always refers to rest or peace with the faith community, it would be difficult to avoid this intent. The ending phrase was an identity mark for Jewish graves. The sleep referred to continued existence within the boundaries of the community, likely even the specific synagogue that used that catacomb. The quality of sleep with the righteous was, it was hoped, *shalom*.

Likewise, *in pace* became the identifying mark of a Christian burial (plate 21). Of the 350 examples in *SICV*, 107 utilize *in pace* at some point. The origin and meaning of the phrase has been much debated.[12] Like *vivas*, it appears as an acclamation, used perhaps at meals or other times of conviviality. *In pace* offers a wish that the person will find joy and satisfaction in the corporate (meal) setting. Christians followed the Jews by using the term *shalom*.[13] Instead of seeing death as a time of individual wandering, Jews and Christians expressed faith in a continued existence (*depositus*) among the believing community.

Conclusion

In regard to language the picture differs from that of symbols. Jews did take on the language of the Romans and they used Roman names. Although Hebrew or Aramaic never became a significant element in the language of the Western world, the Jews did contribute many personal names.

Christians likewise adopted the language of the Roman world. They used Roman names, but not the name system. Dissolution of the Roman name system reflected a strong democratization created by the nascent Jesus movement. Christians apparently contributed very few personal names to the Western world.

In both Judaism and Christianity burial language assumed a continued presence of the deceased family members. Neither signified that the deceased lived in a spirit world.

---

12. For references see Bruun, "Symboles, Signes et Monogrammes," 76–79.

13. Dinkler ("Shalom-Eirene-Pax") doubts that early Christians derived their acclamation "in peace" from Jewish burial practices. He prefers a separate development that depends on early Christian worship (e.g., John 14:27; 20:19, 26; Eph. 2:14). In any case, the original source for the peace acclamation and its communal meaning would have been Judaism.

10

Calendar

A culture cannot exist without language and a calendar. The first Christians did not have a calendar that they could designate their own. Eventually a Christian calendar did emerge from the Roman Julian calendar.

We have here a clear instance of inculturation, but the process may be so complex as to render historical reconstruction impossible.

Lunar and Solar

There are, of course, two types of calendars: lunar and solar. The lunar depends on the observable waning and waxing of the moon (approximately twenty-eight days). Because it is based on the visible regularity of the moon's phases, the lunar calendar serves well to establish calendar units larger than a day (week, month) and to establish the date for festivals on a recurring basis.[1] The solar calendar is based on the time it takes for the earth to circle the sun (365.25 days). Universally a day is measured by the rotation of the earth. Seasons occur because of the tilt of the earth as it rotates around the sun. Both calendar systems are necessary. Unfortunately they are incompatible. There is no way to factor the lunar twenty-eight with the solar 365.25. Cultures based on the lunar calendar inevitably lose track of the seasons and must resort to ad hoc intercalations. Cultures based on the solar calendar have no easily observable units of time smaller than a year and larger than a day. Invariably they too must resort to ad hoc intercalations in order to fill out the year. Few cultures depend exclusively on one or the other, but also, history is littered with attempts to combine the two.

---

1. Roger T. Beckwith, *Calendar and Chronology, Jewish and Christian: Biblical, Intertestamental and Patristic Studies* (Leiden: Brill, 1996); *Encyclopaedia Britannica*, 15th ed., s.v. "calendar," 3:599.

Jewish Calendar

The calendar of the Hebrew Scriptures was primarily lunar. But much like the earlier Mesopotamian culture, both calendars were used. God placed both the sun and the moon in the sky, and God said, "Let there be lights in the dome of the sky to separate the day from the night; and let them be for signs and for seasons and for days and years" (Gen. 1:14). Although the lunar year is explicitly mentioned as the means of measuring time (Ps. 104:19, 89:37), in other instances the solar month must have been intended. For example,

> and the waters gradually receded from the earth. At the end of one
> hundred fifty days the waters had abated; and in the seventh month,
> on the seventeenth day of the month, the ark came to rest on the
> mountains of Ararat. (Gen. 8:3–4)

The five months from the seventeenth of the second month to the seventeenth of the seventh month came to 150 days or five thirty-day (solar) months. Jewish festivals invariably followed the lunar calendar. Because a lunar calendar was used, from time to time an intercalary month (number thirteen) was required. Priests and rabbis could determine the need for such a month primarily by the grain harvest. The harvest was necessary for the proper celebration of the Passover and the Feast of Unleavened Bread (Exod. 12:33–13:10; Josh. 5:10–12). Passover came on the fourteenth of Nisan, a regular lunar date, though quite variable in a solar calendar. Presumably, though not certainly, the fourteenth of Nisan must fall after the vernal equinox.

The lunar month was divided into four phases, or weeks, of seven-day duration. The last day of the week was a day of rest called the Sabbath. Although the origin and rationale for the Sabbath were variously stated (Exod. 20:8–11; 23:12–13; Deut. 5:12–15), keeping the Sabbath became a primary mark of what it means to be a Jew.

During the intertestamental period elements of Judaism shifted more sharply toward a solar calendar. Though the astronomical book of *1 Enoch* 72–82 discusses the lunar calendar, its primary intent is to establish a twelve-month year of 354 days to which are added ten days to match the solar year. The Essene community spent considerable effort to perfect such a calendar (the *Temple Scroll*, 11QTemple).

The Jesus Tradition and the Jewish Calendar

The Jesus tradition makes very few references to the calendar. Indeed, the few references are negative. Jesus seemed not to hold to the Sabbath rest. He cast out an unclean spirit on the Sabbath (Mark 1:21–28). He defended his disciples' act of plucking heads of grain on the Sabbath (Mark 2:23–28). He healed a man with a withered hand on the Sabbath (Mark 3:1–6). He healed a crippled woman on the Sabbath (Luke 13:10–17). And, finally, he healed a man with dropsy on the Sabbath (Luke 14:1–6). In answer to his critics he insisted that the Sabbath was made for the benefit of humankind, not humankind for the Sabbath (Mark 2:27). There are no positive statements about the Sabbath or any indications that Jesus took special care. He did visit the synagogue on the Sabbath (Mark 6:1–2a; Luke 4:16). He hoped that the end time would not come on the Sabbath, because that would hinder end-time flight (Matt. 24:20).

Jesus did not follow the liturgical calendar. Although he did not oppose prayer and fasting, he did suggest that it be done without any public display of piety. The disciple of Jesus should pray in a closet (Matt. 6:5–6) and fast in such a way that no one notices (Matt. 6:16–18). He himself had the reputation of not observing fast days at all (Matt. 9:14–15; 11:18–19).

In the Synoptic Gospels Jesus does celebrate the Passover, but even then the calendric problems are staggering. There is no satisfactory explanation for the activities that seemingly occurred on his final Passover. Nor is there a satisfactory explanation for the Passover date of Nisan 15 in the Gospel of John. One must conclude that the story is so coated with liturgical tradition that we can never hope to know the attitude of Jesus toward the Jewish Passover.

It is clear that the Jesus tradition shows little use for the Jewish calendar. Perhaps "disdain" might better describe the situation. We are left then with several critical problems. Is the apathy toward calendar a reflection of the historical Jesus or a reflection of the Gospel churches? Or put another way: if the attitude toward calendar stems from Jesus, what made the early church keep it as part of the Jesus tradition? If Jesus did not display apathy for the calendar, why did the early church make it part of the Jesus tradition?[2]

One could easily understand that any religious hero would step to the music of a different drummer. But Jesus did more than ignore — he attacked. The notion of attack offers yet another possibility. In addition to lunar and solar calendars there was also the option of anarchy. One popular philosophy did indeed deliberately attack the common conception of time. Cynics wore clothing inappropriate to the season, ignored night and day, and carried out activities at unusual times. For them the calendar was enslaving. We cannot determine here whether, and to what extent,

---

2. See Rordorf, *Sunday: The History of the Day.*

Jesus might have been a Cynic or have been influenced by the Cynics. Perhaps it does not really matter whether the historical Jesus was a Cynic, or a calendric anarchist.[3] What does matter is that the Jesus tradition kept the disdain for the Jewish calendar. The earliest churches, though at first Jewish, eventually could not follow a Jewish calendar without compromising their faith system.

In terms of the Gospels, the first break with the Jewish calendar occurs at the resurrection. Very early on "the first day of the week" the women went to the tomb of Jesus (Mark 16:2 [16:9 is secondary]; likewise Matt. 28:1; Luke 24:1; John 20:1). John goes further yet by having the first meeting of Jesus' disciples on the evening of the "first day of the week" (20:19), and then yet another meeting eight days later (20:26). The Gospel churches of the first century knew the tradition that Jesus rejected the calendar, kept that tradition alive because they too had to reject the Jewish calendar, yet dared not live by the Roman calendar, and finally began to form a new calendar with the "first day of the week" after Passover as the keystone.

Paul and the Calendar

As we have seen, Paul had a strong tendency to keep the status quo but, in an eschatological manner, to relativize everything cultural. That is likely true also of the calendar, but one cannot be certain. Paul is certainly not without a sense of occasion. He urges the Corinthian Christians to laugh at weddings and cry at funerals, but not to take such events seriously (1 Cor. 7:30). On the other hand, he was deadly serious about the Lord's Supper. Failure to recognize the meaning of the occasion was an invitation for illness, even death (1 Cor. 11:30). We do not know the date of the Lord's Supper or its frequency. He repeats the Passover institution of the Eucharist as if it were simply an adaptation of the Jewish meal (1 Cor. 11:24–27). Within the letters of Paul there is only one, quite problematic, hint of the new calendar:

> On the first day of every week [κατὰ μίαν σαββάτου ἕκαστος], each of you is to put aside and save whatever extra you earn, so that collections need not be taken when I come. And when I arrive, I will send any whom you approve with letters to take your gift to Jerusalem. (1 Cor. 16:2–3)

At first glance one supposes that Paul intended for the collection to be made during the meeting on the first day of the week. But a second glance does not sustain that interpretation. Each family is to put aside some money on the first day of the week and then offer what has been saved when the collection is made. It would be ridiculous to suppose that each family gave to the collection at the "first day" meeting and then took it home for a later time. Although one cannot easily explain how the collection was to be made, there is no reason to believe that we have here a change in the Jewish calendar.

Paul and the Pauline tradition were in a serious cultural quandary. To become a follower of Jesus means rejecting the old way of life. The old way of life is deeply embedded in the Julian calendar. In order to change religious allegiance, the Julian calendar, with its solar-determined festivals (πτωχὰ στοιχεῖα), had to be rejected. In writing to the Galatians, Paul expresses in sharp terms his unhappiness with those converts who are slipping back into the solar calendar:

> Formerly, when you did not know God, you were enslaved to beings that by nature are not gods. Now, however, that you have come to know God, or rather to be known by God, how can you turn back again to the weak and beggarly elemental spirits [πτωχὰ στοιχεῖα]? How can you want to be enslaved to them again? You are observing special days [ἡμέρας], and months, and seasons, and years [μῆνας καὶ καιροὺς καὶ ἐνιαυτούς]. I am afraid that my work for you may have been wasted. (Gal. 4:8–11)

At the same time, he scolds those who keep to the Jewish lunar calendar (ἡμέρας παρατηρεῖσθε καὶ μῆνας καὶ καιροὺς καὶ ἐνιαυτούς). With both the solar and the lunar calendar there is a serious problem for the first Christians.

At the same time, Paul, or Deutero-Paul, has a different problem.[4] Leaving the Julian calendar means either anarchy or accepting the available lunar calendar, the Jewish one. Some members of the community, who hold to the solar calendar, condemn others for holding to the lunar, or Jewish, one:

> Therefore do not let anyone condemn you in matters of food and drink or of observing festivals, new moons, or sabbaths [ἑορτῆς ἢ νεομηνίας ἢ σαββάτων]. These are only a shadow of what is to come, but the substance belongs to Christ. (Col. 2:16–17)

Paul advises those following the lunar to ignore the criticisms. His reasoning follows precisely the Pauline attitude toward culture: it does not

---

4. See Troy W. Martin, *By Philosophy and Empty Deceit: Colossians as Response to a Cynic Critique* (Sheffield: Sheffield Academic Press, 1996).

matter anyway. The calendar is merely a shadow of things to come. Whatever his formula "neither Jew nor Greek" means otherwise, it also surely means that neither solar nor lunar calendar is ultimate. Nevertheless, there is no sign of Cynic anarchy in the letter of Paul. His style is end-time relativization, not end-time destruction.

The Paul of Acts follows the pattern we have discerned in the letters. Acts 13:44–46 to the contrary, Paul always went first to the synagogue on the Sabbath. The one exception, Acts 20:7, may not be so much an exception as it appears:

> On the first day of the week ['Εν δὲ τῇ μιᾷ τῶν σαββάτων], when we met to break bread, Paul was holding a discussion with them; since he intended to leave the next day, he continued speaking until midnight. (Acts 20:7)

The language certainly sounds formal. It was the first day of the week; they gathered together and they broke bread. We assume from Acts (2:42, 46) that the breaking of bread was a fellowship meal, not necessarily the Lord's Supper (1 Cor. 11:20) or the Eucharist. There is no reason to suppose anything other than that Paul was speaking at a fellowship meal on the day after the Sabbath.

In the Jewish calendar the days of the week were known by numbers except for the Sabbath and pre-Sabbath (Friday). The day after the Sabbath was the first day. However, in the Hebrew Scriptures, "first day" normally referred to the first day of the month (see 2 Chron. 29:17) or the first day of a festival (e.g., Lev. 23:39). Although all the Gospel writers know that Jesus was raised on the first day of the week, it seems to have no significance for Paul. Granted that a Sunday tradition is starting, the burden of proof lies on those who claim that Sunday was already established in the New Testament period. There is only one incontrovertible witness:

> I was in the spirit on the Lord's day [κυριακῇ ἡμέρᾳ], and I heard behind me a loud voice like a trumpet. (Rev. 1:10)

The "Lord's Day" must be a term for the primary Christian day, the day after the Sabbath. Presumably it reflects the apocalyptic expectation of a day of the Lord (e.g., Joel 1:15; 1 Thess. 5:2).[5]

---

5. D. A. Carson, ed., *From Sabbath to Lord's Day: A Biblical, Historical and Theological Investigation* (Grand Rapids: Zondervan, 1982). *Encyclopaedia Britannica*, 15th ed., s.v. "calendar," 3:600–601.

Calendar in the Fourth Gospel

If Paul relativizes the Jewish calendar, we would expect, from our previous discussion, that John would deconstruct the calendar. That does indeed appear to be the case. The first element of deconstruction appears in the form of timekeeping confusion. The progression in chapters 1 and 2 demonstrates the style. After the Pharisees encounter John the Baptist (1:19–28) there are three successive occurrences of "the next day" (1:29, 35, 43). On what should have been the fifth day, we are informed that the wedding of Cana was on the third day. That means the wedding occurred either on the seventh day after the narrative began, or else it is the third day of the week quite unrelated to the previous "next days." John gives considerable temporal information, but confusion arises because he seldom offers a firm point of reference. On the final Passover visit Jesus goes to Bethany six days before the Passover (12:1), but makes the triumphal entry on "the next day" (12:12). Efforts to rationalize the system have proven unproductive.

In addition to the confusion that arises, John has sharply altered the assumed calendar. Matthew and Luke place the birth of Jesus in what might have appeared to the readers as a firm historical context. John has no birth of Jesus. While other dramatis personae in the Fourth Gospel have names and introductions, the mother of Jesus has no name and no introduction. If by 90 c.e. there was a nascent celebration of the birth of Jesus with honor given to Mary, his mother, John has completely erased it.

By 90 c.e. the churches must have known that the Jewish Passover was no longer celebrated by Christians. They must have known that the fellowship meal derived from or was described by the feeding of the five thousand. John not only deconstructs the Passover, but also deconstructs its replacement. He does include the feeding story (6:1–14), but after crossing the Jordan, his Jesus chastises his listeners for depending on the food in the wilderness. With him they can celebrate the real Passover (Josh. 5:10–12). His very existence is the bread of life (6:35). Moreover, even the cup and the bread themselves must be deconstructed. In 6:51b–58, verses often rejected as late sacramentalism, he eradicates the Eucharist and replaces it with his own blood and flesh, that is, his own reality.

Of course, there is no Passover meal in the Gospel of John. The meal described in 13:1–30, a meal that occurs at the same time (Thursday evening) and with the same personnel as the Passover in the Synoptics, cannot be the Passover in John, because he has shifted it to the fifteenth of Nisan. Jesus is crucified at the same time the lambs are slaughtered for Passover. If John was willing to alter a known, set calendar date in order to make a theological statement about the death of Jesus, then we see what little regard he had for the calendar as a whole. The Jesus of the Gospel of John comes with very little in the way of cultural trappings. To deconstruct the calendar must have been a primary objective of the author.

The Roman Calendar

Before the first century B.C.E. Rome utilized a lunar calendar. In order to make the calendar seasonal a number of intercalations was required. About 46 B.C.E. Julius Caesar asked the astronomer Sosigenes to develop a more stable system. The result was a solar calendar with twelve months that were only approximately lunar.[6] Before the advent of the Julian calendar the Romans had used a nine-day week or *nundinae* period (actually eight, not nine). Somehow (!) at the time of Julian reform a seven-day week was adopted. Eventually this seven-day week became a planetary week with this improbable order: Saturn, Sun, Moon, Mars, Mercury, Jupiter, Venus.

At this juncture the issue of inculturation becomes vitally important. Why did the Romans shift to a seven-day week? Calendar alterations do not come easily. Was it the phases of the moon? But then there are not four lunar weeks in a solar month. Apparently the Jewish seven-day week was so popular that it was adopted by the empire.

Even more critical is the meaning of Saturn, the first day of the week, but identical with the Jewish seventh day, Sabbath. Saturn began to take on the characteristics of the Sabbath; primarily it became a day of rest. Jews argued that the Romans copied their Sabbath. Romans argued that the Jewish Sabbath derived from an earlier Roman practice.[7]

The Calendar of the Early Church

While our survey of symbols, art, and inscriptions would indicate that the Jews accepted some elements of the Roman culture but in return contributed little of their own, the formation of the calendar shows quite the opposite. Even though causes and historical antecedents are difficult to determine, it appears that the Jewish lunar calendar played an important

---

6. Samuele Bacchiocchi, *Anti-Judaism and the Origin of Sunday* (Rome: Pontifical Gregorian University Press, 1975); *From Sabbath to Sunday: A Historical Investigation of the Rise of Sunday Observance in Early Christianity* (Rome: Pontifical Gregorian University Press, 1977).

7. Bacchiocchi, *Anti-Judaism and the Origin of Sunday; From Sabbath to Sunday.*

role in the formation of the Roman week. And the influence of the Sabbath day on the day of Saturn made possible the formation of a Christian calendar. In the planetary calendar, the day after the Roman day of rest was the day of the sun — *dies solis*. Whether or not the *dies solis* had a special meaning, and even though it was the second day, it became the Christian "first day of the week." Early Christians sought to diminish the importance of the Sabbath and its observance. At the same time, they fought the astrological importance of the planetary week. Eventually they made the Roman day of the sun their first day of the week. We cannot be absolutely certain that this was a direct attack on sun worship, but it was an alteration of the Roman calendar for Christian purposes.

In the year 321 Constantine made the day of the sun the official rest day. Presumably this was done for political purpose (calendric unity) rather than to establish the Christian Sunday.

The Birth of Jesus

The most marvelous and striking piece of art discovered beneath St. Peter's by the excavators has to be the yellow and green mosaic showing Christ as Apollo crossing the sky in his biga (plate 22). Whatever we say about the day of the sun, one can hardly doubt that the first Christians struggled with the Roman worship of the sun god. The chariot of Elijah on the doors of St. Sabina (plate 23) probably has the same intent as the mosaic under St. Peter's. There are several frescoes showing the three wise men, or astrologers, approaching Mary, with or without the baby Jesus. Since early Christian art by definition is not illustrative, one assumes that the three astrologers point to the calendric importance of the birth of Jesus. In fact, one later representation (on a fourth-century sarcophagus in Arles) has the three astrologers pointing to the heavenly phenomenon (sun / planet / star? [plate 24]).

While it may be true that the early fathers of the church defended the date of Jesus' birth using internal (biblical) data, still, the generally assumed explanation cannot be ignored. The church redefined the winter solstice as the birth date of Jesus rather than the birth date of the sun god *(natalis solis invicti)*.

The early Christians invaded the Roman solar calendar at the point of the winter solstice. The vernal equinox is another matter. While some Christians insisted on celebrating Easter on the day of the Passover, the fourteenth of Nisan (Quartodecimians), most Christians celebrated it on the first Sunday after the Passover (and presumably after the vernal equinox). Following the lunar calendar for Easter meant that a fixed solar date became impossible and so did a Christian celebration of the vernal equinox.

The Martyrs Calendar

As we have seen in the section on architecture, the earlier Christians adapted the Greco-Roman custom of eating with the dead on their birthday. They extended the sense of family to the church family much as the non-Christian society shared around the tombs of heroes. *Martyria* appeared by the third century (figure 8.3) It is my contention that the large buildings of Constantinian Christianity are actually extended *martyria* called *coemeteria subteglata* (figure 8.4). They were built to house the agape fellowship of the faith community around the graves of the significant dead. These covered cemeteries were eventually converted to basilica style churches.

In any case, eating with the martyrs created another aspect of the Christian calendar. The first literary reference to continued celebration of a martyr's death is recorded in the *Martyrdom of Polycarp* (18:3). Eventually the Christian calendar was nearly filled with significant days based on martyr deaths. The first Christians changed the deep-seated custom of honoring significant dead with the custom of honoring those who died for the faith. Along with Sunday, Christmas, and Easter, the martyr days became the basis for the Western calendar.

11

Food and Meals

The Meaning of Food

The meaning and use of food reflect primary components of a culture. That fact has been recognized only in this century. The sociology of food — a burgeoning field — has much to offer in the study of inculturation. Unfortunately for the historian, the field of study has no unified methodology, and even if it did, the possibility of ascertaining the food habits of an older culture is problematic. Nevertheless, the issue of food cannot be avoided. What we learn from the use of food in a culture will be as valuable as any other indicator.

Methodology

Three approaches to the semiotic use of food have been utilized by social scientists. In *functionalism* researchers (Durkheim,[1] Merton[2]) examine the production and use of food as an integral part of the corporate enterprise. Much as the arm functions as a necessary part of the body, so food functions as a necessary part of any given culture. The advent of *structuralism* as a method of analysis brought among social scientists a significant interest in food (Lévi-Strauss, Douglas). The culinary enterprise manifests deeper, underlying cultural structures that, if correctly deciphered, signal the organization of the human mind and society. While the Lévi-Strauss system of "raw / cooked" may confound many,[3] the adaptation of structuralism by Mary Douglas has been widely used by biblical scholars.[4] A third method, *developmentalism*, actually serves

---

1. Emile Durkheim, *The Elementary Forms of the Religious Life,* trans. J. W. Swain (New York: Free Press, 1965), 13–33, 366–92; Emile Durkheim and Marcel Mauss, *Primitive Classification,* trans. Rodney Needham (London: Cohen and West, 1963).
2. R. K. Merton, *Social Theory and Social Structure* (Glencoe, Ill.: Free Press, 1968).
3. Claude Lévi-Strauss, *The Raw and the Cooked,* trans. John and Doreen Weightman (New York: Harper & Row, 1969).
4. Mary Douglas, "Deciphering a Meal," in *Implicit Meanings: Essays in Anthropology* (London: Routledge and Kegan Paul, 1975), 249–75; *Purity and Danger: An Analysis of the Concepts of Pollution and Taboo* (London: Routledge and Kegan Paul, 1966). Among biblical scholars a good example would be Halvor Moxnes, "Meals and the New Community in Luke," *Svensk Exegetisk Årsbok* 51–52 (1986–87): 158–67.

as something of a catchall of the remaining styles. Normally, developmentalists are interested in the history of food use in a particular environment.[5]

All three methods have something to offer for studies in inculturation. Since structuralism assumes an inherent relationship of food to basic structure (kinship), we will sometimes use the ideas of structuralism, but develop a more sociological, functional approach.

There are several subtopics that are useful for consideration: (1) the meaning of food language; (2) the function and alteration of the menu; (3) the use of meals to include and exclude; (4) the role of gender in the food enterprise; (5) food for the dead; (6) food for the poor.

Jewish Food Symbolism[6]

Judeo-Christian covenant language often makes metaphorical or symbolic use of food, family, meals, and sexuality. God creates the food supply for all creatures:

> These all look to you to give them their food in due season; when you give to them, they gather it up; when you open your hand, they are filled with good things. When you hide your face, they are dismayed; when you take away their breath, they die and return to their dust. (Ps. 104:27–29)

After the flood God proclaimed that everything living, except flesh with blood in it, was available for human consumption:

> Every moving thing that lives shall be food for you; and just as I gave you the green plants, I give you everything. Only, you shall not eat flesh with its life, that is, its blood. (Gen. 9:3–4)

God fed the Israelites after bringing them out of the land of Egypt (Exod. 16:32) and promised to bring them into a land flowing with milk and honey where they would eat and be satisfied (*Jub.* 1:7–8). God promises end-time food. When the Jews return from the exile Jerusalem will be their mother:

---

5. Gillian Feeley-Harnik, *The Lord's Table: Eucharist and Passover in Early Christianity* (Philadelphia: University of Pennsylvania Press, 1981), 16–17; Robert Alter, "A New Theory of *Kashrut*," *Commentary* 68, no. 2 (1979): 46–52.

6. Jean Soler, "The Semiotics of Food in the Bible," in *Food and Drink in History*, Selections from Annales Economies, Sociétés, Civilisations, vol. 5, ed. Robert Forster and Orest Ranum (Baltimore: Johns Hopkins University Press, 1979), 126–38; Roy C. Wood, *The Sociology of the Meal* (Edinburgh: Edinburgh University Press, 1995),1–45; Stephen Mennell, Anne Murcott, and Anneke H. van Otterloo, *The Sociology Of Food: Eating, Diet And Culture* (London: Sage Publications, 1992), 1–19.

> Rejoice with Jerusalem, and be glad for her, all you who love her;
> rejoice with her in joy, all you who mourn over her — that you
> may nurse and be satisfied from her consoling breast; that you may
> drink deeply with delight from her glorious bosom. (Isa. 66:10–11)

At the end time the Jews will all sit under their own vines and under their
own fig trees (Mic. 4:4). The end itself is sometimes characterized by a
banquet (Isa. 25:6–8), to the point that eating together, especially in a
ritual context, foreshadows the end:

> Truly I tell you, I will never again drink of the fruit of the vine until
> that day when I drink it new in the kingdom of God.
>
> (Mark 14:25)

God's care for the people of Israel and even the end time are signified
by food. Various foods implied particular, significant meanings. Bread,
water, wine, and meat are among the foods that carry divine symbolism.

Bread

Faith in God took the form of dependence on God for manna, or bread,
from heaven furnished during the wilderness generation (Exod. 16:4; cf.
Hos. 2:14–15; John 6:31–34).[7] That dependence on God (bread) could
and did include, metaphorically, God's word or God's wisdom. However,
throughout the biblical period the symbolic action of "the breaking of
bread" refers to eating a meal, often sharing a meal (Exod. 2:20; Luke
24:30; Acts 2:42). Just as community was established and maintained by
the breaking of bread, so sharing bread with God maintained the divine
covenant. Bread was a part of the sacrificial system, both leavened (Lev.
7:13) and unleavened (Exod. 29:2).[8] Loaves of bread, called "bread of
the Presence," were placed in the sanctuary of the temple next to the
holy of holies. Both the metaphorical and symbolic significance of bread
can be found through the New Testament and early Christian periods.
However, the author of the Gospel of John rejected the importance of
physical bread in favor of divine reality as found in the presence of Jesus:

> I am the bread of life. Your ancestors ate the manna in the wilder-
> ness, and they died. This is the bread that comes down from heaven,
> so that one may eat of it and not die. (John 6:48–50)

---

7. Peder Borgen, *Bread From Heaven: An Exegetical Study of the Concept of Manna in the Gospel of John and the Writings of Philo* (Leiden: Brill, 1965); Bertil Gärtner, *John 6 and the Jewish Passover*, Coniectanea neotestamentica, no. 17 (Lund: C. W. K Gleerup, 1959); Bruce Malina, *The Palestinian Manna Tradition: The Manna Tradition in the Palestinian Targums and Its Relationship to the New Testament Writings* (Leiden: Brill, 1968), 94–106.

8. Normally, breaking bread refers to the formation of community and the cutting of bread to sacrifice. See Paul Fieldhouse, *Food and Nutrition: Customs and Culture* (London: Croom Helm, 1986), 174.

Although John is the first to refer to Jesus as the bread, Judaism, as we have noted, had already made bread a metaphorical symbol of God's word (Deut. 8:3) and God's wisdom (Prov. 9:1–6).[9]

Bread was not only a staple food among early Christians and all others, but the breaking of bread signified and actualized the formation of community. There are few universals, but bread consistently carries the semiotic value of community with God and within the human community. In the Christian community the breaking of bread commemorated the death of Jesus as that death created and creates the faith community.[10] Bread was an essential part of the Agape and the Eucharist. In early Christian art bread appears in all meals, either as separate loaves or in baskets. Bread could also appear with fish or as an isolated symbol.

Because the breaking of bread was a divine symbol, bread could become a punishment, and inappropriate consumption of bread could lead to judgment rather than covenant life. In a dialectical, apocalyptic pronouncement Isaiah says,

> Though the Lord may give you the bread of adversity and the water of affliction, yet your Teacher will not hide himself any more, but your eyes shall see your Teacher. (Isa. 30:20)

In the same way, those who take the bread and cup of the Christian meal without perceiving the meaning of the event may become ill or even die (1 Cor. 11:29–30).

Water

While water may not formally belong to a food chain, its value as a divine symbol cannot be overstated. God sends the water that gives growth to everything; it symbolizes God's goodness to creation (Pss. 87:7; 104:10; 107:35; 114:8; Isa. 41:18; 58:11). In a semiarid land God's gift was absolutely essential. Israel's memory was that God cared for them with bread and water in the wilderness generation:

> The people quarreled with Moses, and said, "Give us water to drink." Moses said to them, "Why do you quarrel with me? Why do you test the Lord?" But the people thirsted there for water; and the people complained against Moses and said, "Why did you bring us out of Egypt, to kill us and our children and livestock with thirst?" So Moses cried out to the Lord, "What shall I do with this people?

---

9. Borgen, *Bread from Heaven*, 147–78.
10. Breaking bread was a private, family matter that created community. Public uses of bread did not involve breaking. See A. Hamman, *Vie liturgique et vie sociale: repas des pauvres, diaconie et diaconat, agape et repas de charité* (Paris: Desclée, 1968), 55.

They are almost ready to stone me." The Lord said to Moses, "Go on ahead of the people, and take some of the elders of Israel with you; take in your hand the staff with which you struck the Nile, and go.

I will be standing there in front of you on the rock at Horeb. Strike the rock, and water will come out of it, so that the people may drink." Moses did so, in the sight of the elders of Israel.

(Exod. 17:2–6; cf. Isa. 58:11)

The water metaphor signifies God not only as the giver of food, but also as a continuous source, a "fountain of living water" (Jer. 2:13), and, as a result, Israel "shall be like a watered garden, like a spring of water, whose waters never fail" (Isa. 58:11). When there is alienation between the people and God, then God withholds "all support of bread, and all support of water" (Isa. 3:1), or even sends poisonous water:

Why do we sit still? Gather together, let us go into the fortified cities and perish there; for the Lord our God has doomed us to perish, and has given us poisoned water to drink, because we have sinned against the Lord. (Jer. 8:14)

Water is a essential part of the diet. Granted that wine must have been used as a drink, bread and water are a menu pair. In Exod. 23:25 God says he will respond to their worship of him by, in turn, blessing their bread and water. Hosea's adulterous wife says, "I will go after my lovers; they give me my bread and my water, my wool and my flax, my oil and my drink" (Hos. 2:5). At the time of the exile, the Lord speaks extensively with Ezekiel about bread and water. A major threat will be "to break the staff of bread in Jerusalem; they shall eat bread by weight and with fearfulness; and they shall drink water by measure and in dismay. Lacking bread and water, they will look at one another in dismay, and waste away under their punishment (Ezek. 4:16–17). To be sure, as in 1 Kings 22:27, a menu of just bread and water could also be used as punishment. (We are not told there what food was being withheld.)

Water was a food. It was an essential food. But it was more than a food. It was a gift of God that enabled life. That gift was not the water itself but the conquering of original chaos. In the creation narrative God overcame the waters of chaos in order to form the earth (Gen. 1:1–2). According to the psalmist, God took charge of the water and created flowing streams for the dry land God created (Ps. 74:13–15). Although waters do not symbolize evil, they do represent a world that is unproductive and out of control. Using water under control, God created life and civilization as we know it. But God could withdraw that creative power and use the waters to destroy an unfaithful world:

> For my part, I am going to bring a flood of waters on the earth, to destroy from under heaven all flesh in which is the breath of life; everything that is on the earth shall die. (Gen. 6:17)

Uncontrolled waters are, metaphorically, like the chaotic threat of the nations around Israel:

> Ah, the thunder of many peoples, they thunder like the thundering of the sea! Ah, the roar of nations, they roar like the roaring of mighty waters! The nations roar like the roaring of many waters, but he will rebuke them, and they will flee far away, chased like chaff on the mountains before the wind and whirling dust before the storm. (Isa. 17:12–13)

God can control them as he did the Ur-chaos.

Just as bread signifies and effects community, so water signifies and creates social order. When, in Gen. 1, the chaos of the water was overcome, a calendar was formed (sun and moon), agriculture was made possible, and humans became self-conscious. Failure of the human consciousness (sin) eventually resulted in the formation of urban culture (Gen. 4:17), a culture that God threatened to return to the original chaos (Gen. 6:5–7; 7:4).

In the New Testament water takes on more of the chaos symbol than goodness. To be sure, there are some positive uses of water (Matt. 5:44–45; John 4:13–14; 7:37–39). The one who gives a cup of water is lauded (Matt. 10:42). In the story of the rich man and Lazarus even a drop of water would be a sign of mercy (Luke 16:24). But use of water as God's goodness appears only in the book of Revelation:

> Then he said to me, "It is done! I am the Alpha and the Omega, the beginning and the end. To the thirsty I will give water as a gift from the spring of the water of life. (Rev. 21:6)

> Then the angel showed me the river of the water of life, bright as crystal, flowing from the throne of God and of the Lamb.
> (Rev. 22:1)

> The Spirit and the bride say, "Come." And let everyone who hears say, "Come." And let everyone who is thirsty come. Let anyone who wishes take the water of life as a gift. (Rev. 22:17)

Otherwise, water refers to chaos, or else it is upstaged. A storm on Galilee threatens the safety of Jesus and the disciples. Jesus not only calms the water, but he is able to walk on it.[11] The Fourth Gospel also alters the nature of water as a food. At the wedding in Cana Jesus transforms purification water into wine for the feast.[12] At the well in Samaria, Jesus offers himself as living water to replace the stagnant cistern water of Judaism. Perhaps the very absence of references to water indicates a shift in symbolism. It never occurs in the letters of Paul except for yet another alteration: the church is washed by the water of the word of God (Eph. 5:26). The author of 1 Timothy complains about those who still hold to water as the gift of God (1 Tim. 4:3–4; 5:23).[13] For some, bread and wine may have been replaced by bread and water.

Apart from the food cycle we might note here that water was upstaged also as a purifying medium. In Luke 7:44–46 Jesus rebuked Simon the Pharisee for his attitude when Simon failed to furnish water to wash Jesus' feet, while the woman washed his feet with her tears. But most importantly, the baptism of John was with water, while the baptism of Jesus was with the Holy Spirit (Mark 1:8). The baptism of Jesus himself has from the beginning been a problem. Why would Jesus need to be baptized, i.e. purified? Semiotically speaking, much of the church moved in a different direction. Water initially was evil or chaotic. So for Paul, the initiate was baptized in the death of Jesus (Rom. 6:1–4). Typologically, Paul compares baptism with God's parting of the Red Sea (1 Cor. 10:1–2). Ignatius first stated that Jesus cleansed the water ἵνα τῷ πάθει τὸ ὕδωρ καθαρίσῃ (Ign. *Eph.* 18:2). Typologically, the baptism of Jesus was compared to the creation, and to the crossing of the Red Sea and the Jordan — all victories over the forces of evil (see especially Isa. 43:1–2; 51:9–11).[14]

Little wonder, then, that early Christian art shows scenes of victory over the water: symbols such as the anchor, the boat, and the fish portrayed a Christian existence in the cultural chaos. Even more significant

---

11. Raphael Patai assumes that the narrative of Jesus walking on water was built on the Jonah story. See his *Children of Noah: Jewish Seafaring in Ancient Times* (Princeton, N.J.: Princeton University Press, 1998), 117–21. See also the fascinating review by Jenny Diski, "Did Jesus Walk on Water because He Couldn't Swim?" *London Review of Books* (20 August 1998): 18–19.

12. On water as a religious symbol see E. S. Drower, *Water into Wine: A Study of Ritual Idiom in the Middle East* (London: J. Murray, 1956).

13. Those drinking water might be ascetics. But they also might be Christians who have come under the influence of a Jewish menu symbolism and have not yet accepted Christian semiotics. In the Jesus tradition John the Baptist, with a vow of asceticism, came μὴ ἐσθίων ἄρτον μήτε πίνων οἶνον, while Jesus was known as a φάγος καὶ οἰνοπότης (Luke 7:33–34).

14. See André Benoît, *Le baptême chrétien au second siècle: la théologie des pères*, Études d'histoire et de philosophie religieuses de l'Université de Strasbourg publiées sous les auspices de la Faculté de Théologie Protestante 43 (Paris: Presses universitaires de France, 1953), 59–82; Per Lundberg, *La typologie baptismale dans l'ancienne église*, Acta seminarii neotestamentici upsaliensis 10 (Uppsala: Lundequistska, 1942), 135–45.

are representations such as the Jonah cycle, Noah in the ark, and the fisherman — all of which proclaim the possibility of Christian existence in the watery morass of Roman culture.

As Jesus conquered evil through immersion in the water, so the first Christians overcame cultural entrapment by their baptism (see Maria Antiqua sarcophagus [plates 14, 13]).

Wine

The vineyard and its components are a very significant symbol of the God relationship. Israel is a vineyard, as portrayed in the popular song in Isa. 5:

> Let me sing for my beloved my love-song concerning his vineyard: My beloved had a vineyard on a very fertile hill. He dug it and cleared it of stones, and planted it with choice vines; he built a watchtower in the midst of it, and hewed out a wine vat in it; he expected it to yield grapes, but it yielded wild grapes. And now, inhabitants of Jerusalem and people of Judah, judge between me and my vineyard. What more was there to do for my vineyard that I have not done in it? When I expected it to yield grapes, why did it yield wild grapes? And now I will tell you what I will do to my vineyard. I will remove its hedge, and it shall be devoured; I will break down its wall, and it shall be trampled down. I will make it a waste; it shall not be pruned or hoed, and it shall be overgrown with briers and thorns; I will also command the clouds that they rain no rain upon it. For the vineyard of the Lord of hosts is the house of Israel, and the people of Judah are his pleasant planting; he expected justice, but saw bloodshed; righteousness, but heard a cry! (Isa. 5:1–7)

The parables of Jesus refer to the vineyard in such a way that those who heard them must have assumed that the Jesus tradition implied a metaphor for Israel: the parable of the wicked tenants (Mark 12:1–11) and the parable of the vineyard laborers (Matt. 20:1–16). Apart from the parables, in the rest of the New Testament the vineyard plays no role. As a divine symbol it references Israel, but not the church (though note 1 Cor. 3:5–9). Instead, as in Judaism, the symbol has shifted to the vine and grape or wine. Israel is a luxuriant vine that yields its fruit (Hos. 10:1; cf. Ps. 80:8), and the end time will be marked by everyone having their own vine and fig tree (Mic. 4:4; Zech. 3:10).[15] The Synoptic

---

15. Although the vine and fig tree are, in the Hebrew Scriptures, an important symbol for the end time, it did not carry over into the Jesus tradition except for Johannine composition in 1:48–50.

Gospels use the eschatological vine in the Last Supper: "I tell you, I will never again drink of this fruit of the vine until that day when I drink it new with you in my Father's [landless] kingdom" (Matt. 26:29). The author of the Gospel of John uses the eschatological vine as a sign of God's presence: ἐγώ εἰμι ἡ ἄμπελος (John 15:1, 5).

The vine did not disappear from Christian art (plate 22). It had been a consistent decoration in Roman art and from time to time reappears in later Christian art. For example, one thinks of the remarkable "Stem of Jesse" designs on painted churches of Romania. But the real shift was to wine. Wine as a divine symbol was hardly new to early Christianity. Early in the pentateuchal narrative we recognize that wine belongs to priestly actions:

> And King Melchizedek of Salem brought out bread and wine; he was priest of God Most High. (Gen. 14:18)

Wine could be part of the sacrificial system:

> Moreover, you shall offer one-fourth of a hin of wine as a drink offering with the burnt offering or the sacrifice, for each lamb.
> (Num. 15:5)

Wine was also known as "the cup." It could be a cup of salvation (Ps. 116:13), but more often, especially in Jeremiah, it symbolized the wrath or punishment of God:

> For thus the Lord, the God of Israel, said to me: Take from my hand this cup of the wine of wrath, and make all the nations to whom I send you drink it. They shall drink and stagger and go out of their minds because of the sword I am sending among them. So I took the cup from the Lord's hand, and made all the nations to whom the Lord sent me drink it. (Jer. 25:15–17)

And it was, of course, the cup of God's wrath that Jesus prayed might pass (Matt. 26:39).

On the positive side, the Passover meal in the Synoptics and in 1 Cor. 11 use the terms "bread" and "the cup." As the breaking of the bread creates the body, so the drinking of the cup (the wine) releases the Spirit. Put more graphically, the bread is flesh and the wine is blood. The imagery is powerful. As we will see, the blood of a person or an animal was life, and life belonged only to God. A Jew could not eat an animal with the blood (life) in it, nor an animal that itself was carnivorous. To drink blood would be an absolute break with Judaism. But actually it is not a break. As they drank the wine with each other, the first Christians spoke of the life (Spirit/blood) of God present with them.

For both Judaism and the Jesus tradition wine was a divine signifier. But the analogy was not the same. As a divine symbol wine was a sacrifice parallel to the sacrifice of blood and bread (Hos. 9:4). Amos complained that some drank the wine without the sacrifice (Amos 2:8). In the end-time punishment there will be no wine to sacrifice to God (Joel 1:13; 2:14). And in contrast there will be wine, even brandy (?), at the end-time banquet:

> On this mountain the Lord of hosts will make for all peoples a feast of rich food, a feast of well-aged wines, of rich food filled with marrow, of well-aged wines strained clear. (Isa. 25:6)

In Christianity wine was more the sign of God's presence, Spirit, in the community, a community that was itself the sacrifice (Rom. 12:1–3). The vineyard referred to the people and the land. Wine referred to the people without a land. This centrality of wine in the Passover and in the Agape / Eucharist / Mass helped make wine and its production a major element in the Mediterranean food chain.[16]

The use of wine as a food was not new, of course, to the Greco-Roman world. The Greco-Roman meal was divided into two distinct parts. Consumption of food occurred at the δεῖπνον, as, for the most part, the participants reclined at a table, either three-sided or an arc. Following the δεῖπνον proper, the scene shifted to some form of entertainment or learning (the συμπόσιον). At more lavish meals the men were entertained by dancers, musicians, and prostitutes (actually all the women were designated by the term πόρνη). At more intellectual συμπόσια, such as those described by Plato, the entertainment was a learned dialogue. At the religious meal the συμπόσιον was the religious or cultic rite expressed by the believers. Almost invariably the συμπόσιον involved consumption of wine (often mixed wine, depending on the occasion). The Greco-Roman use of wine may have been a serious detriment to table fellowship between Jews and non-Jews. At the συμπόσιον particularly wine was ceremonially mixed with water in a bowl, a μετανιπτρίς, and a libation made.[17] In some groups it was expected that all present would drink from this same bowl. Others might pour from the initial bowl. In any case, commensalism depended on drinking from the same "cup" that contained dedicated wine. For the Jew this was impossible. *Mishnah 'Abod. Zar.* 5 details how to manage the situation. Essentially the Jew

---

16. For example, it may well have so thoroughly replaced beer in Egypt that it destroyed the breweries. See Roger S. Bagnall, *Egypt in Late Antiquity* (Princeton: Princeton University Press, 1993), 32.

17. James N. Davidson, *Courtesans and Fishcakes: The Consuming Passions of Classical Athens* (London: HarperCollins, 1997), 46.

could drink the wine if it came from a sealed jar, that is, could not have been involved in a libation. The Mishnah recognizes full well that in the temporary absence of the Jew, the Gentile might dedicate the wine (see especially *m. 'Abod. Zar.* 5:5). Since commensalism depended on drinking together, the Jew was seriously limited. It may well be that the crucial conflict in Gal. 2 had more to do with the use of wine, so essential for table fellowship, than with delimiting foods.[18]

The Christian use of wine (or the Jewish, for that matter) at its συμπόσιον, the Eucharist, would hardly have been an innovation. The religious use of the wine as a libation was also not new. What was new, the inculturation, was the use of wine as a symbol for Spirit / blood. This was so offensive that the non-Christians accused the Christians of cannibalism. In the many early representations of the Agape the cup of wine (or, krater, the equivalent of the μετανιπτρίς [?]) is always present (plate 5).

Meat

The semiotics of meat is the most complex of the divine food symbols. Comparable to the methodological issues raised at the beginning of this chapter, it has also been suggested that there are three approaches to *kashrut:* (1) pragmatic — food rules were given for health and identity reasons; (2) symbolic — food references a deeper sense of reality; (3) therapeutic — food rules promote a healthier race. We assume here the symbolic nature of *kashrut.*[19]

Deep in "repressed" memory of the Jews must have been the notion that they were a vegetarian people. The P and J accounts of the creation affirm the use of plants for food, but not meat. According to P the animals were given only plant food to eat. The J account tells of a garden in which there was every plant and tree that might be pleasing to the man:

> [God said,] "And to every beast of the earth, and to every bird of the air, and to everything that creeps on the earth, everything that has the breath of life, I have given every green plant for food." And it was so. (Gen. 1:30)

> Out of the ground the Lord God made to grow every tree that is pleasant to the sight and good for food, the tree of life also in the

18. E. P. Sanders, "Jewish Association with Gentiles and Galatians 2:11–14," in *The Conversation Continues: Studies in Paul and John in Honour of J. Louis Martyn.*, ed. Robert T. Fortna and Beverly R. Gaventa (Nashville: Abingdon, 1990), 178; Philip F. Esler, *Community and Gospel in Luke-Acts* (Cambridge: Cambridge University Press, 1987).

19. Alter, "New Theory of *kashrut*," 47.

midst of the garden, and the tree of the knowledge of good and
evil. (Gen. 2:9)

After the fall, God cursed the ground with thorns and thistles and left
only plants for Adam and Eve to eat (grain for the bread?).

> And to the man he said, "Because you have listened to the voice
> of your wife, and have eaten of the tree about which I commanded
> you, 'You shall not eat of it,' cursed is the ground because of you;
> in toil you shall eat of it all the days of your life; thorns and thistles
> it shall bring forth for you; and you shall eat the plants of the field.
> By the sweat of your face you shall eat bread until you return to
> the ground, for out of it you were taken; you are dust, and to dust
> you shall return." (Gen. 3:17–19)

Meat first enters the picture with the sacrifices of Cain and Abel. Cain
offers grain, the actual food for humans. Abel offers meat, the food of
God. God rejected the offering of Cain because grain was not God's food.

According to the E narrative God relented after the flood. Humans
could have animals just as they had eaten plants. However, the life of
the animal belonged to God, so humans could eat the meat, but not
the blood:

> God blessed Noah and his sons, and said to them, "Be fruitful
> and multiply, and fill the earth. The fear and dread of you shall
> rest on every animal of the earth, and on every bird of the air, on
> everything that creeps on the ground, and on all the fish of the sea;
> into your hand they are delivered. Every moving thing that lives
> shall be food for you; and just as I gave you the green plants, I give
> you everything. Only, you shall not eat flesh with its life, that is,
> its blood. For your own lifeblood I will surely require a reckoning:
> from every animal I will require it and from human beings, each
> one for the blood of another, I will require a reckoning for human
> life. Whoever sheds the blood of a human, by a human shall that
> person's blood be shed; for in his own image God made humankind.
> (Gen. 9:1–6; cf. Lev. 17:10–14)

Based on the assumption that blood is life and life belongs to God, the
decree in Gen. 9 has become the primary food regulation of the Jews. For
humans to use meat the God signifier must be absent. Or put another way,
meat is only acceptable, כשר, when the blood has been (ritually) drained
from the animal. Two other regulations remain. First, Jews may not eat
animals that have themselves eaten other animals. That is, draining the
blood from carnivores still does not take away the blood of the animals

they have consumed. Consequently, only animals with hoofs, rather than claws, may be eaten by humans (Lev. 11:3–26). Second, animals, fish, and fowl that do not recapitulate the natural or created order are also forbidden. Taxonomic consistency is required. Although that is not always absolutely clear in Lev. 11, it logically follows. Only an animal that has a cloven foot (not carnivorous) and chews cud (demonstrably vegetarian) can be considered clean (Lev. 11:1–8). Only fish that have fins and scales are accepted (Lev. 11:9–12). All others are variations from normal. Birds that are carnivorous, or even appear to be, are also forbidden (Lev. 11:13–19). Although the reasoning is not always explicable, the Jewish meat regulations were built on the belief that blood / life belonged to God only, and that usable meat must recapitulate a created order.

This theological perception regarding blood and natural order (food holiness), placed alongside the practice of circumcision (sexual holiness) and the keeping of the Sabbath (calendar holiness), made of the Jews an acutely separate people. Eating together at the same table reinforced present communities and created new ones. But Jews could not eat with non-Jews (note Gen. 44:32!), a fact most noticeable in the Diaspora (e.g., Dan. 1:8–10) or during severe oppression (2 Macc. 6:18–22; 7:1–9).

The Jesus Tradition

In the New Testament the Jesus tradition made it clear that defilement was not a matter of eating unclean food:

> Then [Jesus] called the crowd again and said to them, "Listen to me, all of you, and understand: there is nothing outside a person that by going in can defile, but the things that come out are what defile." (Mark 7:14–15)

It is not really clear what Jesus, or the Jesus of the tradition, actually ate. We know only that he ate at formal dinners and was called a φάγος καὶ οἰνοπότης.[20] Since there is no indication that Jesus ate more than he should have, it seems possible that the epithet refers to eating and drinking at inappropriate times and consuming food unacceptable to the Jews.

The Problems of Food for Paul

The issues involving food nearly destroyed the early Christian communities. At first the issue was Jew and Gentile. Because all the first Christians were Jews, there was no way to share the "good news" with Gentiles and

---

20. According to Dennis Smith, Jesus actually enjoyed formal dinners and banquets. See Dennis E. Smith and Hal E. Taussig, *Many Tables: The Eucharist in the New Testament and Liturgy Today* (Philadelphia: Trinity Press International, 1990), 46.

develop new churches without eating together at the same table. Paul was furious with Peter for refusing to eat with the Gentile converts in Galatia (Gal. 2). Out of this conflict came the primary Pauline "slogan:" justification by faith, that is, the good news that satisfactory life depends more on trust relationships than even very appropriate directives regarding God and life — works of the law (Gal. 3:5) — works that create division and boundaries. Paul does not identify the food (i.e., meat with blood in it) as the problem, but he does strongly associate "justification by trust" with boundary-free eating. Justification has come to us because God in Christ has shared the (God's) blood with us (Rom. 5:9).

But the issue was not that simple. To be sure, the problem of eating food in common almost destroyed the Jewish church as it became more non-Jewish. Shortly before the conflict with Peter and the writing of Galatians, Paul had encountered yet another eating problem. If the first followers of Jesus ate according to the Jewish pattern, they would be excluded from normal Greco-Roman social intercourse. If they were excluded from everyday relationships, they would not be able to share the Jesus tradition in either word or deed.

In Corinth some Christians (I think the "Christ group") were concerned about several such issues. They wrote a letter to Paul about their problem, and he responded. First Corinthians 7:1–16:21 contains his answers. In 8:1 they have asked about food sacrificed to idols, and he responds with his epistolary formula: περὶ δὲ τῶν εἰδωλοθύτων. In all these cases Paul must have given instruction that now has gone astray. Paul must have told the Corinthian disciples that it was permissible to eat food offered to idols. The logic, not totally expressed in the letter, would make any philosopher wince. The non-Christians who sacrificed the meat (making the food idol-specific) knew nothing of the Jewish perception of God as the giver of all life and therefore the one to whom life blood should be given. They did not know that the sacrifice for their god was futile. Because the sacrifice was futile, there was no need to avoid eating the resultant meat. Put another way, it was permissible to eat with people who did not, in the Jewish sense, know what they were doing (1 Cor. 8:10; 10:25–30). To obfuscate an already convoluted argument, Paul added the great confession of faith of 8:4–6. Because idols had no real existence, sacrifices offered to them had no theological significance. Blood or no blood, כשר or not, go ahead and eat the meat (food) offered to idols. Within the same letter Paul changed his mind. As we will see, and as everyone recognizes, eating together forms community. Paul had violated his own yet-to-be articulated "justification by trust." It is the eating together in community that creates life, not the giving of life blood to God. So in chapter 10 of the same letter to the Corinthians he comes to his senses. It does not really matter whether the idol exists or not; it does not really matter whether the meat has blood in it or not. What matters is the focus of those who sit at the same table. If you eat at a table with those who *do* believe in idols, then you have become a part of that community that believes in idols.[21] Paul then must thread a very complex path between exclusive Jewish meals and entrapping pagan meals.

Early Christian Food

While Paul may not have found the path, early Christians may indeed have engineered a compromise. The meat meals of the New Testament are not repeated in early Christianity. We cannot say when Christians stopped eating according to *kashrut*. We do know that the menu of the Passover meal was not the menu of the early church. However it might have happened, the feeding of the five thousand set the menu for the first Christians. Bread, fish, and wine always appear (plate 6). Although some fish could be unclean by Jewish standards, there is no life blood involved. The feeding itself deliberately describes a spontaneous eating event where no priestly function could have been involved. The issue of clean and unclean has been bypassed. Furthermore, bread and fish comprised a common meal in the Mediterranean world. That common meal (like coffee and doughnuts, or a cola and a sandwich) of the early Christians became the religious meal of the new faith. The fish signaled separation from this world (water), though eventually it became a key symbol for the faith: ΙΧΘΥΣ, Jesus Christ, Son of God, Savior. Did it not also serve as the compromise meat? It could be eaten by Jew and Gentile alike without the issue of life blood.

Food in the Greco-Roman World

For the Gentiles, that is, Greco-Romans, fish was also a part of the meal. A common meal consisted of bread, wine, and, with the bread, ὄψον, a cooked relish often made of fish bits. One form of the relish was called

---

21. There are two exceptions: if the Christian buys for private consumption and the seller of the meat does not mention the sacrificial element, or if a non-Christian invites the Christian to dinner and does not note where the meat comes from (1 Cor. 10:25–30). "Don't ask!" See Wendell Lee Willis, *Idol Meat in Corinth: The Pauline Argument in 1 Corinthians 8 and 10* (Chico, Calif.: Scholars Press, 1981), 24–245. Somewhat in contrast to my position Willis and Gooch (Peter D. Gooch, *Dangerous Food: 1 Corinthians 8–10 in Its Context* [Waterloo, Ont.: Wilfred Laurier University Press, 1993], 95–97) argue that Paul rejected eating idol meat because he could not and would not abandon his Jewish sense of "one God with his own covenant people" (Willis, *Idol Meat*, 222). From another perspective Hans-Josef Klauck (*Herrenmahl und hellenistischer Kult: Eine religionsgeschichtliche Untersuchung zum ersten Korintherbrief* [Münster: Aschendorf, 1982]) attributes the shift to Paul's fear that the Corinthians would experience a "Rückfall in der Götzendienst" (265–74).

by the diminutive, ὀψάριον.[22] In fact, the author of the Fourth Gospel uses the Greek term for this fish dish in his account of the feeding (John 6:9–11) as well as of the Agape-like meal with Jesus on the side of the lake (John 21:9–13): ἔστιν παιδάριον ὧδε ὃς ἔχει πέντε ἄρτους κριθίνους καὶ δύο ὀψάρια· ἀλλὰ ταῦτα τί ἐστιν εἰς τοσούτους; (John 6:9). Although the word ὀψάριον probably meant a fish relish or sauce, it could actually refer to any relish placed on the staple, bread. Another popular form of fish at the meal was γάρος, a sauce made of fish bits in brine. Though such a meal preceded the bread, fish, and wine of the early Christian Agape, it had no religious implications.[23]

Summary

Any summary of this data will, perforce, be an oversimplification. But generalizations are necessary in order to proceed (functionalism).

- Bread universally signifies the communion of eating together. In the Jewish tradition breaking bread refers not only to human table fellowship, but also marks the covenant relationship with God. The metaphorical use of bread (word and wisdom) continued in the Christian tradition, but more significantly, the breaking of the bread signified the openness of the community (body) instead of exclusiveness. Breaking bread created κοινωνία in the house church. When the church became public the bread was broken by leaders as a sign of Jesus' sacrifice.

- Water signifies Ur-chaos. Only by God's action does water become beneficial. As God's gift it offers the possibility of creating a fertile land, making civilization, and quenching our thirst. On the other hand, water remains the source of chaos, even evil. As in life and culture itself, that ambivalence never disappears. As seen in their symbols and art, the early Christians understood that they could exist in Roman waters.

- Wine evolves from the vineyard and the vine. The vineyard signified Israel and the land. More abstractly, the vine referred to God's people without necessarily including the land. In the New Testament the vineyard appears only as a negative reference to Israel,

---

22. The three proper elements of a Greek meal were σῖτος, ὄψον, and οἶνος. See Andrew Dalby, *Siren Feasts: A History of Food and Gastronomy in Greece* (London: Routledge, 1996), 23.

23. Marcel Detienne and Jean-Pierre Vernant, *The Cuisine of Sacrifice among the Greeks* (Chicago: University of Chicago Press, 1989). There is "an absolute coincidence of meat-eating and sacrificial practice" (p. 3), but the food itself has no particular semiotic value.

while the vine may include the new people of God. But actually the relationship of God to the people ultimately shifts to the fruit of the vine, wine, with its rich reference to the Spirit as the life of the community (the blood of the body).

- Meat belonged to God. Theologically the Jewish people understood that all life came from God, and that life was located in blood. Though originally vegetarian, the Jews came to use meat as a food only when the blood was first given to God. Meat appropriately prepared became a mark of God's people. At the same time, proper, acceptable meat signified God's original order. The semiotic value of meat was obliterated by the first Christians.

- Fish had little semiotic meaning in the Hebrew Scriptures. It was a basic food that, like plants and meat, had a created form that had to be recapitulated. In that sense, fish too represented created order, except that it lived in the chaos symbol, water. Fish, or fish relish, along with bread, was the common meal of the Mediterranean world. In the New Testament, fish became highly symbolic. First, by making fish and bread the religious meal, the first Christians symbolically proclaimed a community that had no cultural barriers. Second, because the fish lived in chaos, the fish, over against Jewish kosher meat that was true to natural law, symbolized life lived or redeemed in/from an alien environment or culture.

Menu and Table Arrangement

Under the rubric "menu" we ask what meaning the type of food eaten has for a given culture. As for the problem of inculturation, we are particularly interested in how the Judeo-Christian menu affected the Greco-Roman world.

The Roman Menu

Although, in contrast to the Jews, the Greco-Roman world had no ethnic identifying menu, they did use the menu to make sharp class distinctions. Presumably the evening *cena* was not likely always a banquet,[24] but when it was a banquet, the wealthy could indeed offer menus that staggered the imagination.[25] One of the most famous was the incredible meal of the nouveau riche Trimalchio, who, among other things, served a "delicacy"

---

24. Florence Dupont, *Daily Life in Ancient Rome* (Oxford: Blackwell, 1992), 272.

25. Emily Gowers rightly warns that meals described in Roman literature may not be factual. (*The Loaded Table: Representations of Food in Roman Literature* (Oxford: Clarendon, 1993),1–3.

on each segment of a zodiac platter: beef, kidney, figs, lobster, goose, to name a few.[26] The distinction between the wealthy and others was that between "soft" and "hard" foods.[27] The wealthy served soft foods that had been delivered quickly to the banquet and had to be consumed immediately (before putrefaction). Fish was a particularly desirable item because it could be prepared and served without concern for sacrifice. The sacrifice of the animal limited the types of cuts available for the banquet. So, in earlier years, at least, the fish eater, ὀψοφάγος, was one who preferred dainty or delicate eating. Presumably the appellation might also have served as a term of derision for lower class people who ate hard food (salt fish) that could be stored and would not need immediate attention.[28]

Furthermore, the patron offered the meal; the client had no choice but to attend. Once there, guests were seated according to their value to the host. The honored seats were those on the couch opposite the empty section of the triclinium (the *lectus medius*). Sometimes a table in the form of an arc was used (the *lunar sigma*, as normally seen in early Christian art [plate 26]).[29] In that case the honored positions were at each end. Following the meal there was invariably a συμπόσιον of some type — dancing, music, presentations, or discussion.

A usual meal in the Greco-Roman world, other than a banquet, consisted of bread, mixed wine, some relish or sauce, and cheese. While such a menu might serve as a "lunch" for most people, as a steady diet it would indicate that the consumer was not of the wealthy or noble class. The differences in menu apparently did not also mark an ethnic, racial, or religious boundary (i.e., had no semiotic value).[30] While food itself may not have served as an ethnic or religious signifier, there were religious associations where meals served as moments of festivity in the name of a particular divinity (1 Cor. 10:20).

The Jewish Menu

The basic Jewish meal was fairly simple. While in the wilderness, the Jews complained about leaving Egypt, where they sat by the kettles of flesh and ate their fill of bread (ὅταν ἐκαθίσαμεν ἐπὶ τῶν λεβήτων τῶν κρεῶν καὶ ἠσθίομεν ἄρτους εἰς πλησμονήν, Exod. 16:3 LXX). Besides bread, the Israelites yearned for water (Exod. 15:24; 17:2). Not only did the Lord

---

26. Jérôme Carcopino, *Daily Life in Ancient Rome*, trans. E. O. Lorimer (New Haven: Yale University Press, 1963), 267–68.

27. Dupont, *Daily Life*, 276.

28. James Davidson, *Courtesans and Fishcakes*, 21.

29. Carcopino, *Daily Life*, 266.

30. Dupont, *Daily Life*, 270–72.

give them water, but also meat in the evening and bread in the morning
(Exod. 16:12). Later the Israelites continued to murmur, remembering
the fish they used to eat in Egypt for nothing, the cucumbers, the melons,
the leeks, the onions, and the garlic (Num. 11:5). We can assume that
these yearnings in the wilderness reflect a typical menu for this area of
the Mediterranean world.[31]

The Jewish menu eventually became embroiled in two serious problems: the distinction between classes, and the distinction between clean
and unclean. As early as the eighth century B.C.E., preexilic prophets
were quick to note the difference between wealthy Jews and those less
prosperous:

> Alas for those who lie on beds of ivory, and lounge on their couches,
> and eat lambs from the flock, and calves from the stall; who sing idle
> songs to the sound of the harp, and like David improvise on instru-
> ments of music; who drink wine from bowls, and anoint themselves
> with the finest oils, but are not grieved over the ruin of Joseph!
> Therefore they shall now be the first to go into exile, and the revelry
> of the loungers shall pass away. (Amos 6:4–7)

Amos describes wealthy Jews reclining on triclinia made of ivory and
covered with fine pillows. They eat succulent dishes made from lambs and
calves, soft foods that parallel Greek the Greek menu. After the meal, like
other wealthy citizens of the Mediterranean world, they offer entertaining
συμπόσια, where idle music is played and improvisation occurs. During
the συμπόσια they drink large amounts of wine and have themselves
massaged with the finest oil. Such a banquet is described in Esther 1:1–
12. Queen Vashti was not present because she followed the Greek custom
of eating separately with her guests. To her credit, and misfortune, she
refused to provide entertainment for the customary συμπόσιον.

There were alternate or counterculture menus that had more sociological significance than actual prophetic protests or alternative symbol
systems. The Nazirite vow entailed abstinence from wine (Judg. 13:4),
and likewise, the Rechabites refused to drink from the fruit of the vine
(Jer. 35:6–7). Bread and water signified life without land. John the Baptist was placed under the same vow to abstain from wine or strong drink
(Luke 1:15). His menu of locusts and wild honey (Matt. 3:4), without
bread and wine (Luke 7:33), does not imply an alternative symbol system, but characterizes John as an ascetic, even a recluse, over against

---

31. Actually the list in Num. 11:5 is strange. In extant Egyptian papyri the bread and
fish are well attested, especially the kettles of fish or γάρος; however, cucumbers, onions,
and garlic are seldom mentioned. Oddly, enough after fish, pork was the meat of choice.
See Bagnall, *Egypt in Late Antiquity*, 23–32.

Jesus, who enjoyed parties and was known as a glutton and a drunkard (Luke 7:34).

Menu in the Jesus Tradition

There are in the New Testament descriptions of meals that maintain the same class distinction condemned by the prophets.[32] After a fine δεῖπνον the daughter of Herodias furnished entertainment for the συμπόσιον (Mark 6:14–29). Even more pertinent to Jewish class problems is the parable of the rich man and Lazarus (Luke 16:19–31), where the rich man, who had a banquet every day (!), does not even share scraps from his magnificent table with the poor Lazarus. Class differentiation is a serious matter, but to leave nothing for the poor is even worse.

The issue of clean and unclean presents more difficulties. Sometime about the sixth century B.C.E., perhaps during or even after the exile, the Jews developed a sharp distinction between foods that were acceptable and foods that were not. In terms of semiotics, we have seen that meat with blood in it, or even carnivorous animals, was not acceptable food, because life / blood belonged to God only. Moreover, plants and animals that were not true to type also were classified as unclean (e.g., fish without scales and fins). In structural, or kinship, terms the dietary or menu laws became a very strong point of identity. During the exile and in subsequent centuries dietary laws, along with Sabbath laws and circumcision, became the social marks of a Jew. While such dietary regulations may be defended for environmental, health, or theological reasons, in fact, they define a people and prevent the crossing of boundaries. In addition to the menu itself (clean or unclean food), there were other considerations that could block table fellowship. First, the participants must have clean hands.

> Now when the Pharisees and some of the scribes who had come from Jerusalem gathered around [Jesus], they noticed that some of his disciples were eating with defiled hands, that is, without washing them. (For the Pharisees, and all the Jews, do not eat unless they thoroughly wash their hands, thus observing the tradition of the elders.) (Mark 7:1–3)

According to this puzzling notice Jesus and the disciples were κοινοί because they failed to wash their hands before eating their bread. The text is problematic.[33] The "tradition of the elders" is nearly impossible to

---

32. Kathleen E. Corley, *Private Women, Public Meals: Social Conflict in the Synoptic Tradition* (Peabody, Mass.: Hendrickson, 1993), 93–95.

33. Marcus J. Borg, *Conflict, Holiness, and Politics in the Teachings of Jesus* (Harrisburg, Pa.: Trinity Press International, 1998), 96–99.

identify. To be sure, the Mishnah describes in great detail the washing of hands (*m. Yad.* 1–2), but there is no way to determine if this was in force at the time of Jesus.

Second, there was the problem of tithing vegetables. Apparently extending the law of Deut. 14:22–23 (note Lev. 27:30), the Jews tithed the vegetables they ate, even rather insignificant seeds:

> "Woe to you, scribes and Pharisees, hypocrites! For you tithe mint, dill, and cummin, and have neglected the weightier matters of the law: justice and mercy and faith. It is these you ought to have practiced without neglecting the others." (Matt. 23:23)

The Jesus tradition rejected the Jewish menu and accompanying blocks to table fellowship. Jesus said that there was nothing outside a person that could defile by going in; it is what comes out (behavior) that defiles (Mark 7:14–23). A similar saying occurs in the harsh Matthean "Woe" passage (Matt. 23:25–26), though food is not specifically mentioned.

Paul continues the rejection of clean and unclean. In a sense it is the same Pauline process of relativization: neither food nor the human body (stomach) has any ultimate value.

> "All things are lawful for me," but not all things are beneficial. "All things are lawful for me," but I will not be dominated by anything. "Food is meant for the stomach and the stomach for food," and God will destroy both one and the other. (1 Cor. 6:12–13)

John's Gospel, on the other hand, characteristically, destroys the menu. Jesus himself is the ἄρτος (6:41, 51), the σάρξ (6:53), the drink (πίνων μου τὸ αἷμα, 6:56), and the ὕδωρ ζῶν (4:14). People do eat in the Gospel of John but there is no positive value placed on it (4:8) John even rejected the standard menu for the early Christians (the fish and bread of 6:1–14; see 6:26, 35, 53).

Why did the Jesus tradition bother to attack the Jewish menu system and Jewish regulations regarding eating together? Did the early churches include in their congregations sufficient Jews that the Gospel writers had to state firmly the policy that menu and table traditions will not block the unity of the early church? Or was the early church more of one mind, and these controversies made clear the position of the nascent Jesus movement over against the neighboring synagogue? One can assume that it was an interior problem for Paul, a problem he had attempted to solve with the words πάντα μοι ἔξεστιν, but failed. That may very well have been the issue for the later Synoptic churches.

Although the early Christians struggled against the Jewish menu and table regulations, at the same time, they strictly denied the Greco-Roman class structure. As early as the writing of 1 Corinthians Paul attacked the Roman double standard. Even at the κυριακὸν δεῖπνον some would eat their soft food, which had to be consumed quickly while others (late-comers?) ate ἄρτος and ὀψάριον. The ones with soft food must also have consumed more wine than the others. In any case, a class-specific meal was severely rejected by Paul.[34]

The early Christian meal — bread, fish, and wine — as seen in the feeding of the five thousand and all the portrayals of early Christian meals, served two functions (plate 26). It opened the boundaries of Judeo-Christianity. Being a common meal in the Mediterranean world, as a menu it did not serve to exclude anyone. Perhaps even Jews might participate without offending their sense of life blood. But even more important, the simple meal of the Christians democratized the Greco-Roman class system. Luxurious banquets, with their ranking of clients, were no longer acceptable.[35] The author of Revelation made it clear:

> And the merchants of the earth weep and mourn for her, since no one buys their cargo anymore, cargo of gold, silver, jewels and pearls, fine linen, purple, silk and scarlet, all kinds of scented wood, all articles of ivory, all articles of costly wood, bronze, iron, and marble, cinnamon, spice, incense, myrrh, frankincense, wine, olive oil, choice flour and wheat, cattle and sheep, horses and chariots, slaves — and human lives. "The fruit for which your soul longed has gone from you, and all your dainties (λιπαρός) and your splendor are lost to you, never to be found again!" (Rev. 18:11–14)

The Jesus Tradition and Seating Arrangements

The Jesus tradition also criticized the Greco-Roman seating arrangements. Seating at the meal had to be democratized. James and John asked if they would sit a the right and left sides of Jesus during the banquet. Jesus said they could drink his cup, but he himself was not in charge of the dinner (host) — he could not grant their request (Mark 10:35–40). In further explanation Jesus says the Gentiles use the banquet as a means of exercising and demonstrating authority, but the honorable ones among the disciples will be those who serve the table:

> So Jesus called them and said to them, "You know that among the Gentiles those whom they recognize as their rulers lord it over them, and their great ones are tyrants over them. But it is not so among you; but whoever wishes to become great among you must

---

34. Smith and Taussig, *Many Tables*. Smith (p. 63) notes the similarities between the style of Roman banquets and the κυριακὸν δεῖπνον.
35. Tertullian, *Pud.* 8; Clement, *Paed.* 2.1.

be your servant, and whoever wishes to be first among you must be slave of all. For the Son of Man came not to be served but to serve, and to give his life a ransom for many." (Mark 10:42–45)

Despite the apparent validity of this criticism, at least two narratives make us pause. Surely the author of the Fourth Gospel knew that we would read the Last Supper in terms of a Roman seating arrangement. By placing the beloved disciple at the chest of Jesus and Peter outside of hearing distance, the author knew we would recognize the beloved disciple as the most honored guest and Peter as one of the least honored (John 13:23–24). The narrative is not ironic. To the contrary, the author deliberately uses a class-oriented seating arrangement to convey the primary importance of the beloved disciple. A second text shows the same attitude. In Luke 14:1–14, Jesus goes to a dinner with a leader of the Pharisees. Noticing how the other guests sought to be placed at the seat of honor, Jesus told an important parable:

> "When you are invited by someone to a wedding banquet, do not sit down at the place of honor, in case someone more distinguished than you has been invited by your host; and the host who invited both of you may come and say to you, 'Give this person your place,' and then in disgrace you would start to take the lowest place. But when you are invited, go and sit down at the lowest place, so that when your host comes, he may say to you, 'Friend, move up higher'; then you will be honored in the presence of all who sit at the table with you. For all who exalt themselves will be humbled, and those who humble themselves will be exalted." (Luke 14:8–11)

The Jesus tradition uses a parable about the Roman tradition of seating, without criticism, to set up one of the best known of the Jesus sayings, that regarding who will be first and who will be last (verse 11).

In early Christian art the first community never sits at a triclinium, but always at a *lunar sigma*. The honored guests are much more difficult to determine — or at least moving "up" is more complex. When there is no clear head of the table, it is impossible to tell who is first and who is last.

Meals, Community Formation, and Table Fellowship

There are few things on which one finds universal agreement. The function of meals in the formation of community is one. One set of sociologists leave little room for exceptions:

> Food brings people together, promotes common interests, and stimulates the formation of bonds with other people and societies.

Almost everywhere, a food offering is a sign of love, affection and friendship. Withholding it may be seen as an expression of anger or hostility, or as a form of punishment. Likewise, to accept food from someone signifies the acceptance of his or her offer and the reciprocity of feelings expressed, while refusal may be viewed by some as a rejection of their kindness or an expression of hostility.[36]

One of the earliest users of the sociological approach to culture, William Robertson Smith, wrote,

> Those who sit at meat together are united for all social effects, those who do not eat together are aliens to one another, without fellowship in religion and without reciprocal social duties.[37]

Even a graffiti scribbler in Pompei knew the truth: at quam non ceno, barbarus ille mihi est.[38]

Jewish Commensalism

The meal as a builder of community would be true in any society, though it seems especially true for the Judeo-Christian tradition. The formation of the Jewish people occurred at the Exodus, which was celebrated by a group meal, the Passover, in each home (Exod. 12:1–11). The meal was exclusive. No foreigner or uncircumcised was allowed to participate. On the other hand, meals were a critical part of hospitality. When the messengers appeared to Abraham and Sarah (Gen. 18:1–8), they offered their guests a meal of cakes, curds and milk, and calf (though the messengers apparently ate alone). Likewise, when the messengers appeared to Lot, he prepared a feast for them with unleavened bread (Gen. 19:3).

There was nothing better than to eat with one's friends. Even the dour author of Ecclesiastes, who saw little of value in life, found in eating together a refuge from what was otherwise a continuing time of toil:

> So I commend enjoyment, for there is nothing better for people under the sun than to eat, and drink, and enjoy themselves, for this will go with them in their toil through the days of life that God gives them under the sun. (Eccl. 8:15)

Eating and intimacy were closely aligned. Boaz "flirted" with Ruth by sharing his relish bowl (Ruth 2:14). The Song of Solomon reader could not easily distinguish between lovemaking and eating:

---

36. Carol Bryant et al., *The Cultural Feast: An Introduction to Food and Society* (St. Paul: West Publishing Co., 1985), 150.

37. William Robertson Smith, *Kinship and Marriage in Early Arabia* (Cambridge: Cambridge University Press, 1885), 251.

38. Cited in Gowers, *The Loaded Table*, 26.

Awake, O north wind, and come, O south wind! Blow upon my garden that its fragrance may be wafted abroad. Let my beloved come to his garden, and eat its choicest fruits. (Song of Sol. 4:16)

On the other hand, because eating together was intimate, it was quite possible to abuse its significance. David tried to persuade Uriah to eat and to lie with his wife, Bathsheba, in order to conceal that her pregnancy was the result of relations with David. Uriah was horrified that David would even suggest such a violation of holy war (2 Sam. 11:11). Even more pernicious was Amnon's seduction and rape of Tamar, which he accomplished by asking her to eat privately with him (2 Sam. 13:1–14). There was also political value in the family table. David made some peace with the followers of Saul by inviting Saul's grandson, Mephibosheth, to eat at his table with all the king's sons (2 Sam. 9:11).

As we have seen, about the sixth century B.C.E. the Jews codified a diet system that essentially identified them as Jews and excluded others from eating at the same table. In the New Testament the story of Peter and Paul in Gal. 2 sets well the problem of Jewish exclusivism. There are four questions that need to be addressed: (1) Could Jews eat the same food as Gentiles and eat at the same table? (2) Could Jews eat in the same room with Gentiles? (3) Does eating in the same room constitute table fellowship? (4) Is the food issue due to dietary laws or idolatry?

Jews and Gentiles at the Same Table

As we have already seen in our earlier discussion of Cornelius, the Gentile mission began with the revelation to Peter that eating with the Gentile Cornelius was appropriate. The assumption of the author must have been that such table fellowship was not only forbidden, but perhaps even repugnant. Certainly it was the general assumption among non-Jewish writers that Jews could not eat with non-Jews.[39] Tacitus notes,

They sit apart at meals and they sleep apart, and although they are a race most given to lust, they abstain from intercourse with foreign women; among themselves nothing is unlawful. (*Hist.* 5.5.2)

Jewish sources are not quite as clear. The author of Daniel portrays Daniel as not wishing to eat the food of King Nebuchadnezzar:

But Daniel resolved that he would not defile himself with the royal rations of food and wine; so he asked the palace master to allow him not to defile himself [ἵνα μὴ συμμολυνθῇ]. (Dan. 1:8)

---

39. See examples in Philip F. Esler, *Galatians* (London: Routledge, 1989), 95.

It is not certain whether Daniel and the young Jewish men ate alone, nor is it absolutely clear that συμμολύνω refers to the defilement of unclean food or the disgrace of eating with idolators. Other Jewish sources are not more precise. When Judith ate with Holofernes she ate her own food. Her rationale was indeed avoidance of disgrace (σκάνδαλον) rather than defilement.

> Then he commanded them to bring her in where his silver dinner-ware was kept, and ordered them to set a table for her with some of his own delicacies, and with some of his own wine to drink. But Judith said, "I cannot partake of them, or it will be an offense [σκάνδαλον]; but I will have enough with the things I brought with me." (Jth. 12:1–2)

Of course, she would not tell the man she was about to murder that his food was unacceptable.

Jews Eating with Gentiles in the Same Room

Despite our earlier discussion of Cornelius, it would appear that the answer is yes to the question of eating in the same room. In a document approximately contemporary with the New Testament, *Joseph and Aseneth*, Joseph ate with his prospective parents-in-law (non-Jews), but at a separate table:

> And Joseph entered the house of Pentephres and sat upon the throne. And they washed his feet and set a table before him by itself, because Joseph never ate with the Egyptians, for this was an abomination to him. (*Jos. Asen.* 7:1)

The *Letter of Aristeas*, also contemporary with the New Testament, gives us a different slant. After a lengthy philosophical discussion of unclean food, the Jewish sages participate in a great banquet with the king. However, the king honors the dietary laws of the Jews: "Everything of which you partake ... will be served in compliance with your habits; it will be served to me as well as to you (*Let. Aris.* 181). Jew and non-Jew ate in the same room and possibly at the same table. But the king agreed to eat kosher food.

One Table

In a sense the issue of meals and the intent of this study rest here. Speaking in terms of structuralism, it could appear that the dietary laws and meal restrictions signified a Judaism closed to outside relationships. As we have seen, the calendar contributed to that exclusivism (e.g., the Sabbath), but the real issue must have been table fellowship. Since Jews could not eat with non-Jews, there was little opportunity for Jewish inculturation of non-Jewish cultures. And to be sure, as we have seen, there was minimal inculturation coming from Judaism. Are the structuralists correct? Was there no table fellowship even if Jews and non-Jews were in the same room? Was the situation described in Galatians one where there were two menus and two tables? Did Paul see that community could only be formed when there was only one table? Did he see that two cooks, two waitstaffs, and two tables could never result in the kind of community envisaged by the Jesus movement? Can inculturation occur only when genuine table fellowship can be enjoyed?

In recent days, poststructural perhaps, some scholars have insisted that Jews were not so exclusive. Based, to some extent, on the same evidence we have amassed in chapter 1, these scholars suggest that there was more fluidity than has been proposed. Fredrik Barth argues that no group can maintain its own ethnic distinctiveness without social interaction with other groups and cultures.[40] Boundaries are not so tightly fixed that individuals cannot move back and forth. Indeed, the identity of the group is not diminished by individuals coming and going. Some scholars have applied this to the Antioch dispute and other New Testament material.[41] They argue that some social intercourse with non-Jews is prescribed and some proscribed. Despite this difference between structuralists and post[non]structuralists, most do agree that the issue at Antioch was the inability to develop community if Jews and non-Jews had to sit in the same room but at separate tables with separate menus. We can be fairly certain that individual Jews did move in Hellenistic circles, such as in civic activities. We can also be fairly certain that non-Jews joined with Jews in the doing of good works. It does not seem likely, however, that Jews and Gentiles ate at the same table. This limited the impact of cultural Judaism on neighboring cultures. It was the Jesus movement within Judaism that changed the nature of table fellowship. Despite the importance of theology, the death and resurrection of Jesus, and an ethic of caring, the real alteration in Judaism occurred (and Christianity clearly emerged) when table fellowship was not blocked by dietary obligations or the rejection of food dedicated to idols.

---

40. Fredrik Barth, *Ethnic Groups and Boundaries: The Social Organization of Culture Difference* (Boston: Little, Brown and Company, 1969).

41. E. P. Sanders, "Jewish Association with Gentiles and Galatians 2:11–14," in *The Conversation Continues*, 170–88; Craig C. Hill, *Hellenists and Hebrews: Reappraising Division within the Earliest Church* (Minneapolis: Fortress, 1992).

Kashrut *or Idolatry*

Esler has suggested that the issue at Antioch was idolatry not defilement.[42] The argument has merit and should not be easily dismissed. If the Jews and the Gentiles could sit in the same room and have a meal together, either with separate cooks or all kosher, then what was the problem? Although the New Testament deals with unclean food, it does not mention the problem of wine. In the non-Jewish world wine was frequently made usable by offering a small libation to the gods. Presumably (only presumably) the problem of food offered to idols was a problem only in the Diaspora. In Palestine the issue must have been clean or unclean. Regarding Diaspora adherents, the council of Jerusalem (Acts 15:20) prohibits food offered to idols. The issue of defiling foods is not mentioned. Paul would permit the use of food offered to idols (1 Cor. 8), but eventually qualifies his remarks, especially when it involves mixed table fellowship (1 Cor. 10:23–30). Was wine offered as a libation one of the foods in question? From the mishnaic material it would appear that the use of wine was not to be trusted unless the Jew knew for certain that it could not have been offered to the gods. And since the wine jar was open, or could be opened and closed, that was very difficult (*m. Abod. Zar.* 5:5). It is possible that the issue of defilement had been settled, and in this city of Antioch, in the Diaspora, the problem finally came down to idolatry — wine offered to the gods. It is one thing to overcome the exclusivism of clean / unclean regulations, but quite another to eat and drink food dedicated to idols. The Jesus movement had to overcome both barriers in order to move freely in the Mediterranean world.

The Jesus Tradition

The Jesus tradition shattered Jewish exclusivism. Jewish leaders complained that Jesus ate with tax collectors and sinners (Matt. 9:10–13; Luke 5:30). In the parable of the great banquet the outcasts are invited to the meal after the upstanding citizens of the town refuse the invitation (Luke 14:16–24). In Matthew's harsh allegorical interpretation of the parable, the good citizens are obviously the Jews and the "street people" are the Christians (Matt. 22:1–10).

In order for the Christian meal to be inclusive, the menu had to change. As we have seen, the very fact that in the feeding story it was a boy who furnished the loaves and fishes would indicate that it was a common, everyday meal (σῖτος, ὀψάριον [ὄψον], οἶνος).[43] The first Christians

---

42. Esler, *Galatians*, 104–8.
43. Davidson, *Courtesans and Fishcakes*, 21.

avoided the exclusive nature of the Jewish diet-menu. At the same time, they thoroughly repudiated the Roman use of the menu for class distinctions, for establishing the relationship between patron and client, and for distinguishing between first and last. As in many other ways, Christianity was a faith for the people, not the elite. And it was available to all the people. The menu of bread, fish, and wine became the Agape, the religious meal of the earliest Christians. It is portrayed that way in many pictorial representations of the Agape. Even when Jesus was first portrayed at the Last Supper (Ravenna), the menu was still bread, fish, and wine rather than lamb.

Commensalism and Gender

The roles of men and women at mealtimes are extraordinarily diverse and informative. In my opinion, any discussion of the role of women in the early church should include, perhaps even start with, men and women at the table. At the same time, I must admit that the table customs in Judeo-Christian tradition are as complex as they are informative.

Women at Jewish Meals

There is little in the Hebrew Scriptures to help us. When the messengers came to see Abraham and Sarah, Abraham was in the charge of the meal. He asked Sarah to fix the cakes while he procured a calf. A servant was told to prepare the calf. As the three messengers ate, Abraham stood nearby, while Sarah was in the tent. She was close enough, of course, to hear what the messengers had to say (Gen. 18:1–15). In the account of the Passover, women and children were present at the meal (Exod. 12:47). One assumes that they reclined at the table with the husbands. Other eating scenes from the Hebrew Scriptures follow somewhat the Passover pattern. On feast days the sons and daughters of Job ate together (Job 1:4). The book of Job ends with the happy note that his brothers, sisters, and friends came to his house and ate bread with him (Job 42:11).

I do assume that a story-based society like Judaism retained excellent memories of prior practices. At the same time, such memories will have been updated. So, for example, the descriptions of meals in the New Testament often reflect a Roman style that might not have been the actual custom at the time of Jesus. Likewise, I assume that negative portrayals could reflect a later criticism of earlier customs. So the reader does not necessarily know which culture is being reflected by a given narrative, and whether it is positive or negative. It would appear that the narratives of the Hebrew Scriptures, even the story of Esther, indicate more freedom for women than found in the Greco-Roman world.[44]

Roman Background

To gain a more certain understanding of the role of Jewish women we need to turn to Roman customs and Roman criticism of Jewish women. For the most part, women in the Greco-Roman world were private persons. Or, perhaps more accurately, in private women related to women, but in public did not relate to men. Consequently, proper women were not present at formal meals, or meals where guests were involved. Women who did appear at such meals were usually categorized by the term πόρνη, prostitute. Women who were slaves or freedwomen were automatically prostitutes because they were or had been available to a man or men on demand. Women who performed for or entertained men during the συμπόσια were prostitutes. Learned women who participated in public discussions (also the symposium) fell in the same category. Women who reclined at the table with men became public persons and also were prostitutes. Apparently, women who cooked food and served it were also labeled πόρναι. Women who were legitimate could be only those born free or noble women. They did not appear in public with men. There were short times in Roman history when the attitude toward women was not so stringent, but for the most part, rules of privacy were upheld.[45]

When we turn to the Judeo-Christian population several things, by reverse deduction, become clear. Since women born slaves were πόρναι, it stands to reason that many Christian women were, in the eyes of Roman society, prostitutes. Women who reclined at meals with their husbands, women who participated equally in the religious activities after the meal, women who served the meals — such women would have been seen as prostitutes in Roman eyes. Obviously, many Eastern table fellowship religions did include women who were called prostitutes. The Romans named three such groups: Mithraism, the cult of Isis, and Judaism. Since Jewish women were not necessarily born slaves, it stands to reason, by reverse logic, that Jewish women and men did eat together, as we had supposed from the uncertain data found in the Hebrew Scriptures.[46]

---

44. Corley, *Private Women*, 66–67.
45. Corley, *Private Women*, chapter 2.
46. Balch, *Let Wives Be Submissive*; Winter, *Seek the Welfare of the City*.

The Jesus Tradition

In early Christianity the interplay between Jewish and Roman customs can be seen in a number of situations. Following the clues of Corley,[47] one can see in the Synoptic Gospels quite different adaptations of the Jesus tradition. Mark has women present at meals with Jesus, but the Markan tradition seems to have little feel for what that means. Matthew tends to have women fully and deliberately present in the Jewish manner, as we described. Luke has women present even more than Mark and Matthew, but tends to protect them from the Roman opprobrium πόρνη.

The Healing of Peter's Mother-in-Law (Mark 1:29–31; Matt. 8:14–15; Luke 4:38–39)

Although the method of healing varies in each of the Gospels, the end result is the same. She serves. In all three narratives the word διακονέω is used. Mark is unaware of any problem; for Matthew the behavior of the mother-in-law is assumed. Why did not Luke save the situation by using another word? He knew it was derogatory for a woman wealthy enough to own her own home to serve these five men. The answer is relatively clear. The Jesus tradition tends to use healing stories for a purpose other than the healing itself. For the man with the unclean spirit (Mark 1:21–28) it was teaching (διδάσκω); for the healing of the paralytic (Mark 2:1–12) it was preaching (κηρύσσω) the word (though teaching in Luke 5:17). The healing of Peter's mother-in-law establishes the importance of the diaconate in the early churches. Luke did not wish to eliminate from association with Jesus an office that later in the story would become quite important (Acts 6:1–6).

If this analysis is correct, we have seen an important piece of data. The early Christians were aware that women served as caregivers, as διάκονοι, and as ones who served, even officiated, the tables at the agape meal (plate 26).

In Acts 6:1–6, which describes how the early Jerusalem church established the diaconate as a formal office, Luke did his best to save women from the πόρνη nomenclature. He indicates that the Twelve were serving the tables until such a time that it became a burden for them to preach the word and serve the tables at the same time. So they agreed to appoint seven others to wait on tables (διακονεῖν τραπέζαις). According to Luke these seven Hellenists, appointed to appease the Hellenist widows, immediately became evangelists. There is no reason to suppose that they ever served the tables. We can hardly believe that any of the Twelve waited on tables. Surely the tables were served by men and women who were

47. Corley, *Private Women*, 182–83.

not primarily responsible for the mission of the Jesus movement. Why did the Hellenist widows fail to receive their share of the food? Was it not likely that they were serving the tables, and failed to receive a full share? In such a case the appointment of the Hellenist men as deacons would be a literary diversion to cover the fact that it was the Hellenist women who were overly occupied with serving (διακονεῖν) the tables. The diversion may have worked in the first century, but modern scholars still puzzle over the call of the deacons in Acts.

The Woman Who Came to Dinner

One of the most extensive New Testament descriptions of a meal follows the accusation that Jesus is a glutton and drunkard and eats with, or is friends with, tax collectors and sinners (ἰδοὺ ἄνθρωπος φάγος καὶ οἰνοπότης, φίλος τελωνῶν καὶ ἁμαρτωλῶν, Luke 7:35). In response Luke narrates the story of Jesus at the house of Simon the Pharisee (7:36–50). Sometime in the course of the meal a woman came into the house (open or outdoor triclinium?) and, in an emotional scene, washed the feet of Jesus with her tears and with ointment. It was a scandalous scene in any culture. The Pharisee Simon and his guests were dumbfounded. Their response to the scene was epistemological. If this man were from God he would have known that the woman was a ἁμαρτωλός (not a πόρνη). To be sure, their emphasis is on prior knowledge about the woman, but we are left with the sensation that Jesus did not care whether the woman was an ἁμαρτωλός, nor did he acknowledge that her action categorized her as a πόρνη. Luke did nothing to save her reputation. She could not be saved.

Matthew and Mark changed the story completely. The story occurs as part of the Passion narrative in the home of Simon the leper rather than Simon the Pharisee (Matt. 26:6–13; Mark 14:3–9). Again, a woman comes into the eating area, but this time anoints the head of Jesus for burial. There is no mention of her as a ἁμαρτωλός or a πόρνη. Instead the guests complained about the excessive cost of the ointment. In contrast to Luke, Mark and Matthew assumed the legitimacy of the woman's presence. Mark ignores the issue, and Matthew follows the Jewish custom that women were present at a meal.

John takes the anointment part of the Matthean and Markan story, but picks up some elements of the Lukan story. The woman anoints the feet of Jesus and wipes them with her hair. Again, a scandalous act. But the woman was neither a ἁμαρτωλός nor a πόρνη. Quite the contrary: she was Mary of Bethany, the most important female friend of Jesus. Again without any apology, Mary was serving the table, but apparently was not reclining at the table with Jesus. Like for Luke, for John her action was scandalous. As in Matthew and Luke, in John the concern for excessive expense was expressed — but only by Judas. How could John have told this incredible story to a Greco-Roman audience? Did he intend to leave us with the teasing impression that Mary was the wife of Jesus? Should we not assume that the Mary Magdalene of chapter 21 actually, in the Gospel of John, be identified as Mary of Bethany? This Mary, as a woman, parallels the masculine Beloved Disciple — two persons who had received the divine reality from Jesus and who therefore were intimate friends, especially at mealtime (ἐν τῷ κόλπῳ τοῦ Ἰησοῦ, John 13:23). In the case of a woman, Mary, that intimacy took on a strong sexual quality. Still we are astounded that John could relate this narrative to a Greco-Roman audience.

The Feeding of the Five Thousand

Because of the frequency of this feeding narrative (six times in the four Gospels) and the frequency of artistic representations of the feeding (plate 19) and/or the related Agape (plate 25), the story must be taken seriously as data for meals in the early church.

In Mark's account of the feeding of the five thousand (6:30–44) he refers to the crowd by means of the masculine plural pronoun (6:34, 41). Only in verse 44 does he identify the five thousand as men (καὶ ἦσαν οἱ φαγόντες [τοὺς ἄρτους] πεντακισχίλιοι ἄνδρες). Since the great crowd surely consisted of families going up to Jerusalem for a festival, there must have been women and children present. Mark does not mention women, though his method of counting might have been to number only the men. In the feeding of the four thousand (8:1–10) there is no indication of gender. The masculine pronoun is used (verse 3), but otherwise it is a crowd, a plural verb or masculine plural noun ending (in Greek a masculine plural does not necessarily define gender; a feminine plural does).

Luke, like Mark, refers to the crowd with corporate words like λαός or pronouns (9:10–17), except that the disciples estimated the number of people to be five thousand men (ἦσαν γὰρ ὡσεὶ ἄνδρες πεντακισχίλιοι, verse 14). Women do not recline and eat with the men.

In Matthew the feeding stories (Matt. 14:13–21; 15:32–39) are similar to Mark and Luke, except that both times, when the number is mentioned, the obvious is also stated: women and children ate with the men (οἱ δὲ ἐσθίοντες ἦσαν ἄνδρες ὡσεὶ πεντακισχίλιοι χωρὶς γυναικῶν καὶ παιδίων, 14:21; likewise, οἱ δὲ ἐσθίοντες ἦσαν τετρακισχίλιοι ἄνδρες χωρὶς γυναικῶν καὶ παιδίων, 15:38). True to other narratives, Matthew does not hesitate to have men and women eat together and does not hesitate to infer that in the early Christian Agape men and women reclined together at the table.

In John's account of the feeding (6:1–14), that which we suspected is made evident. At issue is the number count. All the men and women (ἄνθρωποι) were told to sit down, and their number was five thousand men (εἶπεν ὁ Ἰησοῦς· ποιήσατε τοὺς ἀνθρώπους ἀναπεσεῖν. ἦν δὲ χόρτος πολὺς ἐν τῷ τόπῳ. ἀνέπεσαν οὖν οἱ ἄνδρες τόν ἀριθμὸν πεντακισχίλιοι).

When all six stories are considered we must conclude that at common meals in the first-century churches men and women ate together. Of course, each account has been edited to fit the theme of the redactor. John wants no cultural inhibitions to the relationship between men and women (so Mary at the table of Jesus). Matthew follows Jewish custom — men and women together. Luke eliminates women in order to avert Roman criticism, and Mark simply uses the word ἄνδρες to set the total number.

Mary and Martha

Jesus comes to a meal at the home of Mary, Martha, and Lazarus in Bethany (Luke 10:38–41; see John 12:1–3).[48] At the meal Mary sat at the feet of the Lord and listened (παρακαθεσθεῖσα πρὸς τοὺς πόδας τοῦ κυρίου ἤκουεν τὸν λόγον αὐτοῦ, 10:39). While this remarkable narrative bristles with data, two items contribute to the matter of gender and meals. It is difficult to picture the position of Mary, regardless of the assumed table arrangement. Jesus was reclining at either a triclinium or an arc. In either case Mary would be sitting on the edge of the table at the feet of Jesus or even on the floor behind the table. How such a position would enable Mary to hear the words of Jesus is inexplicable. If we are to take this as a proper description of an early Jewish-Christian meal, then women were not reclining with men. Otherwise, Mary has the position of a submissive wife invited to a usually male event (sitting at a place somewhat apart from the table). Any attempt by Luke to prevent the appearance, in Roman eyes, of a πόρνη seems absent.

There is yet another possibility. Just as healing narratives have been used to develop the leadership of the faith community, so the intent of this story may be to describe the training of early Christian (women?) teachers. Mary takes the traditional stance of a student-disciple at the feet of the master.[49]

The latter suggestion leaves Martha in limbo. Historically, Mary has been taken as a contemplative and Martha as a practitioner. While there is no basis for this ancient interpretation, there can be no doubt that Martha acts as a server. It is Martha's house; she issued the invitation

---

48. Corley, *Private Women*, 133–44.

49. Elisabeth Schüssler Fiorenza, "Theological Criteria and Historical Reconstruction: Martha and Mary; Luke 10:38–42," *Colloquy* 53 (Berkeley, Calif.: Center for Hermeneutical Studies in Hellenistic and Modern Culture, 1987), 1–12.

to Jesus. While, in Roman eyes, by serving the table she also might appear to be a πόρνη, in early Christian worship practice the owner of the house church also serves the Eucharist / Agape. That is, the owner is the minister (διάκονος). Taken this way, the story has meaning in the Jesus movement: Mary is becoming a διδάσκαλος (teacher) by sitting at the feet of Jesus and hearing the word, while Martha acts as a διάκονος (minister) as she serves the table (ἡ δὲ Μάρθα περιεσπᾶτο περὶ πολλὴν διακονίαν ἐπιστᾶσα δὲ εἶπεν, κύριε, οὐ μέλει σοι ὅτι ἡ ἀδελφή μου μόνην με κατέλιπεν διακονεῖν;). This leaves us with a serious problem. Why is only one ministry needed, in contrast to πολλὴν διακονίαν, and why is Mary's μερίς better than Martha's? Does the narrative reflect a time when the tasks of the διάκονος are overwhelming, so that specialization has become necessary (Acts 6:1–6)?

Archaeological Evidence

However difficult it might be to work through the nature of the influences on how men and women ate at the same table, we can be fairly certain of the result. In artistic representations of the early Christian Agape, men and women are seated at the same table. We can mention the *fractio panis* in the catacomb of Priscilla (plate 25). Even more explicitly female are some characters sitting at the table found in the crypt of Gaudentius (catacomb of SS. Peter and Marcellinus, plate 26). The woman in the lower right holds a glass of wine with the eucharistic bread directly on it. She not only participates in the meal but apparently is officiating. Though difficult to discern, the words in the upper right-hand corner appear to me as "IRENE, MISC," that is, "Irene, mix some water with the wine [for us]." I assume they are the words of the man to the right of Irene the officiant. The hostess, Irene, would do the mixing. In the same catacomb we find two other agape meals with inscriptions. In one the feminine name Agape appears to the left (plate 27). She is asked to mix the wine (*nobis*, for us). The inscription to the right reads, I believe, "PORCIA, BIBA," that is "Portia, live well," a drinking salute to deceased Portia, who apparently was buried in the *loculus*. In another scene (plate 28) the names Irene and Agape appear.[50] Irene is asked to pass the hot food ("IRENE DA CALDA"), while Agape is asked to mix the wine. The words to Agape are addressed to the woman on the right who apparently has already mixed the water and wine and is distributing it with the help of a young servant (artistic representations in antiquity could show successive actions in the same picture).

---

50. Pierre du Bourguet, *Early Christian Painting*, trans. S. W. Taylor (London: Weidenfeld & Nicolson, 1965), plates 87, 89, 100.

Women are reclining at the arc with men. In these three examples women are in charge of the meals and are mixing the wine and distributing both bread and wine. Women are at least equal in early Christian table fellowship.

Some inscriptions lead to the same conclusion. For example, in the triclia under St. Sebastiano, early Christians sat at tables and scribbled prayers on the wall. Many of the prayers inscribed come from one person (eating alone?). Others include several people, presumably a whole family. Primus, for example, eats with his wife Prima, his daughter-in-law Saturnina, and Victorinus, his father (?).[51] It would be unreasonable to suppose that the women and men first ate at separate tables, then came together to scratch graffiti on the wall.

The Meal for the Dead

In recent years there has arisen a massive amount of literature on this subject. The problems involved and the volume of the literature forbid a thorough treatment of the subject. Here we can only give a brief synopsis of the function of the meal for the dead in early medieval Christianity and the early church. Despite the breadth of research and the controversies that have arisen, a general consensus about the meal for the dead is emerging. That consensus would include, among others, the studies of Lionel Rothkrug on medieval shrines and relics;[52] Peter Brown on the cult of the saints;[53] Richard Krautheimer on early Christian architecture, especially covered cemeteries;[54] and the work of Theodor Klauser,[55] André Grabar,[56] Ejnar Dyggve,[57] and J. B. Ward-Perkins[58] on the relationship of pre-Christian cultic practices to the cult of the saints and meal for the dead.[59]

---

51. Snyder, *Ante Pacem*, 43. See Orazio Marucchi, "L'ipogeo con i graffiti degli apostoli Pietro e Paolo scoperto sotto las basilica di S. Sebastiano," *NBAC* 27 (1921): 14.

52. Lionel Rothkrug, *Religious Practices and Collective Perceptions*, Historical Reflections, vol. 7, no. 1 (Waterloo, Ont.: Historical Reflections Press, 1980).

53. Peter Brown, *The Cult of the Saints* (Chicago: University of Chicago Press, 1981).

54. Richard Krautheimer, *Early Christian and Byzantine Architecture* (Harmondsworth, England: Pelican, 1975); *Rome: Profile of a City, 312–1308* (Princeton: Princeton University Press, 1980).

55. Theodor Klauser, "Christliche Märtyrerkult, heidnischer Heroenkult und spätjüdische Heiligenverehrung," in *Gesammelte Arbeiten* (Münster: Aschendorf, 1974), 221–29; "Von Heroon zur Märtyrerbasilika," in *Gesammelte Arbeiten*, 275–91.

56. André Grabar, *Martyrium: recherches sur le culte des reliques et l'art, chrétien antique* (Paris: College de France, 1946).

57. Ejnar Dyggve *Dødekult, Kejserkult og Basilika* (Copenhagen: P. Branner, 1943).

58. J. B. Ward-Perkins "Memoria, Martyr's Tomb and Martyr's Church," *JTS* 17 (1966): 20–38.

59. The distinction is made here between the kinship community, which depends on relationships for personal reputation, and the moral community, which depends on tran-

Consensus Position

Briefly, the consensus would look like this:

1. Speaking methodologically, it would be inappropriate to refer to the feast for the dead as superstition or ignorant folk religion. While there may be considerable truth to the two-level religion described by David Hume in his work on natural religion, one may not use this distinction to render theological disdain toward popular practices or to cast such practices into historical occultism. Popular religious practices must be taken seriously theologically and historically.

2. In the ancient world there probably was no more important popular religious practice than that associated with the cult of the dead and eating with the dead.

3. The main sociological function of eating with the dead, or of the cult of the dead in general, was community formation. The dead simply were the "ultimate age bracket" of the local community. By visiting the place where they were buried one would enjoy fellowship with them and share in a continued conviviality. The location of family tombs was normally around that of some "special dead." The special dead could be clan or community leaders, or, in pre-Christian times, persons of some renown.

4. The psyche of the special dead was limited geographically by the burial place, so that the function of such a person was to create social cement in local kinship communities. All stable communities had a cult of the special dead.

5. This cult of the dead was so powerfully ingrained in popular religion and so critical for social stability that it could be utilized for political or ecclesiastical purposes. Once that is understood, it is possible to see that some of the most important political and ecclesiastical formations in the Western world were handled by management of the cult of the dead.

Cult of the Saints

We can sketch briefly some examples.[60] Inculturation of the Jesus tradition into pagan Europe, north of Italy, required extraordinary measures

---

scendent values for reputation. I prefer and will use the term "ideological community" for moral community. See Rothkrug, *Religious Practices*, 25.

60. The following thesis has been taken from Rothkrug's work.

as far as Christian formation was concerned. For the most part this formation among pagans was accomplished by means of the cult of the
saints. Where Christian community did not exist, the elevation of a local
saint with shrine and relics, often at a pagan holy place, created a sense of
community with the Christian past that enabled certain Christian community virtues to be expected and a certain amount of loyalty or kinship
with the community where this special dead had resided. In southern
Germany sufficient indigenous saints were produced to develop a fairly
complete cult of the saints. In eastern France the production of saints was
much slower. In order to compensate for this lack, the papacy translated
abbots and bishops into sainthood. Their graves were elevated and the
relics translated into shrines where the community could meet in celebration of appropriate feast days. Of course, burials were encouraged
around these shrines. In being buried close to the shrine one continued
in the kinship community of the special dead.

In northern Germany, on the other hand, there were few indigenous
saints. As a consequence, in order to foster Christian community, saints
and their relics had to be imported from southern Europe. Apparently
such imported saints failed to gain the popularity of either indigenous
saints or translated bishops. In any case, when the papacy strove to unite
the various local communities of Europe into a catholic, translocal community around the Virgin Mary, who could have no strictly local shrine,
there was considerable success except in northern Germany. It was there
that Protestantism, with its ideological community (as opposed to kinship
community), eventually developed.

The Beginnings of Christian Meals for the Dead

Returning to Rome, we can see exactly the same procedures at an earlier
date. Prior to Constantine the Christians had developed a cult of the
special dead, normally the martyr. It would be difficult to determine when
this started. Certainly the description in the *Martyrdom of Polycarp*,
about 156, cannot be interpreted other than as a cult of the martyr (*Mart.
Pol.* 18).[61]

It also seems probable that Ignatius of Antioch, rather than having an
idée fixe on his own death, actually anticipated that his martyrdom would
become a source of unification for the church of his time. He speaks of
himself becoming bread by means of the beasts.[62] At least, when the
fathers of Israel no longer could serve as ancestry for the new Christian

---

61. See the discussion by Bernhard Kötting, *Der frühchristliche Reliquienkult und die
Bestattung im Kirchengebäude* (Cologne: Westdeutscher Verlag, 1965), 10. Kötting's work
is useful throughout.
62. *artos tou christou*, Ign. *Rom.* 4:1 (some MSS).

communities, then there must have been a need to create kinship communities by means of a new special dead, the Christian martyrs. One would expect that by the turn of the first century the Gentile church would have to be seeking such new ancestry. In fact, one would suppose that the Gentile church had to deal with the issue from the very beginning. In any case, pre-Constantinian Christians in Rome and elsewhere had such cults. In Rome the most famous is the *memoria apostolorum* underneath the floor of present day St. Sebastiano. Here one finds a large edifice where clearly many, many Christians ate together and made prayers to the special dead, especially Peter and Paul.[63] Other *memoriae* can be found at St. Lorenzo, St. Agnese, and SS. Marcellino e Pietro. When Constantine became emperor he tried to consolidate the Christian church at Rome. One major way he did this was by building edifices in the cemeteries over or near to the *memoriae* of the saints. As we have seen in our discussion of architecture, most of what we call Constantinian basilicas are actually *coemeteria subteglata* (figure 8.4).[64] All the covered cemeteries, including St. Peter's, were built to continue the cult of the dead. It was Constantine's method of increasing the strength of Christian communities in the urban areas. These buildings did not function as churches. They had no altars and no priests.[65] We know from the literature of the time that these buildings were used for burial places, funeral meals and ceremonies, meals for the dead, and large festivals on the days of the special dead and saints, all of which also served as a form of welfare for the poor of the city.[66] Following this move by Constantine to strengthen the Christian church as the national religious institution, it fell upon at least two princes of the church, Augustine and Ambrose, to unify the local communities and consolidate the power of the church. It was these two in the late fourth and early fifth century who insisted that the cult of the dead outside the walls cease.[67] As an alternative the relics or remains of the special dead were brought into the city and placed in the crypt of local community churches. By this means the community that had developed outside the walls would now be formed inside the walls. Inside the city, inside authorized churches, the excesses of the cult of the dead could be regularized by the priesthood and the hierarchy. At the same time, the psychic effect of the presence of the special dead would create new community life within the city, with its attending virtue of *caritas*. It

63. Graydon F. Snyder, "Survey and 'New Thesis' on the Bones of Peter," *BA* 32 (1969): 1–24.
64. Krautheimer, *Rome*, 25.
65. Ibid., 21–24.
66. For example, Paulinus of Nola, *Epist.* 13.11f. On the welfare function of the agape meal see Reicke, *Diakonie, Festfreude und Zelos*.
67. Augustine, *Conf.* 6:2

was an original urban renewal program. At its deepest level the presence of the dead now inside the city created a much more powerful sense of extended community. Such a move was surely one of the sharpest social revolutions in the ancient world.[68] The connection of tomb with altar brought ultimate kinship values into the life of the city. If what has been observed here is correct, then one might rightly ask whether the same phenomenon appeared at other times in Judeo-Christian history. When serious disruptions occurred, how was new community formed?

Jewish Meals for the Dead

There can be no doubt that the new community of Hebrews in Palestine needed the graves of the special dead. We can see in Gen. 23 the amusing, but absolutely essential, account of Abraham securing graves for himself and the community mother, Sarah, at Mamre. Similarly the carrying of the bones of Joseph from Egypt to Palestine served the same function of holding together the Jewish community in Egypt as well as creating new community in the promised land (Exod. 13:19). There are other examples of the special dead in the Hebrew Scriptures. Apparently, Rachel's tomb could be remembered and her presence imagined or felt (Jer. 31:15). Jewish women made a special pilgrimage to the grave of Jephthah's daughter (Judg. 11:39–40). So there can be no doubt about honoring the special dead and the importance of that for the Jewish community.[69]

However, there is no meal for the dead mentioned in relation to these graves. There is a meal for the dead in the Hebrew Scriptures and in late Judaism. It occurs primarily as the bread of mourning, as in Jer. 16:7–8. But there is no reason to suppose that the meals for these dead occurred at any time other than the normal mourning period. The meal that created catholic community in ancient Israel was the Passover meal.[70] It was an ideological community meal, celebrating the Exodus liberation, rather than strictly a kinship meal. But it certainly allowed for and promoted the kinship function. Like Augustine's incorporation of the meal for the dead in Christian liturgy, the Passover meal, a universal ideological meal, incorporated in its celebration the function of the major harvest kinship

68. Brown, *Cult of the Saints*, 4–5. J. Guyon describes the same revolution on the basis of inscriptions. The catacombs now belonged to the church. See "La vente des tombes à travers l'épigraphie de la Rome chrétienne," *Mélanges de l'école française de Rome, Antiquité* 86 (1974): 549–96.

69. Joachim Jeremias, *Heiligengräber in Jesu Umwelt (Mt. 23,29; L. 11,47)* (Göttingen: Vandenhoeck & Ruprecht, 1958).

70. For a structuralist analysis of the meal for the dead, see Salvatore D'Onofrio, "A las mesa con los muertos," in *Antropología de la alimentación: Ensayos sobre la dieta Mediterranea*, ed. Isabel González Turmo y Pedro Romero de Solís (Almería, Spain: Consejería de cultura y medio ambiente de la junta de Andalucía, 1993), 147–77.

meal. Even though the Passover incorporated the harvest meal, the Jews changed its date to a nonharvest period.[71]

Paul and Meals for the Dead

In the New Testament there are two major meals or communions.[72] The one is called the Agape and the other the Eucharist. The Agape is well known in Acts as the breaking of bread (2:42).[73] As we have seen, the Agape took its dominical institution from the feeding of the five thousand (Mark 6:30–44). Certainly in catacomb art and later ecclesiastical art, the point of reference would be the miraculous feeding with its symbols of fish, loaves of bread, wine, and baskets filled with rolls (plate 25). Before the seventh century there is no portrayal of a Christian meal, or even the Last Supper, that shows any Passover elements in it. They all refer back to the feeding of the five thousand. The early church celebrated this bread and fish meal for many centuries. The Agape was either identical to that meal, or else the Agape disappeared.

The Eucharist, on the other hand, is an ἀνάμνησις meal relating to the death and resurrection of Christ. Although it is true that the eucharistic meal celebrates a death and likely has taken on elements of the Jewish meal for the dead, it cannot be maintained that the ἀνάμνησις Eucharist is a meal for the dead Jesus. Rather, like the Passover meal, it is a universalized community commemoration with great ideological power. It is not only a translocal (catholic) kinship meal, but an ideological meal. Jesus cannot be localized.

The clearest instance of community formation in the New Testament can be found in 1 Corinthians. There we find Paul struggling with local community formation that threatens catholicity; or, perhaps, Paul has learned at Corinth that local formation, even as fostered by an apostle, can move in directions counter to the universal expectation. Three times he reminded them that a particular practice was being done in all the churches (7:17; 11:16; 14:33). Among other divisive problems, a cult of the hero has formed around such fabled persons as Peter, Apollos, and Paul himself. Against such local formations Paul wrote the first four chapters of 1 Corinthians, stressing a *theologia crucis* that knows no local concretizations. Of even greater importance, in chapters 5–15 he must deal with competitive cult practices in Corinth. In chapter 8 he turns to their

---

71. Pedersen, *Israel: Its Life and Culture*, 3/4: 384–88.

72. Hans Lietzmann, *Mass and the Lord's Supper: A Study in the History of the Liturgy*, trans. Dorothea H. G. Reeve (Leiden: Brill, 1979).

73. Andreas Lindemann, "The Beginnings of Christian Life in Jerusalem According to the Summaries in the Acts of the Apostles (Acts 2:42–47; 4:32–37; 5:12–16)," in *Common Life in the Early Church*, ed. Julian V. Hills (Harrisburg, Pa.: Trinity Press International, 1998), 202–18.

question regarding εἰδωλόθυτος, meat offered to idols. He assures them that idol meat has no importance since there is no God save one. He does admit there are many θεοί and κύριοι (apparently synonyms for εἴδωλον) available to them, but actually there is only one God and one Lord (8:5–6). Without giving value to the εἰδωλόθυτος, he suggests that they act lovingly toward each other by not creating divisions over practice (8:7–13).

In light of our previous discussion, one must make two observations at this point. The prejudicial term εἰδωλόθυτος need not refer only to meat made available at shops connected with a given god or goddess. To be sure, it can refer to such meat (1 Cor. 10:25). And, although the Judeo-Christian term εἰδωλεῖον is rare, there are references to a *ser-apeion*, which must refer to places where food is offered to Serapis.[74] Still, we should not limit the word εἰδωλόθυτος strictly to such practices. The term εἴδωλον did not mean false gods and goddesses to the Gentiles. It referred positively to the presence or images of the special dead. There is no reason to exclude this meaning, that is, for the special dead, from the term εἰδωλόθυτος as Paul used it. To the contrary, the discussion of the table of δαιμονίων in 1 Cor. 10:14–22 requires it. Secondly, the opposition of one God to many gods and lords simply states the conflict between local and catholic in a theological way. Polytheism, as a configuration of local divinities, corresponds roughly to local autonomy. Advocacy of one God opposes the ultimate value of local structures. It calls for an ideological community over against kinship communities. Paul was attacking idolatry as noncatholic.

However ambiguous he might have been in chapter 8 of 1 Corinthians, Paul speaks plainly in chapter 10. There he recognizes that a cultic meal around a local deity could be very damaging to the new Christian. He cites as evidence the damage wrought by the Israelites when they ate around the idol at the foot of Mount Sinai. Now he urges them not to participate in such meals, not simply because they might injure a brother or sister, but because such meals effectively build kinship community. In 10:16–17 he reminds them of their agape meal together and the faith formulas they use on that occasion: "The cup of blessing that we bless, is it not the κοινωνία of the blood of Christ?" and "The bread that we break, is it not the κοινωνία of the body of Christ?" These formulas stress κοινωνία rather than ἀνάμνησις. The offering is the community's bread and wine, not the body and blood of Christ. The people bless the bread and the cup.

In verses 10:18–22 Paul makes it clear that the problem is not the true God versus false gods, but two competing fellowship meals. He cites

---

74. See J. H. Moulton and G. Milligan, *The Vocabulary of the Greek New Testament* (Grand Rapids: Eerdmans, 1949), for the Koine use of these terms.

once more the κοινωνία formed by the Israelites around the altar, and then shifts to the κοινωνία created by Gentiles when they eat εἰδωλόθυτος around the table of δαιμόνια. Paul shifted from the word εἴδωλον to the more specific term δαιμόνιον, which refers to the power and presence of the special dead.[75] Paul strictly forbids them to eat εἰδωλόθυτος at the table of the special dead. One cannot drink of the cup of the δαιμόνιον, the special dead, and the cup of God at the same time. One cannot eat at the table of the special dead and eat at God's table at the same time. One cannot adhere to two cultic communities simultaneously.

Following a further discussion regarding possible divisions in the community, Paul describes the agape meal as a means of healing such problems (11:17–22). He concludes his argument for unity with a rehearsal of the words of the ἀνάμνησις eucharist (11:23–27). In other words, he offers in place of the δαιμόνιον a resurrected special dead, Jesus Christ, who cannot be localized. Paul countered the effectiveness of the Corinthian cult of the dead by joining the Christian κοινωνία meal, the Agape, with the Christian memorial of the universal special dead, Jesus Christ. Like his Jewish ancestors before him, he tried to develop local kinship community on an ideological basis. Paul failed. There remained in early Christianity two celebrative meals, the ἀνάμνησις Eucharist and the Agape. The ἀνάμνησις was based on the Passover and Jesus' farewell meal. The Agape was based on the feeding of the five thousand; its symbols were bread, fish, and wine. The Agape was the kinship meal of early Christianity. Eventually it did not compete with the table of δαιμόνια; it became the table of δαιμόνια, not of pagan heroes, but of Christian saints and martyrs. It was their presence and power that built new kinship structures throughout European cities. The evidence is unmistakable. However much patristic literature may reflect on the meaning and practice of the ἀνάμνησις meal, the art and architecture of early Christianity portray more often the agape meal with the dead, with its bread, fish, wine, and baskets. It was Augustine and Ambrose who finally succeeded where Paul failed; they brought together in one meal the ἀνάμνησις Eucharist of the universal church and the Agape with its δαιμόνιον of the martyr.

Meals and the Poor

Jewish Charity

According to the Hebrew Scriptures, the poor are fed from excess food deliberately assigned to them. In the well-known example from the book

75. O. Waser, "Daimon," *Paulys Realencyclopädie der klassischen Altertumswissenschaft* (Stuttgart: J. B. Metzler, 1901), 4.2:2010–12.

of Ruth, Boaz instructed the workers to leave extra grain for Ruth. Although there was surely a romantic intent in this order, leaving food for those in need was the custom (Ruth 2; cf. Exod. 23:11; Lev. 19:10; 23:22). Closer to the New Testament period, Tobit says that he would share his bread with the hungry:

> I would give my food to the hungry and my clothing to the naked; and if I saw the dead body of any of my people thrown out behind the wall of Nineveh, I would bury it. (Tob. 1:17)

The author of Sirach says much the same: "The bread of the needy is the life of the poor; whoever deprives them of it is a murderer" (Sir. 34:25; ἄρτος ἐπιδεομένων ζωὴ πτωχῶν ὁ ἀποστερῶν αὐτὴν ἄνθρωπος αἱμάτων, Sir. 34:21 LXX).

Feeding the Poor in the Jesus Tradition

The same Jewish expectation can be seen in the New Testament. In Luke's parable of the rich man and Lazarus, it is assumed that the rich man and his brothers ought to have known from scriptures and tradition that sharing with the poor was expected (Luke 16:31). Zacchaeus, a Jew (Luke 19:9), sharing a meal with Jesus felt compelled to share with the poor, especially those whom he himself had impoverished (Luke 19:1–10). Similarly James condemns those who wish well for others, but do not actually share their food with them (James 2:15–16). The Jesus tradition throughout the Synoptic Gospels portrays Jesus as one who ate with all types of people, who by eating together indeed developed community across boundary lines. But even more, he urged his followers to invite the poor to their meals:

> He said also to the one who had invited him, "When you give a luncheon or a dinner, do not invite your friends or your brothers or your relatives or rich neighbors, in case they may invite you in return, and you would be repaid. But when you give a banquet, invite the poor, the crippled, the lame, and the blind. And you will be blessed, because they cannot repay you, for you will be repaid at the resurrection of the righteous." (Luke 14:12–14)

Paul does not directly utilize the Jesus tradition and does not often speak of meals. But Paul's complaint about the celebration of the Lord's Supper, the Agape, in 1 Cor. 11 presumably was based on the fact that the rich did not share equally with the poor.

True to his program of deculturization, the author of John seriously depreciates sharing with the poor. As we have seen, John devaluated the feeding of the five thousand, a story that stresses the sharing of food, presumably with the poor. In John, Jesus says that the multitude was interested only in the food and not the faith significance of Jesus as the bread of life (John 6:26). Even more significantly, Judas is criticized for sharing with the poor after a meal. After the dinner with Mary, Martha, and Lazarus (John 12:1–8), Mary uses an expensive ointment to anoint Jesus. Judas was scandalized by the failure to share with the poor. In order to cover over the omission, the redactor claims that Judas was actually a thief rather than a compassionate Jew (12:6). Likewise at the meal in John 13, when Judas leaves the room the disciples rather automatically assume he is buying something for the poor (13:29). These strange accusations about Judas, who consistently misunderstands Jesus, are directed toward members of the Johannine church who have failed to share with the poor after the community meal, the Agape.

There are other hints in the New Testament. The story of the deacons in Acts 6 would leave the impression that equality of distribution was to be expected. So, according to Luke, deacons were appointed to distribute food and resources.

The Agape in Early Christian Literature

We find references to the Agape in later literature, although association with distribution of food does not occur as often.[76] In Jude the opponents are indeed accused of sharing in the Agape without concern for sharing with others:

> These are blemishes on your love-feasts [ἀγάπαις], while they feast with you without fear, feeding themselves. They are waterless clouds carried along by the winds; autumn trees without fruit, twice dead, uprooted. (Jude 12)

Second Peter probably reflects the same problem (assuming a reference to the Agape), though failure to share with the poor is not specifically mentioned:

> They count it a pleasure to revel in the daytime. They are blots and blemishes, reveling in their dissipation while they feast with you.
> (2 Pet. 2:13)

Soon after the problem raised in Jude, Ignatius of Antioch referred more explicitly to a similar problem in Smyrna. It is at the Agape that compassion is shown. The opponents do not show that compassion:

---

76. *EEC*, s.v. "Agape," 16–17 .

They have no regard for the Agape; no care for the widow, or the orphan, or the oppressed; for the bond, or for the free; for the hungry, or for the thirsty. (Ign. *Smyrn.* 6:2b)

In fact, it may be that the opponents do not even attend the Agape:

They abstain from the Eucharist and from prayer, because they do not confess the Eucharist to be the flesh of our Saviour Jesus Christ, who suffered for our sins, and whom the Father, of his goodness, raised up again. Those, therefore, who speak against this gift of God incur death in the midst of their disputes. But it were better for them to celebrate the Agape, that they also might rise again.

(Ign. *Smyrn.* 6:2c–7:1)

The Agape as Social Concern

The function of the Agape as a means of social concern continued through the second century.[77] In Hippolytus (*Trad. ap.* 26) we find care for the widows. In Tertullian (*Apol.* 39) the food is used to help the poor.

In the New Testament story of the feeding of the five thousand, no practical reason is given for collecting the leftover fragments of food. Nor can one say with any certainty whether the feeding gave rise to a particular form of the Agape or whether the earliest churches, celebrating an Agape, formed the narrative that we call the feeding of the five thousand. But the constant appearance in early Christian art of the baskets around a table cannot be simply a memory of the biblical story, nor should one suppose that it took seven baskets of bread to feed seven people (plate 25). To be sure, the pictorial representation is symbolic. It reflects the practice of the early church as it shares its agape meal with outsiders, marginal people, and the poor.[78]

---

77. Reicke, *Diakonie, Festfreude, und Zelos.*
78. A. Hamman, *Vie liturgique et vie sociale.*

12

Gender Meaning and Roles

The problem of gender inculturation may be the most complex and yet the most significant way in which the Jesus tradition affected the Greco-Roman world. It is complex because the data are not consistent in themselves and therefore have led to vastly differing secondary evaluations.

Gender as Divine Symbol

The symbol system of gender comprises a significant aspect of any culture. It is the symbol that, for the most part, energizes human action, though one must always ask whether economic and political considerations have influenced the formation of the gender symbol. Invariably, ultimate language about gender utilizes icons and words from the culture, but normally does not simply mimic human sexuality.

Greco-Roman Gender Symbolism

In the Greco-Roman world the divine world operated like a human family with father, mother, and child deities. The divine family was arbitrary, if not chaotic, so the life of the gods did not serve as moral examples. Male deities ruled the Olympic family, while powerful goddesses guided creativity and fertility. With such ultimate gender definitions the human roles would be clear. Men are the ultimate authorities and must succeed in making ultimate, public decisions. Women create cultural values and future generations. They do that privately. Roman homes had fertility symbols (e.g., Venus), but the household altar also often held small statues of the emperor, who represented at the human level the masculine, political power. The incursion of Eastern religions altered the Greco-Roman symbols of gender. None were family-oriented. Some (e.g., Isis, Dionysius) elevated the feminine experience to ultimate significance (music, dance, ecstasy). Others (e.g., Mithra) elevated the masculine experience (bonding, sacrifice).

Jewish Gender Symbolism

In the Jewish tradition there was one God, who was masculine. Or better stated, the functional God, יהוה, was described as one and masculine
("Hear, O Israel: יהוה is our אלהים, יהוה is one" [Deut. 6:4]). The more
general God, אלהים, the universal God, was plural and therefore not
strictly male or female ("Let us make male and female in our image"
[see Gen. 1:26–27]). In Hebrew semiotics the masculine is the creator.
There is no divine family. Although many suppose that the predominance
of the masculine deity creates or supports a patriarchal society, the symbolic meaning does not necessarily support that supposition. In Hebrew
semiotics the masculine creates and the feminine is created. More specifically, though not exclusively, יהוה is the husband and Israel, the people,
is the wife. Men in the society of this feminine people must be just as receptive to the masculine word of God as are women (note Eph. 5:23–24;
1 Cor. 11:3). Kings and leaders who refuse to hear and obey the word
are soundly punished — they along with the feminine people, Israel. The
"sons of God" are masculine, but the word may be brought to kings and
the people by male or female prophets-messengers. Since gender signifies
a symbiotic relationship between divinity and people, one cannot easily
alter society by changing the gender of the god. That is, a goddess of
Israel would result in a divinity receptive to the words of the masculine
people, rather than a feminine people that receives the words of the masculine god. Such a gender symbol would be very close to Eastern fertility
religions like that of Isis. Because a masculine people can manipulate
goddesses (female), fertility religions have not particularly resulted in a
symbol of equality for the sexes.[1]

The interaction between Greco-Roman and Jewish symbol systems can
be fairly well documented. There is none. In Greco-Roman art there are
frequent manifestations of the divinities. Of particular interest is Venus
in her conch, Neptune with his trident, Selene the moon goddess, Apollo
the sun god. In Jewish art there are no pictorial manifestations of יהוה
or אלהים. God may be in command, but there is no symbolic gender
definition.

Because Jesus was a male Jewish person, there was no reason for early
Christians to shun artistic representations. At first Jesus was a wonder
worker, much like Hercules, but eventually he took on the characteristics
of a philosopher, then an emperor.[2] That is, Jesus replaced the *lares* of the
family altar. In addition to the emperor, *filius dei*, he invaded the symbol

---

1. Judith Plaskow, "Jewish Theology," in *Feminist Perspectives on Jewish Studies*, ed.
Lynn Davidman and Shelly Tenenbaum (New Haven: Yale University Press, 1994), 62–84.
2. P. Beskow, *Rex Gloriae: The Kingship of Christ in the Early Church* (Stockholm:
Almquist and Wiksell, 1962).

of Apollo, the sun god (plate 22). Eventually the masculine picture of Jesus was known as God, particularly the Pantocrator. These semiotic shifts necessarily caused a shift in the way gender was seen.

Gender Roles in the Greco-Roman World

In regard to meals we have already noted the strict distinction between private and public in Hellenistic society. Women were not permitted to appear at meals, unless the meals were private (with the immediate family). Women who did cook, serve, and entertain could be considered public women, or πόρναι. Women who were slaves or had been slaves and women who had public professions were automatically πόρναι.[3] The role of women did change during the late republic and early empire of the Roman world, marked perhaps by the repeal of the restrictive Oppian Law in 195 B.C.E.[4] Women were more free to act in public, to own property, and to be educated. Much of the attack on women during this period comes from intellectuals who resented this new-found freedom.

Gender Roles in Judaism

Although few societies have seriously altered the private nature of women and the public nature of men, still, the Jewish society did not practice the same strictures as the Greco-Roman. To be sure, women were subordinate to male authority. Male offspring were preferred to female (Gen. 19:31–38). Daughters were given in marriage by their fathers (Gen. 29:21–30; *m. Ketub.* 4.4–5).[5] Because of their sexual function, women could be unclean (Leviticus). But women were not excluded from public meetings (e.g., *m. Ker.* 1.3–7; Luke 2:41).[6] In the temple there was a court for women through which the men would pass. Although there were no female hierarchical leaders in Israel, there were women leaders (Miriam, Deborah) and women heroes (Judith, Jael, Tamar, Rahab, and Esther).[7] Men and women shared the same Passover table and eventually worshiped in the same synagogue.

---

3. Luise Schottroff, *Let the Oppressed Go Free: Feminist Perspectives on the New Testament* (Louisville: Westminster/John Knox, 1993).

4. Schottroff, *Let the Oppressed Go Free*, 80–87; Corley, *Private Women*, 12.

5. Tal Ilan, *Jewish Women in Greco-Roman Palestine* (Peabody, Mass.: Hendrickson, 1998), 49.

6. Ilan, *Jewish Women*, 180.

7. Tikva Frymer-Kensky, "The Bible and Women's Studies," in *Feminist Perspectives on Jewish Studies*, 16–39; Susan Niditch, "Portrayals of Women in the Hebrew Bible," in *Jewish Women in Historical Perspective*, ed. Judith R. Baskin (Detroit: Wayne State University Press, 1991) 25–45.

Judaism at the time of the New Testament was much more flexible. Again, in terms of cause and effect, one cannot determine whether the more open attitude toward gender derived from earlier Judaism or the influence of a more liberal Roman attitude.

There are two major resources for determining the role of women in Judaism in the first century: the presence of God-fearers (especially in the writings of Luke) and the evidence of inscriptions.

God-fearers

Along with the consensus about God-fearers as the bridge between Jew and Gentile (see chapter 1), another consensus assumes that Luke has a deep compassion for the poor and the marginalized. Among the marginalized he includes women, so that he mentions women far more often than the other Synoptics. In the Gospel of Luke there are forty-two passages that concern women or female motifs. Of these, twenty-three are peculiar to Luke. It is true that Luke does not place the same emphasis on women in his second book, Acts.[8] Nevertheless, generally speaking, the consensus runs as follows: (1) Luke corrects the picture of Mark and Matthew by including women in the narrative; (2) the inclusion of women reflects the compassion and equanimity of Luke; (3) in fact, however, many of the God-fearers were indeed women; (4) for several reasons the God-fearing women could not become proselytes; (5) prevented from being Jews many female God-fearers heard Paul gladly and responded positively; (6) many of the God-fearing women were wealthy or influential; (7) the Jews were angry with Paul and Barnabas for "stealing" their highly prized, wealthy, God-fearing women. In the Lukan speeches of Paul in Acts 13, we should assume that the masculine plural addresses ἄνδρες Ἰσραηλῖται and ἄνδρες ἀδελφοί, υἱοὶ γένους Ἀβραάμ include women.[9]

Women Leaders in Jewish Inscriptions

Proof for the presence of women can also be derived from inscriptions that include women as leaders. Trebilco notes four early synagogue inscriptions from Asia Minor that mention women as leaders:[10]

1. Smyrna, Ionia: Rufinia, a Jewess is identified as the ἀρχισυνάγωγος at Smyrna.

---

8. Ivoni Richter Reimer, *Women in the Acts of the Apostles: A Feminist Liberation Perspective* (Minneapolis: Fortress, 1995).

9. Jacob Jervell argues that the term does refer only to men, even though Jewish women are present; the men represent the women, so only they are addressed ("Daughters of Abraham," in *The Unknown Paul: Essays on Luke-Acts and Early Christian History* [Minneapolis: Augsburg, 1984], 146–57).

10. Trebilco, *Jewish Communities*, 104–13.

2. Myndos, Caria: Theopempte is identified as the ἀρχισυνάγωγος at Myndos.

3. Aphrodisias, Caria: On face A of the stele previously mentioned, lines 9–10 mention a certain Ἰαηλ προστάτης and her son who are members of the δεκανία responsible for building the soup kitchen. Following the discovery of the stele, Jael was at first identified as a man (4 Ezra 10:43), but given the list of famous Jewish names on the stele, it would be much more likely that Jael is the woman of Judg. 4–5.[11] In that case, a Jewish woman was chair (προστάτης) of the building committee commemorated by the stele.

4. Phocaea, Ionia: Tation, daughter of Straton, built a synagogue with her own funds and was honored by the Jewish community with a χρυσῷ στεφάνῳ καὶ προεδρίᾳ. Although the seat of honor likely carried no administrative responsibilities, the inscription does show the presence of a highly influential women in the synagogue.

In addition to these inscriptions from Asia Minor, Bernadette Brooten lists approximately thirty more from the Mediterranean area that mention women as the head of a synagogue.[12] Although the issue of female leadership does not directly impinge on Paul's speeches in Acts 13, there is a corollary argument. It is widely assumed that women played a more prominent social and political role in Asia Minor than in other parts of the Mediterranean world.[13] These inscriptions do verify that women played leadership roles in Asia Minor synagogues as well (note that the Jewish Christian Tabitha was πλήρης ἔργων ἀγαθῶν, Acts 9:36). These inscriptions and others indicate that women were held in high regard for their contribution to the life of the community and especially, in these cases, the life of the synagogue.[14] Capitolina of Tralles (see chapter 2) is, unfortunately, the only non-Jewish God-fearer woman mentioned in

---

11. Bernadette J. Brooten, "The Gender of Ἰαηλ in the Jewish Inscription from Aphrodisias," in *Of Scribes and Scrolls: Studies on the Hebrew Bible, Intertestamentary Judaism, and Christian Origins presented to John Strugnell on the Occasion of His Sixtieth Birthday*, ed. H. W. Attridge, J. J. Collins, and T. H. Tobin (Lanham, Md.: University Press of America, 1990), 163–173.

12. Bernadette J. Brooten, *Women Leaders in the Ancient Synagogue: Inscriptional Evidence and Background Issue* (Chico, Cailf.: Scholars Press, 1982), 23.

13. Trebilco, *Jewish Communities*, 113–26.

14. It is argued that the titles for females are not honorific, but relate to their benefaction: Ross S. Kraemer, *Her Share of the Blessings: Women's Religions among Pagans, Jews, and Christians in the Graeco-Roman World* (Philadelphia: Fortress, 1988), 87; Riet van Bremen, "Women and Wealth," in *Images of Women in Antiquity*, ed. A. Cameron and A. Kuhrt (Detroit: Wayne State University Press, 1985), 236–37; Margaret Y. MacDonald, *Early Christian Women and Pagan Opinion: The Power of the Hysterical Woman* (Cambridge: Cambridge University Press, 1996), 35.

an Asia Minor inscription. She was mentioned, presumably, because she fulfilled her pledge.

Jewish Women in the Book of Acts

Though the evidence is slim, we would assume that there were in the synagogue at Pisidian Antioch Gentile women known as God-fearers, some of whom could be called εὐσχήμονας. However obnoxious the theology of Paul might have been to some, it does seem likely that the obdurate Jews of Acts 13:50 were angry primarily because they were losing the loyalty and beneficence of the God-fearing women and the leading men.

The role of leading women in relationship to a synagogue is mentioned only in Thessalonica where, after speaking in the synagogue, some Jews were convinced as well as τῶν τε σεβομένων Ἑλλήνων πλῆθος πολύ, γυναικῶν τε τῶν πρώτων οὐκ ὀλίγαι (17:4). In this text, though, the leading women are not necessarily identified with the God-fearers, a category that presumably included both men and women. The only God-fearing woman mentioned by name in Acts is Lydia of Thyatira who lived in Philippi. As was his custom, Paul went first to the "synagogue," designated in this case as a προσευχή, a place of prayer, where he spoke to the ταῖς συνελθούσαις γυναιξίν (16:13).[15] The issue here is complex. Were there only women at the place of prayer? Did Paul speak only to the women (and not to the obdurate Jews)? Was the term προσευχή used for assemblies of Jews when there were not enough persons, or men, for a legitimate synagogue? These much debated issues cannot be solved, but, in any case, Paul found there Lydia, a σεβομένη τὸν θεόν. She was not mentioned as a leading citizen or as a wealthy donor,[16] but she did invite Paul to her home, where probably the first house church in Philippi assembled.

Gender Roles in the Jesus Tradition

The Jesus tradition varies from Gospel to Gospel (including the *Gospel of Thomas*), yet there is enough similarity to draw some conclusions. From time to time we notice that the Greco-Roman attitude holds also for Palestine. Just as the book of Esther portrays a society in which highly placed women perform for the symposium, so the story of Herod and the daughter of Herodias reflects the same tradition. Perhaps even the

---

15. Reimer, *Women in the Acts of the Apostles*, 78–85.

16. She had only one name, so was obviously not from a leading family (see Schottroff, *Let the Oppressed Go Free*). Lydia was apparently a worker in an industry known as dirty work (see Reimer, *Women in the Acts of the Apostles*, 101–7).

narrative of the Pharisee and the sinning woman fits the same pattern. Otherwise, in the Jesus movement women do not appear to be severely hindered by the private / public dichotomy. According to Luke women accompanied Jesus on his mission trips.

> Soon afterwards he went on through cities and villages, proclaiming and bringing the good news of the kingdom of God. The twelve were with him, as well as some women who had been cured of evil spirits and infirmities: Mary, called Magdalene, from whom seven demons had gone out, and Joanna, the wife of Herod's steward Chuza, and Susanna, and many others, who provided [διηκόνουν] for them out of their resources. (Luke 8:1–3)

According to Luke the women served as deacons to the missionaries (or to Jesus [against Vaticanus]). Presumably the women left their families and were using their own resources to support the nascent Jesus movement. The notice about supportive women matches the picture of women seen in Acts, and is corroborated by Mark's comment about the women at the crucifixion:

> There were also women looking on from a distance; among them were Mary Magdalene, and Mary the mother of James the younger and of Joses, and Salome. These used to follow him and provided [διηκόνουν] for him when he was in Galilee; and there were many other women who had come up with him to Jerusalem.
> (Mark 15:40–41)

Placed in proper context, women clearly played an important, public role in the Jesus movement through most of the first century. The aforementioned women witnessed the crucifixion (Mark 15:40, 47) and were the first to see the empty tomb (Mark 16:1–8); that is, they were primary sources for the kerygmatic *Heilstatsache* (the absence of the women in 1 Cor. 15:5 still lacks adequate clarification).

The Jesus tradition does not hold to the Jewish sense of female uncleanness. The woman with the flow of blood was not rebuked for touching Jesus (Mark 5:34), nor did Jesus refrain from touching and healing a young girl presumed dead (Mark 5:41). Likewise, peripheral women were accepted. Jesus was categorized as a φίλος τελωνῶν καὶ ἁμαρτωλῶν (Luke 7:34). The saying then is punctuated by Luke with the story of Simon the Pharisee and the woman of the city who makes public appearances (she is never called a prostitute, but given the public / private dichotomy, it does not matter).

Gender Roles in the Letters of Paul

While the Jesus tradition transcended both Jewish and Roman gender mores, Paul is, on the one hand, more directly revolutionary, yet, on the other hand, more concerned that the revolution not be visible to society at large. One starts with the startling passage from Galatians:

> As many of you as were baptized into Christ have clothed yourselves with Christ. There is no longer Jew or Greek, there is no longer slave or free, there is no longer male and female; for all of you are one in Christ Jesus. (Gal. 3:27–28)

Within the Jesus movement basic social divisions — ethnic, economic, and gender — no longer apply. Although Paul did not apply his vision to society at large, he did consistently call for social balance in the church. The letter to Philemon serves as an excellent example of Paul's style. Paul insists that Philemon and Onesimus are brothers καὶ ἐν σαρκὶ καὶ ἐν κυρίῳ (Philem. 16), yet never suggests that Philemon should free Onesimus. Likewise, in 1 Cor. 7:17–24 Paul makes it a rule (or order) that all should stay in the condition in which they were called: (ἕκαστος ἐν τῇ κλήσει ᾗ ἐκλήθη, ἐν ταύτῃ μενέτω (7:20). In Christ it does not really matter (7:22).

Women in Leadership

On the more private level (family and faith community) the radical change is obvious. In the Pauline churches women are not only functionaries, but they also speak publicly and interpret the faith tradition. Although 1 Cor. 11:2–16 has caused considerable conflict for interpreters, the reader must not overlook verse 5a: πᾶσα δὲ γυνὴ προσευχομένη ἢ προφητεύουσα. Public churchwomen may not have dressed as Paul would have liked, but nevertheless, they led the gathered community in prayer and interpreted the faith to them. This was true not only for Corinth. Phoebe was the minister for the church at Cenchreae (Rom. 16:1–2). Like her Palestinian sisters, she supported the Jesus movement with her resources and even contemplated further support in Rome. It was in Phoebe's home that the Cenchreae church met, so she was the designated minister (Συνίστημι δὲ ὑμῖν Φοίβην τὴν ἀδελφὴν ἡμῶν, οὖσαν [καὶ] διάκονον τῆς ἐκκλησίας τῆς ἐν Κεγχρεαῖς, 16:1). One suspects that the same was true for Prisca (or, Priscilla), since she is so often mentioned first in the Prisca and Aquila team. The house where their group met presumably belonged to both of them (τὴν κατ᾽ οἶκον αὐτῶν ἐκκλησίαν, Rom. 16:5), but surely Prisca was equally the minister (Rom. 16:3–4; see also 1 Cor. 16:19; 2 Tim. 4:19; Acts 18:2, 18, 26). Although Paul cannot be responsible for the apostleship of Junia (since she preceded him), nevertheless, only Paul mentions her, or any woman, for that matter, as an apostle (Rom. 16:7) In a church Paul did found, two women, Euodia and Syntyche, own the house where the Philippian community meets. Though they had worked with Paul in the spread of the gospel, now some conflict has arisen. Paul asks another person, likely a woman (σύζυγε, a very close female friend [or Σύζυγε]) to mediate the problem (Phil. 4:2–3).

Family

In regard to family, Paul's sense of the marriage covenant has no peer in the ancient literature. In Hebrew anthropology the body (σῶμα) refers to the corporate group, not necessarily to an individual being. In Pauline literature σῶμα τοῦ χριστοῦ would be the most obvious example. The individual derives identity from the σῶμα (1 Cor. 5:3; 10:17; 11:27–32; 12:12–31). So in marriage the identity of the husband depends on the action of the wife and the identity of the wife depends on the action of the husband. There is no difference:

> The husband should give to his wife her conjugal rights, and likewise the wife to her husband. For the wife does not have authority over her own body [σώματος, corporate identity], but the husband does; likewise the husband does not have authority over his own body [σώματος; corporate identity], but the wife does.
>
> (1 Cor. 7:3–4)

In the difficult eleventh chapter of 1 Corinthians Paul makes the same point. In the body of Christ (the Lord) men and women are not separate from each other (πλὴν οὔτε γυνὴ χωρὶς ἀνδρὸς οὔτε ἀνὴρ χωρὶς γυναικὸς ἐν κυρίῳ, 1 Cor. 11:11).

It is very difficult to live concrete lives "in the Lord" without any social interaction. It is Paul's genius to urge that the first Christians accept cultural norms but live in another social loyalty. Needless to say, dual citizenship can lead to serious misunderstanding — then and now. In the Jesus tradition second marriage was essentially forbidden because the σῶμα identity was formed by the original marriage (Mark 10:2–9; Matthew missed the point [Matt. 19:9]). In his teaching, Paul conveyed that Jesus tradition. Regarding remarriage his slogan, as repeated by some Corinthians, "Better not to touch a [second] woman [at all than to destroy your identity as a man]" (1 Cor. 7:1) was accepted by the Corinthians, but in ways unacceptable to society at large. Some previously married Christians could not discipline their sexual dynamics. Their promiscuous behavior was noticeable. Consequently Paul was forced, reluctantly, to modify the Jesus tradition. Demarried people might do well to marry (1 Cor. 7:2), though they would do better to remain demarried, as he himself is (1 Cor. 7:8). Others chose a more subtle and difficult solution. They lived with companions as man and wife, but did not engage in intercourse. While the presence of families might satisfy public curiosity about the new community, Paul suspected that it had to lead to a more public promiscuity (1 Cor. 7:5).

Marriage

The issue of marriage itself is more complicated. In 1 Corinthians 7, starting in verse 25, Paul shifts from remarriage to first marriage. Of course it is perfectly all right to marry (7:28), though following the "remain as you are" logic even the single person would do well not to marry (7:26–27). Paul argues that the forms of this world are passing away, and one should wait to see the new life. One aspect of the new life is the new relationship between men and women. In the new age, women are not possessions. So, though society expects daughters to be passed to husbands by their fathers, Paul urges fathers in the Lord to allow daughters time to make their own decision:

> If anyone thinks he is dealing inappropriately with his unmarried daughter, since she already is past the age for marrying, and therefore ought to do something, let him do as he wishes. He does not sin; let the couple marry. But the one who can stand firm in his heart, without any distress, having the power to do as he wishes, and has already made up his mind not to pledge his unmarried daughter, he does well. So the one who gives his daughter in marriage does well, but the one who does not give in marriage does even better.[17] (1 Cor. 7:36–38)

There are other borderline instances. Women could pray and preach in the local community, but Paul did not wish the women to dress in a way scandalous to the local society. So he insisted that, when the women spoke, they cover their head. To be sure, his arguments may appear to be so many non sequiturs, but the point is clear: your private role in the church does not allow you to alter your public appearance (1 Cor. 11:2–16).[18]

A more difficult passage is 1 Cor. 14:34–35. If it is genuinely from Paul, it follows the same direction we have already noted. While women

---

17. Cf. the alternate translation of the NRSV, and the notes on 7:36–38 in *The New Oxford Annotated Bible.*

18. "Because of the angels" (1 Cor. 11:10) is the social issue (Snyder, *First Corinthians*, 49).

may take leadership roles, it is inappropriate for them to be involved in the ecstatic, unstructured part of the worship, particularly when outsiders have walked in (14:23). Obviously, for the sake of social — that is, public — decorum Paul is trying to limit the ecstatic expressions (14:12, 19, 26–27). The outside world might assume that the Jesus movement originated in religious hysteria.[19]

Gender Roles in the Gospel of John

Though the stories of the Fourth Gospel are often used to indicate the favorable attitude of Jesus toward women, that would be a misunderstanding of the purpose of the author.[20] In fact, women are not necessarily treated favorably. Jesus speaks quite sharply to his mother (2:4);[21] the Samaritan women never does understand the nature of Jesus, even though she brought others to him (4:29); Martha remained an end-time-oriented Christian (11:24).[22] There were no women in the traveling entourage, nor were there women mentioned as present at significant events like the final supper, the resurrection appearances in the upper room, or the last "Eucharist" beside the lake.

On the other hand, the significant women of the Gospel of John stand apart from the normal roles played by women in contemporary material. Those who may be classified as literary characters (the Samaritan woman, Mary, Martha, and Mary Magdelene) do not act as *oikos* women.[23] They do not have families; there are no children; in encounters they act as men might have; and they seem to be geographically mobile.[24] In any case, there is no woman in the New Testament who matches John's portrayal of Mary of Bethany. Unlike her sister, Martha, Mary does understand the reality offered by Jesus. But even more important, she exhibits that intimacy with Jesus that marks the Johannine believer. In the Gospel there are at least two such believers: the Beloved Disciple and Mary. The Beloved Disciple, chosen first by Jesus, is never named and serves as the implied author (1:40; 21:20–25). On the cross Jesus designates him as the Johannine heir apparent (19:26). In addition to being a permanent

19. MacDonald, *Early Christian Women.*

20. See Robert Gordon Maccini, *Her Testimony Is True: Women as Witnesses according to John,* Journal of the Study of the New Testament Supplement Series 125 (Sheffield: Sheffield Academic Press, 1996), especially the concluding chapter.

21. Judith M. Lieu, "The Mother of the Son in the Fourth Gospel," *JBL* 117 (1998): 61–77.

22. Graydon F. Snyder, "The Social Context of the Ironic Dialogues in the Gospel of John," in *Putting Body and Soul Together* (Valley Forge, Pa.: Trinity Press International, 1997), 3–23.

23. Culpepper, *Anatomy of the Fourth Gospel.*

24. Van Tilborg, *Imaginative Love in John,* 196–99.

member of the disciple band, the Beloved Disciple is called beloved because of the intimacy with Jesus; that is, at the final supper he reclined in the breast of Jesus (13:23). Even more intimate is Mary's washing the feet of Jesus with ointment and drying them with her hair (12:3). The author of the Fourth Gospel wishes to show that appropriation of the Jesus presence comes through intimate involvement rather than belief or service.

Although the primary narrative of the Gospel stresses the intimacy of the Beloved Disciple and Mary of Bethany, one must not ignore another major character, Mary Magdalene. At the empty tomb Mary Magdalene also expresses intimacy with Jesus. She addresses him as Rabbouni, "My dear Master," and moves quickly to embrace him (20:16–17). Who is Mary Magdalene? Some suspect that there is only one "literary" Mary, so that Mary of Bethany and Mary Magdalene are one and the same.[25] To have only one Mary makes the narrative cleaner — only one intimate female, as only one intimate male. But Mary Magdalene has a special role. She is the first to see the resurrected Lord. The contrast between the author of the Fourth Gospel and the accepted kerygma (1 Cor. 15:5) could not be more poignantly stated. In the kerygma the resurrection is a fact first observed by Peter. In the Gospel of John the resurrection is intimacy expressed. But intimacy with the resurrected Jesus cannot be achieved physically, so Mary Magdalene cannot touch the one she loves. From this point on the Johannine intimacy comes through the Spirit (1 John 4:13).

Gender in the Early Church

The cultural impact of gender in the Jesus tradition has been difficult to assess and complex in any case. There are several reasons. First, there is no single pattern. As Christianity became more firm in its variations, the issue of gender was more clearly differentiated. Second, it is difficult to assess the role of gender in the Roman culture at the end of the first century. Third, our attitude has been formed by men writing in the first centuries and by male scholars in this century. Only recently have female scholars begun to give us reevaluations. That process is far from complete.

Household Codes

There can be little doubt that official Christianity softened the radical nature of the earlier interpreters of the Jesus tradition. The presence of

---

25. Sandra M. Schneiders, "Women in the Fourth Gospel and the Role of Women in the Contemporary Church," *Biblical Theology Bulletin* 12 (1982): 35–45.

the *Haustafeln* (household codes) should be interpreted as an attempt to defend nascent Christianity. The household codes call for subordination of citizens to the emperor, of wives to husbands, of children to parents, and of slaves to masters (Col. 3:18–4:1; Eph. 5:21–6:9; 1 Pet. 2:11–3:12; 1 Tim. 2:8–15; 5:1–2; 6:1–2; Titus 2:1–10; 3:1). Although many of these codes do not match Greek codes, such as Aristotle's, still, the similarity is close enough to bear the explanation that Christian leaders adopted them either to maintain order in the churches or to avoid criticism.[26] As an attempt to defend against Christian heteronomy, they infer that there were Christians who did not recognize the authority of the state, did not consider women subordinate to men, did not accept the right of parents to determine the faith of their offspring, and accepted slaves as equal partners in the faith community.[27] Of course, such alternative Christian groups surely did exist. Although it is difficult to extricate structural information from the gnostic materials, it would appear that the gnostic Christians did not recognize a hierarchy and did not differentiate role models for the genders.[28] Likewise, the communities that produced the apocryphal Acts also must have recognized female leadership, stressed the independence of women (chastity), rejected social norms and the authority of the state, advocated poverty, and stressed divine healing.[29] The household codes and Pastoral Epistles could well have been written to counter these early Christian groups. They value authority, assume marriage and family, address persons of wealth, oppose excessive asceticism (e.g., no wine), and disallow the membership of younger women among the organization of widows. If the early Christian writers (especially the Pastorals and 1 Peter) opposed radical Christian groups,[30] can we assume that the radical groups actually reflected the process of acculturation? That is, has the Roman culture moved more toward independence for women, celibacy, rejection of family and wealth? Clearly not. The authors of the apocryphal Acts make it quite clear that they (the women of the Acts) are despised by the Romans. The Romans accused these Christians of being sorcerers. They mean by that epithet that the Christians reject authority and disturb society by rejecting sex and marriage.[31]

---

26. Balch, *Let Wives Be Submissive*. See Edgar Krentz, "Order in the 'House' of God: The Haustafel in 1 Peter 2:11–3:12," in *Common Life in the Early Church*, ed. Julian V. Hills (Harrisburg, Pa.: Trinity Press International, 1998), 279–85.

27. J. E. Crouch, *The Origin and Intention of the Colossian Haustafel* (Göttingen: Vandenhoeck & Ruprecht, 1972); David C. Verner, *The Household of God: The Social World of the Pastoral Epistles* (Chico, Calif.: Scholars Press, 1983).

28. Elaine Pagels, *The Gnostic Gospels* (New York: Random House, 1979), 48–69.

29. Stevan L. Davies, *The Revolt of the Widows: The Social World of the Apocryphal Acts* (Carbondale and Edwardsville, Ill.: Southern Illinois University Press, 1980).

30. Verner, *The Household of God*.

31. Davies, *The Revolt of the Widows*.

On the other hand, the codes may have considerable meaning for the process of inculturation. The codes were ostensibly written for the *oikos* of God. The codes do not reflect a waning of the original Gospel, an acculturation to the Roman world. But instead, the later New Testament materials are attempting to stave off persecution and thereby let the new church be the church. In that way gradual inculturation could occur.[32] Inculturation of the Jesus tradition regarding language, social structure, architecture, food, calendar — all could occur because the faith community was offered relative peace. It gained that peace by appearing to organize the *oikos* according to acceptable Greco-Roman standards. However, gender issues did not fare so well. One might plausibly argue that the strategy of conformity was effective and at the same time disastrous. When the church shifted from a private *oikos,* where women could exercise leadership, to a public *polis,* where female leadership was unacceptable, the church began to adapt the very codes it had earlier feigned to accept.[33]

The Jesus Tradition and Gender Roles in the Early Church

The Jesus tradition deeply affected gender roles in the early church. As long as the faith community met in house churches and only loosely recognized the authority of the state, men and women more or less shared leadership roles. But when the church became the state religion, when Christians met in basilicas, when Jesus became the emperor, then women once again became subordinate or more private. Splinter groups like the Gnostics, the Montanists, and the communities of the apocryphal Acts either disappeared or were forced to dissociate from the mainline Christians. Nevertheless, there were some cultural alterations. The continued interest in virginity and widows by Tertullian, Cyprian, and especially Jerome, meant that women were not to be held subordinate under the *potestas* of the father or the *manus* of the husband. A woman was encouraged to be free. Still, although the majority of Christian women participated freely in a private family life and in the local faith community, their role in public was not likely greatly altered by the Jesus tradition.

---

32. Winter, *Seek the Welfare of the City.*
33. Karen Jo Torjesen, *When Women Were Priests: Women's Leadership in the Early Church and the Scandal of Their Subordination in the Rise of Christianity* (San Francisco: HarperSanFrancisco, 1993).

13

Health and Medicine

Health and Healing in the Hebrew Scriptures

Health and illness in the Hebrew Scriptures is a unilateral matter. God gives health and punishes with ill health. There is no hint of environmental causation and no instance of rational observation of the ill person. Divine causation was not peculiar to the people of Israel. Its roots were deep in Near Eastern culture.[1]

The tradition of Exodus makes it clear that health is a gift to God's people as they heed God's laws and ordinances:

> There the Lord made for them a statute and an ordinance and there he put them to the test. He said, "If you will listen carefully to the voice of the Lord your God, and do what is right in his sight, and give heed to his commandments and keep all his statutes, I will not bring upon you any of the diseases that I brought upon the Egyptians; for I am the Lord who heals you." (Exod. 15:25–26)

The Egyptians were ill because they were not God's people, though God brought disease and health to any who disobeyed:

> See now that I, even I, am he; there is no god beside me. I kill and I make alive; I wound and I heal; and no one can deliver from my hand. (Deut. 32.39)

Despite the threatening posture, however, in the final analysis healing is a product of God's love (חסד) for Israel:

> Yet it was I who taught Ephraim to walk, I took them up in my arms; but they did not know that I healed them. (Hos. 11:3)

And finally, health depends on one's trusting relationship with God:

---

1. Hector Avalos, *Illness and Health Care in the Ancient Near East*, Harvard Semitic Monographs, no. 54 (Atlanta: Scholars Press, 1995); P. Humbert, "Maladie et médicine dans l'Ancient Testament," *RHPR* 44 (1964): 1–29; Claus Westermann, "Heilung und Heil in der Gemeinde aus der Sicht des Alten Testament," *Wege zum Menschen* 27 (1975): 1–12; Joseph Zias, "Death and Disease in Ancient Israel," *BA* 54, no. 3 (1991): 146–59.

Blessed are those who trust in the Lord, whose trust is the Lord.
They shall be like a tree planted by water, sending out its roots by
the stream. It shall not fear when heat comes, and its leaves shall
stay green; in the year of drought it is not anxious, and it does not
cease to bear fruit. . . .

Heal me, O Lord, and I shall be healed; save me, and I shall be
saved; for you are my praise. (Jer. 17:8–14)

Even more powerfully, the prophets portray health as a result of
God's vicarious suffering for us, a precursor of some New Testament
perspectives:

Surely he has borne our infirmities and carried our diseases; yet
we accounted him stricken, struck down by God, and afflicted. But
he was wounded for our transgressions, crushed for our iniquities;
upon him was the punishment that made us whole, and by his
bruises we are healed. All we like sheep have gone astray; we have
all turned to our own way, and the Lord has laid on him the iniquity
of us all. (Isa. 53:4–6)

As we have seen, the prophets also considered health as an end-time state
even for those who otherwise have been disabled or chronically ill. The
catena of Isaiah became an organizational principle for the Gospels and
perhaps some early Christian communities.

Then the eyes of the blind shall be opened, and the ears of the
deaf unstopped; then the lame shall leap like a deer, and the tongue
of the speechless sing for joy. For waters shall break forth in the
wilderness, and streams in the desert. (Isa. 35:5–6)

There are two possible instances of health by observation. The first
would be sanitation near the camp. In Deuteronomy there is a regulation
for disposing of excrement:

You shall have a designated area outside the camp to which you
shall go. With your utensils you shall have a trowel; when you
relieve yourself outside, you shall dig a hole with it and then cover
up your excrement. Because the Lord your God travels along with
your camp, to save you and to hand over your enemies to you,
therefore your camp must be holy, so that he may not see anything
indecent among you and turn away from you. (Deut. 23:12–14)

Obviously it is a health regulation, but even here the rationale is based on
the division between "clean and unclean." Good health is not mentioned.

The other potential health issue has already been considered. Leviticus lists foods that are clean and unclean. Many suppose that these prohibitions are based on health observations. For example, readers have frequently supposed that the prohibition against pork reflects observations about the spread of trichinosis. Actually, the food prohibitions never mention health, and most prohibitions would be difficult to defend on the basis of any potential disease.

There are not many healing narratives in the Hebrew Scriptures. The few we find corroborate the divine dicta and the laws: God gives health and disease. The story of Elisha and the king of Syria, Namaan, illustrates well the Hebrew belief system. Namaan had heard that Elisha could heal, but was reluctant to wash in the Jordan because it seemed so mundane — the only requirement was obedience to God as relayed by God's spokesperson, Elisha. Nevertheless, Namaan did follow directions and was healed of leprosy by God (2 Kings 5; see Lev. 13–14).

Health and Healing in Second Temple Judaism

There is little difference between the Hebrew Scriptures and later Judaism. And there are very few healing narratives. The most striking would be, of course, the strange transformation of Nebuchadnezzar into a composite animal (Dan. 4:28–33) ordered by a φωνή ἐκ τοῦ οὐρανοῦ (4:31). After the ordeal was over Nebuchadnezzar, in his prayer of thanksgiving, blessed and praised the θεὸς τῶν θεῶν καὶ κύριος τῶν κυρίων καὶ βασιλεὺς τῶν βασιλέων (Dan. 4:37 LXX).

The story of Tobit is more bizarre. Tobit was lying in his courtyard with his face uncovered. Bird droppings fell on his eyes and blinded him. He attempted to have the blindness cured through medicine:

> I did not know that there were sparrows on the wall; their fresh droppings fell into my eyes and produced white films. I went to physicians to be healed, but the more they treated me with ointments the more my vision was obscured by the white films, until I became completely blind. For four years I remained unable to see. All my kindred were sorry for me, and Ahikar took care of me for two years before he went to Elymais. (Tob. 2:10)

At the end of the story Tobit is cured by fish gall applied to his eyes, a cure prescribed by Raphael the angel:

> Then Tobit got up and came stumbling out through the courtyard door. Tobias went up to him, with the gall of the fish in his hand, and holding him firmly, he blew into his eyes, saying, "Take

courage, father." With this he applied the medicine on his eyes, and it made them smart. Next, with both hands he peeled off the white films from the corners of his eyes. Then Tobit saw his son and threw his arms around him, and he wept and said to him, "I see you, my son, the light of my eyes!" (Tob. 11:10–14)

Whatever the medicinal value of fish gall, Tobit recognized the source of the healing:

Blessed be God, and blessed be his great name, and blessed be all his holy angels. May his holy name be blessed throughout all the ages. Though he afflicted me, he has had mercy upon me. Now I see my son Tobias! (Tob. 11:14–15)

Raphael the angel says, "And now God sent me to heal you . . . " (12:14). Tobit had consulted physicians. Given the theocentric nature of well-being in the biblical material, physicians seldom appear, and when they do they are ineffective. For example, the woman with the flow of blood had wasted her money on doctors. Health derives from God not medical care (but note one exception: Matt. 9:12). In Judaism a major exception would be Sirach, with the remarkably positive attitude toward physicians:

Honor physicians for their services, for the Lord created them; for their gift of healing comes from the Most High, and they are rewarded by the king. The skill of physicians makes them distinguished, and in the presence of the great they are admired. The Lord created medicines out of the earth, and the sensible will not despise them. Was not water made sweet with a tree in order that its power might be known? And he gave skill to human beings that he might be glorified in his marvelous works. By them the physician heals and takes away pain; the pharmacist makes a mixture from them. God's works will never be finished; and from him health spreads over all the earth. My child, when you are ill, do not delay, but pray to the Lord, and he will heal you. Give up your faults and direct your hands rightly, and cleanse your heart from all sin. Offer a sweet-smelling sacrifice, and a memorial portion of choice flour, and pour oil on your offering, as much as you can afford. Then give the physician his place, for the Lord created him; do not let him leave you, for you need him. There may come a time when recovery lies in the hands of physicians, for they too pray to the Lord that he grant them success in diagnosis and in healing, for the sake of preserving life. He who sins against his Maker, will be defiant toward the physician [ὁ ἁμαρτάνων ἔναντι τοῦ ποιήσαντος αὐτὸν ἐμπέσοι εἰς χεῖρας ἰατρουᾳ]. (Sir. 38:11–15)

If, after prayer and confession, you are still ill, then turn to the doctor. In fact, that could be the only recourse (38:13). The strange verse 15 still leaves us uncertain. It could mean that a person who has sinned against God has nothing left but a physician. Or, as the NRSV translates, the person who sins against God also fails to recognize the gift of God in the physician. Or it might mean that the person who has sinned against God, and therefore has become ill, still has the physician available. Given the positive attitude toward doctors in Sir. 38, the latter seems most likely.

While the people of the Dead Sea Scrolls apparently did not utilize physicians, they did study and utilize various herbs and stones for medicinal purposes (CD 12:11–13:7; see also Josephus, *War* 2:134–36). The awareness of the demonic, as in the Jesus tradition, appears in the Prayer of Nabonidus (4QprNab). But returning to more mainline Judaism, the issue remains that of clean and unclean (unclean are corpses, lepers, spittle, semen, urine, menstrual flow [*m. Kelim* 1.1–3]).[2]

Healing in the Jesus Tradition

The Jewish cultural background makes the Jesus tradition all the more surprising. Granted that our knowledge of Jesus lies in the Jesus tradition, when the reader of the Gospels looks backward into the tradition at least one thing, among others, cannot be denied. Jesus was a healer. In the Jesus tradition itself there is no utilization of disease as simply a matter of clean and unclean. To the contrary, Jesus consistently attacks or ignores the distinction. In Mark 7 Jesus sharply rejects the tradition of unclean food and unclean vessels. Otherwise, in healing narratives, Jesus ignores regulations regarding clean and unclean. He does not react negatively to a woman with a flow of blood touching him (Mark 5:34). He touched a man covered with leprosy before he declared him clean (Luke 5:13). He touched the hand of a girl who had been declared dead (Mark 5:41).

Unlike some of his immediate Jewish counterparts, Jesus had little use for medicines, or healing objects like stones or amulets (note the oil in Mark 6:13). What is new is the causative factor. Jesus never directly mentioned sin as the cause of illness.[3] In the Gospel of John he even

---

2. David M. Feldman, *Health and Medicine in the Jewish Tradition* (New York: Crossroad, 1986); Hannah K. Harrington, *The Impurity Systems of Qumran and the Rabbis: Biblical Foundations* (Atlanta: Scholars Press, 1993); Larry P. Hogan, *Healing in the Second Temple Period* (Göttingen: Vandenhoeck & Ruprecht, 1992).

3. Mark 2:1–12 is surely a conflation of two stories: one healing narrative and one conflict narrative.

directly denies it (9:3; though note 5:14). Nor does the Jesus tradition consider ill health the result of God's unilateral judgment. In contrast to Judaism, in the Jesus tradition a major cause for illness comes from demon possession, or unclean spirits (Mark 1:21–45; 3:7–12; 5:1–20; 6:13; 7:24–30; 9:14–29). Two major questions arise from the tradition about healing. Why is Jesus the Jew remembered as a healer, and why have demons become a causative factor?

Jesus the Healer

For good reason the first question has been answered in many different ways. For some interpreters Jesus fits well with the magical healing practices of the ancient Near East.[4] The importance of this thesis is apparent for this study. Whatever Jesus might have done, the early Christians were in some type of conflict with Greco-Roman culture regarding the use of magic to heal. But there are sharp differences between Jesus the healer and other healers. As we have seen, Jesus did not use magical objects, did not use gestures, and did not call upon magical names.[5] Furthermore, Hellenistic healings did not signal a conflict with the demonic world (note Matt. 8:28–34). Healings did exhibit the power of the magician, and healers may have even acted out of compassion. That is not to say that Jesus did not have compassion (Matt. 14:14), but the major concern is to restore trust, as can be seen in the formulas: ἡ πίστις σου σέσωκέν σε (Mark 5:34) and μὴ φοβοῦ, μόνον πίστευε (Mark 5:36), and in Jesus' frustration over a faithless people: τί δειλοί ἐστε; οὔπω ἔχετε πίστιν; (Mark 4:40); ὦ γενεὰ ἄπιστος, ἕως πότε πρὸς ὑμᾶς ἔσομαι; ἕως πότε ἀνέξομαι ὑμῶν; (Mark 9:19). Some of the healings restore persons to proper function in their society: lame people can walk (Mark 2:1–12); deaf people can hear (Mark 7:31–37); blind people can see (Mark 8:22–26). But even more poignantly, lepers are no longer unclean and can return to their families (Mark 1:40–45); a woman with a flow of blood no longer needs to fear ostracism, but now is a daughter in the faith community (Mark 5:25–34); an uncontrollable, maniacal man goes home to his friends (ὕπαγε εἰς τὸν οἶκόν σου πρὸς τοὺς σούς [Mark 5:19]). An epileptic (?) boy could reclaim his childhood with his father (Mark 9:14–29).

---

4. Though there are magical parallels in the Gospels, Hull assumes the tradition of a magical Jesus first occurred when Christianity became public and had to compete with other healing religions. John M. Hull, *Hellenistic Magic and the Synoptic Tradition,* Studies in Biblical Theology, 2d ser., no. 28 (London: SCM, 1974), 1–4.

5. David Bartlett, *Ministry in the New Testament* (Minneapolis: Fortress, 1993).

Healing and Community Formation

As the Jesus tradition is expressed in particular faith communities, healing expresses even more than restoration of the trust relationship. The healings are attached to various functions in the faith community.[6] The healing of the paralytic has been couched in a teaching framework:

> They went to Capernaum; and when the sabbath came, he entered the synagogue and taught [ἐδίδασκεν]. They were astounded at his teaching [διδαχῇ], for he taught [διδάσκων] them as one having authority, and not as the scribes. Just then there was in their synagogue a man with an unclean spirit, and he cried out, "What have you to do with us, Jesus of Nazareth? Have you come to destroy us? I know who you are, the Holy One of God." But Jesus rebuked him, saying, "Be silent, and come out of him!" And the unclean spirit, convulsing him and crying with a loud voice, came out of him. They were all amazed, and they kept on asking one another, "What is this? A new teaching [διδαχή] — with authority! He commands even the unclean spirits, and they obey him." At once his fame began to spread throughout the surrounding region of Galilee.
> (Mark 1:21–28)

As we have already noted, the healing of Peter's mother-in-law became a call for her to be a "deacon":

> As soon as they left the synagogue, they entered the house of Simon and Andrew, with James and John. Now Simon's mother-in-law was in bed with a fever, and they told him about her at once. He came and took her by the hand and lifted her up. Then the fever left her, and she began to serve [διηκόνει] them. (Mark 1:29–31)

The general healing narrative of Mark 1:32–34 belongs in a preaching structure. According to Matt. 8:16–17 Jesus cured the assembled people with the λόγος. In the Markan account the demons are forbidden to speak a λόγος even though they can correctly proclaim the good news!

> That evening, at sundown, they brought to him all who were sick or possessed with demons. And the whole city was gathered around the door. And he cured many who were sick with various diseases, and cast out many demons; and he would not permit the demons to speak, because they knew him [οὐκ ἤφιεν λαλεῖν τὰ δαιμόνια, ὅτι ᾔδεισαν αὐτόν]. (Mark 1:32–33)

---

6. Herman Hendrickx, *The Miracle Stories of the Synoptic Gospels* (London: Geoffrey Chapman; San Francisco: Harper & Row, 1987).

On the other hand, the healed leper does not refrain from preaching the gospel even though he was admonished not to by the one who healed him:

> A leper came to him begging him, and kneeling he said to him, "If you choose, you can make me clean." Moved with pity, Jesus stretched out his hand and touched him, and said to him, "I do choose. Be made clean!" Immediately the leprosy left him, and he was made clean. After sternly warning him he sent him away at once, saying to him, "See that you say nothing to anyone; but go, show yourself to the priest, and offer for your cleansing what Moses commanded, as a testimony to them." But he went out and began to proclaim it freely, and to spread the word [ἤρξατο κηρύσσειν πολλὰ καὶ διαφημίζειν τὸν λόγον], so that Jesus could no longer go into a town openly, but stayed out in the country; and people came to him from every quarter. (Mark 1:40–45)

The function of the good news in a healing context reaches a climax in the story of the paralytic. The healing narrative begins with Jesus speaking the word (2:2). Then the faith community inserted a controversy story regarding forgiveness of sins. In that way the proclamation of the good news was identified with healing.

> When he returned to Capernaum after some days, it was reported that he was at home. So many gathered around that there was no longer room for them, not even in front of the door; and he was speaking the word to them [ἐλάλει αὐτοῖς τὸν λόγον]. Then some people came, bringing to him a paralyzed man, carried by four of them. And when they could not bring him to Jesus because of the crowd, they removed the roof above him; and after having dug through it, they let down the mat on which the paralytic lay. When Jesus saw their faith, he said to the paralytic, "Son, your sins are forgiven." Now some of the scribes were sitting there, questioning in their hearts, "Why does this fellow speak in this way? It is blasphemy! Who can forgive sins but God alone?" At once Jesus perceived in his spirit that they were discussing these questions among themselves; and he said to them, "Why do you raise such questions in your hearts? Which is easier, to say to the paralytic, 'Your sins are forgiven,' or to say, 'Stand up and take your mat and walk'? But so that you may know that the Son of Man has authority on earth to forgive sins" — he said to the paralytic — [secondary connector, see v. 5] "I say to you, stand up, take your mat and go to your home." And he stood up, and immediately took the mat and went out before all of them; so that they were all

amazed and glorified God, saying, "We have never seen anything like this!" (Mark 2:1–12)

With these few examples we can characterize the Jesus tradition in this way:

1. Jesus was known as a healer.

2. Jesus sometimes healed out of compassion.

3. Jesus healed primarily to restore faith, to enable disabled persons to participate in their community, and to obliterate the divisive category "unclean."

4. The first faith community used the Jesus tradition not only to destroy divisive boundaries, but also to define or establish the functions of the earliest trust community (serving as deacons, teaching, preaching, and forgiving). Jesus healed infirmities that otherwise limited the community participation of those disabled.

Demons and Unclean Spirits

The casting out of demons was another matter. Early in Hebrew theology the functions of אלהים were distributed to subentities, often called בני אלהים, "sons of God." We know these figures primarily as subheads of collective groups, like nations (Deut. 32:8). At the same time, some figures were functionaries. We know Satan (Job 1:6), for example, as the prosecuting attorney for the divine council (ריב). By the time of late Second Temple Judaism the protector of God's law (שטן) had become a problem for God's people. The presence of the law and the law protector led to further disobedience. Although origins are complicated, one can say generally that subentities of the sons of God are what we call angels, while subentities of the (fallen) Satan are what we call demons. The nomenclature is tricky. Negative subpowers can be called angels, spirits, and demons. Positive subpowers can be called angels or spirits. Positive subpowers pull the person toward faith, trust, and involvement in the life of God's people. Negative subpowers individualize the person and therefore create distrust. Distrust and individualism create illness, psychic distress, and eventually, inappropriate action. When the primary positive subentity, Jesus, encounters divisive spirits, the demons are transformed, so to speak, into positive agents for trust and participation in the community.[7]

---

7. Stevan L. Davies, *Jesus the Healer: Possession, Trance, and the Origins of Christianity* (New York: Continuum, 1995); Paul Hollenbach, "Jesus, Demoniacs, and Public Authorities: A Socio-Historical Study," *JAAR* 49 (1981): 567–88.

Public Healing

When the church became more public the healing ministry moved in two different directions.

Diakonia

The church of the second century continued the compassion found in the Jesus tradition. There is no doubt. The call for caring found in Matt. 25 reflects the attitude of the earliest church:

> Then the king will say to those at his right hand, "Come, you that are blessed by my Father, inherit the kingdom prepared for you from the foundation of the world; for I was hungry and you gave me food, I was thirsty and you gave me something to drink, I was a stranger and you welcomed me, I was naked and you gave me clothing, I was sick and you took care of me, I was in prison and you visited me." Then the righteous will answer him, "Lord, when was it that we saw you hungry and gave you food, or thirsty and gave you something to drink? And when was it that we saw you a stranger and welcomed you, or naked and gave you clothing? And when was it that we saw you sick or in prison and visited you?" And the king will answer them, "Truly I tell you, just as you did it to one of the least of these who are members of my family, you did it to me." (Matt. 25:34–40)

The caring was noted by the non-Christian world. Tertullian wrote, "It is our care of the helpless, our practice of loving kindness that brands us in the eyes of many of our opponents. 'Only look,' they say, 'look how they love one another!' " (*Apol.* 39).

Early Christian art verifies the concern for caring. Jesus is pictured healing the paralytic, making the deaf hear, the blind to see, and raising the dead. In the fourth century the healing of lepers also occurs. The frequent symbol of the Good Shepherd surely signified the importance of care and hospitality. Rodney Stark argues that the incredible growth of the early Christian church depended to a large extent on the fact that Christians cared for their members during severe epidemics.[8] He contends that even minimal care would have raised the percentage of those who survived. Likewise, non-Christians saved by Christian care likely joined with the group that healed them.

---

8. Rodney Stark, *The Rise of Christianity* (San Francisco: HarperSanFrancisco, 1997).

Miracle

In contrast to congregational care, the earliest church was also locked into a conflict with the Romans and with other Eastern religions. While the healing tradition of the early church might have been based on compassion and unity formation, placed in the public world of the Roman Empire, it looked like magic. As the Christians were known as sorcerers, in terms of gender, so in terms of healing they were known as magicians. In fact, Wilken claims that a major element in the growth of Christianity was its ability to overpower competitive magicians.[9] One can see the conflict already in the New Testament materials.

A magician named Simon was popular in Samaria, but when Philip began to preach in Samaria he also did many healings ("For unclean spirits, crying with loud shrieks, came out of many who were possessed; and many others who were paralyzed or lame were cured," Acts 8:7). As Philip came into competition with Simon, the people of Samaria began to follow Philip and wished to be baptized. Eventually Simon saw the handwriting on the wall. He, too, asked to be baptized:

> Now a certain man named Simon had previously practiced magic in the city and amazed the people of Samaria, saying that he was someone great. All of them, from the least to the greatest, listened to him eagerly, saying, "This man is the power of God that is called Great." And they listened eagerly to him because for a long time he had amazed them with his magic. But when they believed Philip, who was proclaiming the good news about the kingdom of God and the name of Jesus Christ, they were baptized, both men and women. Even Simon himself believed. After being baptized [ὁ δὲ Σίμων καὶ αὐτὸς ἐπίστευσεν καὶ βαπτισθείς], he stayed constantly with Philip and was amazed when he saw the signs and great miracles that took place. (Acts 8:9–13)

Luke's narrative throughout reflects the competition between the Jesus tradition and the Greco-Roman religious world. In Cyprus Paul encountered a magician, a false Jewish prophet, by the name of Bar-Jesus. Bar-Jesus tried to win the favor of the proconsul, Sergius Paulus. But in that competitive structure Paul blinded the magician temporarily and "When the procounsul saw what had happened, he believed, for he was astonished about the teaching of the Lord" (Acts 13:12).

Or, after Paul healed a lame man in Lystra, the populace compared

---

9. Robert L. Wilken, *The Myth of Christian Beginnings: History's Impact on Belief* (Garden City, N.Y.: Doubleday, 1971); *The Christians as the Romans Saw Them* (New Haven: Yale University Press, 1984).

Paul and Barnabas with Zeus and Hermes (Acts 14:8–18). But more pertinent would be the conflict with the magician in Philippi, where the magician's spiritual mouthpiece actually "converted to Paul" and left her owner without a means of income:

> One day, as we were going to the place of prayer, we met a slave girl who had a spirit of divination and brought her owners a great deal of money by fortune-telling. While she followed Paul [αὕτη κατακολουθοῦσα τῷ Παύλῳ] and us, she would cry out, "These men are slaves of the Most High God, who proclaim to you a way of salvation." She kept doing this for many days. But Paul, very much annoyed, turned and said to the spirit, "I order you in the name of Jesus Christ [ἐν ὀνόματι Ἰησοῦ Χριστοῦ] to come out of her." And it came out that very hour. (Acts 16:16–18)

Competition

The first disciples of Jesus even competed with Jewish healers. In Ephesus Paul discovered Jewish healers who healed in the name of Jesus. Particularly the seven sons of Sceva, a Jewish high priest, used the name. It was not Paul, but an evil spirit, that attacked the sons for their abuse of the Jesus tradition:

> Then some itinerant Jewish exorcists tried to use the name of the Lord Jesus over those who had evil spirits, saying, "I adjure you by the Jesus whom Paul proclaims." Seven sons of a Jewish high priest named Sceva were doing this. But the evil spirit said to them in reply, "Jesus I know, and Paul I know; but who are you?" [ἀποκριθὲν δὲ τὸ πνεῦμα τὸ πονηρὸν εἶπεν αὐτοῖς· τὸν [μὲν] Ἰησοῦν γινώσκω καὶ τὸ Παῦλον ἐπίσταμαι, ὑμεῖς δὲ τίνες ἐστέ;] Then the man with the evil spirit leaped on them, mastered them all, and so overpowered them that they fled out of the house naked and wounded. When this became known to all residents of Ephesus, both Jews and Greeks, everyone was awestruck; and the name of the Lord Jesus was praised. (Acts 19:13–17)

Although the later New Testament does not record such competitive healings, the apocryphal Acts abound with nearly formal power competitions. The *Acts of Peter* (19–29) is famous, of course, for the contest with Simon. Peter finally wins with the resurrection of a young boy. Justin Martyr recounted another story of competition with Magus and the ex-prostitute Helena. Christians rejected the accusation of magic, but nevertheless their attack on the demons of ill health turned them into a healing religion.[10]

Impact on Greco-Roman Healing

As a result of the inculturation of the Jesus tradition caring-healing became a mark of religious piety. Furthermore, the established church developed institutions to care for the ill. In 335 Constantine decreed the building of hospitals in Rome, Ephesus, Constantinople, and elsewhere. The Hôtel-Dieu of Lyons was opened in 542, and the Hôtel-Dieu of Paris in 660. Nevertheless, while the Jesus tradition exhibited compassion, for the most part, it retained the magical approach to healing and even the casting out of demons. Eventually Christianity repressed the observational approach to medicine, so well developed in the Greek world. Briefly stated, the Asclepius movement split about 200 B.C.E. One section moved in the direction of shamanism and the other in the direction of "scientific" medicine. In the nascent Christian Roman tradition both were rejected — shamanism as pagan, and the heritage of Hippolytus as non-theological. The observational part of Greek medicine went underground in to the Arabic world and did not reemerge until the Renaissance. Meanwhile, illness was still considered a divine punishment and health a divine gift.

---

10. Like Hull (*Hellenistic Magic*), Gary Ferngren believes that Christianity became a healing religion only after the rise of Constantine ("Early Christianity as a Religion of Healing," *Bulletin of the History of Medicine* 66, no. 1 (1992): 1–15). See also Eugene V. Gallagher, *Divine Man or Magician? Celsus and Origen on Jesus* (Chico, Calif.: Scholars Press, 1981).

14

Conclusion: The Jesus Tradition and the Formation of Christian Culture

We ought not say that it was useless for scholars to trace the demise of the earliest Christianity. Nor can we say which thesis — loss of eschatology, loss of spirit, loss of democracy — actually is most true to the data. This work is not a rebuttal of previous research. My question is a different one. How did the Jesus tradition so impact Roman culture that a new culture was created? My attempt to investigate this question has been useful, but far from complete. Each topic touched upon has been thoroughly researched by many scholars. The work here has taken that research and asked a different question — that of inculturation rather than acculturation.

The Synoptic Jesus Tradition

According to tradition Jesus did not so much alter culture as rearrange Jewish and Roman values both. "Jesus" celebrated meals as a form of community building, but he did not follow Jewish dietary laws, nor did he observe Roman eating customs. He apparently ate with anyone he wished regardless of sex, occupation, or reputation. That is, the churches of the Synoptic tradition consisted of communities that observed no self-evident boundaries.

The Synoptic communities met in houses (Mark 1:29–31; 14:14–15; Luke 10:38–42; 24:29–30, 33) and used the nomenclature of families — brother, sister, father, mother, son, and daughter. In addition to sharing open meals, Jesus healed persons who were excluded from Jewish communities. He restored the disabled to their proper place in society and cast out demons that caused destructive individualism.

Jesus did not scorn the Jewish calendar, but certainly did not follow it. He did not follow the Sabbath tradition at all times, though he did observe the Passover. In the Synoptic communities, inexplicably, there is little hint of a new calendar (Mark 16:9 would be much later).

Although the Synoptic communities did not share the Roman attitude toward (proper) women, neither do the churches seem to have broken from general Jewish culture. Women played an important role, but not often as leaders. Luke mentions the presence of women frequently, while only Matthew has women present on occasions where in Jewish and Roman cultures they might not have been (Matt. 14:21; 15:38; 22:30).

It is difficult to ascertain nongraphic symbols. They are surely present in Synoptic Jesus tradition. The symbol of water took on unusual meaning at the baptism of Jesus, though it does not occur later in the story (no real origin for water baptism has been established). The symbol remained a part of early Christian symbolism (whether as cleansing agent or as alien force). The Synoptic tradition does not negate the Passover symbols, but nevertheless, the meal symbolism shifts to bread and fish. Bread always symbolizes community formation. The shift from meat, that is, taxonomic order, to fish follows the meaning of the water — existence in alien environment. In early Christian symbolism healing scenes, prophetic existence in water, and eating together dominate the subject matter.

The Pauline Jesus Tradition

There are strong differences between the Pauline tradition and Synoptic tradition. Paul seldom advocates jettisoning either Jewish or Roman culture, but he consistently relativizes cultural values and practices. The *hōs mē* passage of 1 Cor. 7 states the case perfectly: take your place in society, but do not take it seriously. One might call it an eschatological suspension of culture. At the same time, Paul faces the need for a Christian culture, so in his letters one sees a constant leaning toward the establishment of a new order, neither Jewish nor Roman, with new values.

Congruent with the Jesus tradition, Paul also uses the meal as a means of forming the new community. Unfortunately we cannot determine just who ate at the tables. One could assume there were all classes of participants, but the Jesus tradition of eating with sinners is not repeated in the letters of Paul. Nevertheless, the meal is the key agent for building community. In Gal. 2 Paul recounts his attack on Peter for failing to eat with the non-Jews present. From this dramatic incident arose the central Pauline teaching about justification: it is not custom or law that makes us right before God. On the other hand, Paul was nonchalant about meals in general. Because idols had no real existence, eating meals at *idolatreia* was a relative matter. It was not to be taken seriously (1 Cor. 8). Eventually Paul's sociological awareness caught up with him. Relativity of idols not withstanding, meals did create community, so later in the same

Corinthian letter Paul recognized how critically important it was for the faith community to eat together (1 Cor. 11).

The churches mentioned in the letters of Paul met in houses rather than temples or synagogues. The house church was not only practical, but reflected the family orientation of the Pauline communities. Leadership in the Pauline churches derived from the house churches. Owners or hosts of the houses also served as ministers (*diakonoi*) of the local church.

There is no indication that Paul chose to ignore the Sabbath. If it were not for the rare reference to first day of the week (1 Cor. 16:2), the reader would suppose that Paul and his communities still met on the Sabbath. But Paul realizes that the new community is neither Jewish nor Greek. He chastises the Galatians for being tempted to celebrate the Jewish calendar, yet obviously he will not endorse the Roman. Paul offers no new suggestion.

As in the Jesus tradition, women play an important role in the life of the new community. They preach (prophesy), they serve as ministers, they have apostolic rank. Men and women act as equal partners in sexual bonding. Daughters of Christians are encouraged to make marriage decisions for themselves. Nevertheless, it would be difficult to say that men and women were treated with equality. Paul did not want the faith communities to appear subversive. He asked women to cover their heads when they spoke and perhaps even asked them not to disrupt the worship with ecstatic chatter. Normal sex standards were made relative; that is, men and women were treated equally unless it seriously upset current cultural expectations. In Christ there were not to be separate standards for male and female.

The Jesus tradition of healing seems strangely absent from the letters of Paul. There are no references to Jesus healing, to Paul healing, or anyone else for that matter. We know that healing occurs, because he speaks of χαρίσματα ἰαμάτων ἐν τῷ ἑνὶ πνεύματι (1 Cor. 12:9; see also 12:28, 30). Despite the absence of healing narratives, the formation of the Pauline faith community occurs in a way quite parallel to the Synoptic tradition. While healing in the Jesus tradition brings trust, restoration to community, and faith community roles, in Paul's theology the gift of God in Christ and the Spirit do the same thing. At the heart of Paul's faith is the restoration to trust (*dikaiosune* by the loving act of God in Jesus (Rom. 8:2). The life-giving Spirit (ὁ γὰρ νόμος τοῦ πνεύματος τῆς ζωῆς ἐν Χριστῷ Ἰησοῦ ἠλευθέρωσέν σε ἀπὸ τοῦ νόμου τῆς ἁμαρτίας καὶ τοῦ θανάτου [Rom. 8:2]) directs the faith community and raises up those roles necessary for community life and mission (1 Cor. 12:4–7).

The relativity of social classes, as well as of gender roles, affected the church, but not society. True to his unwillingness to attack the larger social structure, Paul has nothing to say about slavery as such. He assumes that in the Lord there is no distinction between master and slave (Gal. 3:28; Philemon). Making relative or suspending a culture value or institution can have devastating results. In this case it did. As the later inscriptions show, the early Christians did not make standard nomenclature distinctions between slaves, freed, and free.

Again, symbols are hard to determine. Water takes on a powerful meaning in Rom. 5. By being baptized the convert dies with Jesus on the cross. Entering the water signifies an encounter with the past that results in death and an anticipation of new life. There is no mention of the loaves and fishes in Paul. Although he uses the paschal lamb as a symbol (1 Cor. 5:7), he does not mention a Passover menu for the early Christian meals. Paul's primary symbols are bread and wine. The bread signifies the participation in the new community (body of Christ; see 1 Cor. 10:14–22) and the openness of the new community (broken; see 1 Cor. 11:23–26). The wine signifies the Spirit of the new fellowship as well as the blood of the broken (open) body that gives new life. Both symbols were highly significant in early Christian art. The life-giving brokenness of the body was accomplished on a cross. Paul surely expressed that centrality. Early Christian literature continued to state the centrality of the cross symbol, even though the more popular early Christian art did not.

The Johannine Jesus Tradition

Writing toward the end of the first century, the author of the Gospel of John approached inculturation in quite a different way. In contrast to the Synoptic Jesus tradition, which brought new life in terms of Jewish values, or the Pauline, which, in search of a new way, relativized or suspended the Jewish and Roman cultures, John tried to deculturize Jesus. We cannot know the extent to which John intended, or was able, to deculturize. Obviously, any written document about any given event in history cannot possibly do away with culture. So the Fourth Gospel is written in Greek in the context of Jewish and Hellenistic culture. But the author wishes to present a Jesus who is free of Jewish and Roman cultural practices — or more, perhaps, present a Jesus who, as nearly as possible, can be transported from place to place without cultural translation. That was accomplished primarily by shifting cultural values to symbols, healings to signs, and downgrading or eliminating basic cultural items.

There are meals in the Gospel of John. The reader would be hard put to find community formation in them. The wedding at Cana does not involve persons who reflect the new community of faith; the meal at the well in Samaria actually occurs off stage; the final supper in Jerusalem, with Peter refusing to participate and Judas doomed to "betrayal," could hardly be called a paradigm of community formation. Even the feeding of the five thousand, a replacement for the Passover in the Gospels, is displaced by the symbol of Jesus as the bread of life. Johannine characters, and therefore the readers of the Fourth Gospel, are chastised for seeking food and drink that does not satisfy (4:13–14;6:26–27), when the symbolic bread of life and living water are available to them. The symbols of bread, water, and wine reference the divine presence available in the Jesus of history. These are available only from Jesus, not in an actual meal.

There is no indication of community building in the meals. The issue is always assimilation of the divine presence. That assimilation is described in terms of love or intimacy. At the great dinner for Jesus (12:1–8) Mary of Bethany becomes "beloved" by washing the feet of Jesus with her hair. At the dinner described in chapter 13 Peter refuses the intimacy of washing feet, while the disciple designated as the Beloved Disciple reclines in the bosom of Jesus. It is not clear how Mary Magdalene became a "beloved disciple," though she also is portrayed as an intimate disciple.

What is true about food and meals is equally true about healing. The healing stories have become *sēmeia*. The healing of the official's son was a second sign that led people to see the divine presence (4:46–54; cf. 2:11). The healing of the man lame for thirty-eight years actually served to attack the calendar (5:1–18). And, of course, restoring sight to the man born blind is a narrative carefully constructed to show, symbolically, that restoration of sight and reception of the divine presence are parallel to faith development. There is no hint of community development or faith community leadership.

The author of John appears to repudiate the calendar even more than does the Jesus tradition itself. The healings deliberately make the "work" of the Father available on the Sabbath (see 5:17). The festivals of the Jews serve as literary devices to set the stage for conflict with the Jews (2:13–22; 5:1–8; 7:10–52; 10:22–39; and the final Passover narrative). At times it seems like the author is playing calendar games with us. He frequently tells us the time and often gives us a succession of days ("and on the next day"). It leads to nothing. His date for the Passover has confounded readers from the second century on. Despite the seeming cavalier attitude toward calendar, it is not that simple. Mary Magdalene came to the tomb τῇ δὲ μιᾷ τῶν σαββάτων; the disciples met that evening for the first time. Eight days later they met again. In the Gospel of John we have the beginning of a Christian calendar.

In fact, beginning on the first day of the week after the resurrection, we see the hints of inculturation. A Christian calendar is established and a minimal liturgy described. Although intimacy was the method of sharing the divine presence, Thomas, who wants to touch Jesus, does not need to. Jesus ends with a blessing on those who can believe without the physical presence. The additional chapter 21 continues the process of inculturation. The disciples share a breakfast with the risen Jesus that consists of bread and fish — the food of the feeding of the five thousand and the food consistently portrayed in early Christian art. Peter is rehabilitated. Eschatological thinking is recognized without criticism. *After the resurrection* the Spirit leads the faith community in the process of inculturation. But the deculturized Jesus still remains in the Fourth Gospel — available for impacting other times and other cultures.

Gender may be a moot point in the Fourth Gospel. Men and women equally fall short of genuine discipleship. Some readers suppose that John's concern for the mother of Jesus, for the Samaritan woman, for Mary and Martha, and for Mary Magdalene indicates a tradition where women are treated with respect and equality. The argument does not hold up. Jesus' treatment of his mother is not even polite. The Samaritan woman fares badly at the hands of Jesus at the well. Martha does not "catch on." Only the female "beloved disciples," Mary of Bethany and Mary Magdalene, receive the approbation of the author. Intimacy creates genuine appropriation of the divine presence in Jesus. Because Jesus is male and the two (?) Marys are female, the intimacy appears very sensual. There is no hint of that in the Johannine narratives. Apparently faith intimacy is identical for men and women. Failure to receive the divine presence also reveals no gender differentiation.

Jesus Tradition Trajectories

There are a number of areas where the Jesus tradition has impacted Roman culture. Exploring all of them seems impractical at this time, so we have selected a few trajectories that will illustrate the process of inculturation.

Symbols

Although Jewish symbols did not impact Roman culture, the Jesus tradition entered and altered the meaning of several Roman symbols. The new symbol system stressed community hospitality, life in an alien culture, community foods, and peace. These new symbols clearly picked up the Jesus traditions of community openness and his prophetic critique of the dominant culture. After the peace of the church most of the basic symbols were either altered in meaning or referenced concrete events. The Good Shepherd became Jesus; the fish became an acrostic; bread

and wine referred to the Eucharist; the boat became the ark. Symbols
that dealt with cultural tension disappeared (anchor, Orante).

Art

Jewish art was too insignificant to be a factor in this discussion. The
Jesus tradition utilized elements of contemporary Roman art to express
primary Christian concerns. Stories from the Hebrew Scriptures were
used to express deliverance from an oppressive culture, state, and even
the environment. The Greco-Roman Orante figure often signified that
deliverance. New Testament stories reflected healings, communal meals,
birth, baptism. Jesus appeared as a Hellenistic divine healer or miracle
worker. About the time of Constantine, pictorial representations shifted
from symbolic art to illustrations. The illustrations (e.g., in Maria Mag-
giore, Rome; or Ravenna) could be used for ecclesiastical propaganda,
educational purposes, or theological persuasion. Jesus became an emperor who ruled and judged the world. The loss of living symbols and
symbolic art meant that the church could no longer live out of the Jesus
tradition, but had to expand and defend its own self-inflicted artistic concretizations. The Jesus tradition permeates Christian art, but no longer
as an effective force for inculturation.

Architecture

For pragmatic reasons (availability) and for communal reasons the
church of the first centuries almost invariably met in house churches.
For much the same reasons, Jewish meetings were held in homes that
eventually evolved into more formal halls. Both were family-oriented.
The early Christians kept the family orientation through the first three
centuries and, somewhat in contrast to the Jews, deliberately kept house
architecture. However, both traditions were reluctant to shift from the
more communal square buildings to those longitudinal buildings that afforded hierarchical leadership. Because of the familial organization of
the church, meals for the dead played an important role in the life of the
church. Such meals were held in triclinium-like cemetery rooms, or circular edifices like the Greek heroon. These *martyria* were elongated, by the
addition of naves, to accommodate larger groups of families. At the same
time, the square house churches were also elongated to accommodate
larger congregations. The two developments eventually ended in longitudinal churches with apses, sometimes domes, and sometimes cruciform
wings at the end. The element of the extended family — the remains of
faith community heroes, the martyrs — was centrally placed before the
apse beneath the table/altar. Although the Jesus tradition of communal
life permeated early Christian architecture and even helped create the

fourth-century Christian basilica, still, the formation of Roman Christian culture changed the family nature of the early church's built form into a hierarchical structure.

Meals

The primary function of meals in the material under discussion is to establish community. Obviously, meals serve to maintain health and life, but that does not come under consideration. Jewish meals not only solidified Jewish community but also tended to exclude non-Jews. In order to preserve the meaning of food, strict dietary laws evolved. It was the dietary laws that prevented table fellowship with non-Jews. Along with the keeping of the Sabbath and circumcision, the dietary laws then became primary marks for what it meant to be a Jew. It is difficult to determine, then and now, whether the dietary laws serve to affirm a certain symbolic faith, or whether they define Jewish identity (or both).

In contrast to Judaism, the meals and food of the Roman world served much more as a sign of class. The nature of food itself signaled class distinctions. Soft, perishable food indicated upper class, while hard, dry, and preserved food indicated low class. In the higher class meals social favor was even more sharply defined by position at the table.

In the Jesus tradition the Jewish meal was radically altered. Boundary lines were dropped. Dietary laws were abolished. Non-Jews came to the table. Men and women ate together, although that might be more of a break with Greco-Roman custom than with Jewish. The primary food shifted to bread, wine, and fish. Bread and wine were elements of common meals, and both were basic foods for developing community. Bread, wine, and fish were the elements of the early Christian common meal, as seen in the story of the feeding of the five thousand and in early Christian art. At the same time, bread and wine were the elements of the major early Christian ritual, the Eucharist. Bread and wine marked the formation of community (1 Cor. 10:14–22), and they also, in terms of semiotics, became symbols of the death and resurrection of Jesus (1 Cor. 11:23–26). As for the fish, also common to Mediterranean meals, it too became a much used symbol. For the more elite it became an acrostic referring to Jesus Christ, Son of God, Savior, but for most early Christians it signified, along with the anchor and boat, the gift of life in an alien environment.

The impact of the Jesus tradition on meals resulted in new traditions. Meals became inclusive means of establishing and continuing the Christian community. The basic foods remained symbols of redemption (fish) rather than creation (meat). Types of food did not distinguish classes, and placement at the table did not establish social status. Even though the fellowship meal coalesced with the larger meal for/with the dead, and even though that became, after Constantine, the more public meal, the Mass, still, participation in the meal was democratic and symbolic of the redemptive act. Eventually, of course, society reestablished social distinctions and exclusivity, but nevertheless, the Jesus tradition did permanently alter Jewish and Hellenistic meal traditions.

Calendar

As far as festivals were concerned, the Jews followed a lunar calendar, although some elements of the calendar were based on solar movements. At the same time, the Romans followed a solar calendar, which frequently had to be adjusted. At the time of the Roman Republic the Romans made an effort to shift to a lunar calendar. Eventually a compromise was made that proved fairly satisfactory. Meanwhile, the Jesus tradition tended to make the Sabbath observance subservient to more humane considerations. Nevertheless, there is little indication that the lunar calendar was rejected. There are slight hints in the New Testament period that the Christian calendar would become a lunar one based on the first day of the week. Early in the life of the church, leaders (Paul) were aware that the first Christians dare not follow either a Jewish calendar or a Roman one. Their earliest calendar did follow a lunar system, but the primary day became the first day of the week rather than the Sabbath. It would also appear that the Romans, for unknown reasons, followed the Jewish calendar and named the seventh day a day of rest. The situation then was set for a public Christian calendar based on the "first day of the week." Nevertheless, in their public struggle with the sun god the first Christians took over solar festivals to create primary festivals such as Christmas and Easter. The Jesus tradition had infiltrated Jewish and Roman calendars in such a way as to create a new cultural basis for keeping time and ordering festival days.

Gender

Gender issues in the early Christian period have been so variously interpreted that a confident statement becomes nearly impossible. In the Greco-Roman world women had to remain private or be known as "prostitutes." That severe role for women was altered at the end of the Roman Republic so that women could, in a limited way, take part in public life. The Jewish background remains even more difficult to ascertain. Women surely did not enjoy equality, yet there is little indication that public appearance was totally inappropriate. At the time of the New Testament period, Jewish women were patrons of synagogues, and even leaders, while non-Jewish women joined Judaism as "God-fearers." The

Jesus tradition may not be all that different from contemporary Judaism. In fact, some modern readers assume that so-called early Christian inequality derived from its predecessor Judaism. But it is not that simple. There is little in the Jesus tradition to indicate that women were not treated evenhandedly. To be sure, often there is no mention of special or equal treatment. It would appear that women were not named or mentioned in order to protect them from possible misunderstanding in the Greco-Roman world. In the letters of Paul we find an eschatological expectation that gender does not matter, while in fact women do take an equal role in the faith community. Paul has men and women equal in matters of marriage, and calls for more freedom in the marriage process.

As the church became more and more public, church writers called for a community structure that would be acceptable to the Greco-Roman world. The submission of women to men, or at least wives to husbands, was made clear. This was the public stance. The private practice might have been something else. Inscriptions show no differentiation between men and women, or slaves and masters. Early Christian art does not show a preference for male figures and certainly not for male-based narratives. In early Christian art women were shown officiating at meals.

Healing

According to the Jesus tradition, Jesus was known primarily as a healer. That tradition stands in contrast to other Jewish leaders and prophets, who could call upon divine power to heal, but did not engage in healing ministries. Indeed, healing stands in contrast to the two other major Jesus traditions: wisdom teacher and eschatological prophet. Healing had one function: to restore the ill and diseased to their rightful community. The lame, blind, and hard-of-hearing were given back those functions that made them whole members of society. On the other hand, according to the Jesus tradition, Jesus also struggled with demonic forces, the power of divine unity transformed by human society into divisive spirits. By casting out demons Jesus restored people to their rightful place in society, but also transformed social structures. In either case, the first Christians saw the tradition of healing as one that not only expressed caring, but made community (society) possible.

For that reason many of the healing stories deal either with persons returning home, or, more likely, with the formation of faith community roles such as preaching, teaching, and serving. The tradition of eating together created new communities without boundaries, led by persons who offered hospitality (elders and bishops). Healing also broke boundaries and resulted in healed persons who found a place in the new community (ministers, teachers, deacons). The healing tradition continued through the first centuries. Christians cared for children, disabled, impoverished in such a way that the Roman culture sensed the contrast. In many ways the Christian care for others created cognitive dissonance in the dominant culture. As a side issue, Christians leaders also battled with demonic forces and with other healers who claimed superior powers. According to Christian narratives the Christian leaders won those battles and, after Constantine, gained the consequent allegiance of the populace.

Private (caring) and public (exorcism) traditions of healing were both central to Christianity, and they continued into the later centuries. However, a price was paid. The Judeo-Christian understanding of health and wholeness, as a divine gift, left no room for the more observational style of the Greek physicians. That rich heritage went underground until the sixteenth century.

Conclusions

The Jesus tradition continued with power, primarily the power of the Spirit, into the life of the earliest faith community. It was variously used, though not necessarily contrary to the original. Boundaries were broken, people were cared for, new open communities of faith were formed, society was challenged. Although the Jesus tradition remained powerful, eventually alterations did occur. Primarily at the end of the third century and the beginning of the fourth, when the heretofore private faith community became public, significant developments can be seen. The church building became a longitudinal basilica. Some symbols became reified (e.g., the Good Shepherd became Jesus), while others were dropped (the Orante). Art no longer reflected the role of the faith community in an alien culture, but became illustrative for educational and promotional purposes. Meals that had been used for family and community cohesiveness became liturgical celebrations. Although the Jesus tradition of caring remained central to the fourth-century church, the casting out of demons became a public competition for adherents.

The Jesus tradition was not destroyed, as has been suggested. In its earliest form it altered the Jewish culture in which it found itself. When a Jesus movement culture was needed, early Christians tried to create something new by weaving between what was Roman and what was Jewish (Paul). One early religious genius (John) recognized the dangers of a new Christian culture and attempted to eliminate cultural specifics from the story of Jesus. The Jesus tradition eventually did become concretized in specific (Roman) cultural garb. The mistake then, and from time to time the mistake now, is to identify the Roman form of Christianity with the Jesus tradition itself. To offer to non-Christians a so-called orthodox Christianity is to offer them a Roman Christian culture inculturated by the Jesus tradition rather than the Jesus tradition itself. By tracing how this was done we have an opportunity to see the Jesus tradition before it became concrete.

Bibliography

Achtemeier, Paul. "The Origin and Function of the Pre-Marcan Miracle Catenae." *JBL* 91 (1972): 199–200.

Aleith, Eva. *Paulusverständnis in der alten Kirche*. Berlin: Töpelmann, 1937.

Alter, Robert. "A New Theory of *kashrut*." *Commentary* 68, no. 2 (1979): 46–
52.

Arens, E. "Was St. Paul Married?" *Bible Today* 66 (1973): 1188–91.

Arrupe, Pedro. "Letter to the Whole Society on Inculturation." *Aixala* 3 (1978):
172 81.

Avalos, Hector. *Illness and Health Care in the Ancient Near East*. Harvard
Semitic Monographs, no. 54. Atlanta: Scholars Press, 1995.

Bacchiocchi, Samuele. *Anti-Judaism and the Origin of Sunday*. Rome: Pontifical
Gregorian University Press, 1975.

———. *From Sabbath to Sunday: A Historical Investigation of the Rise of Sunday Observance in Early Christianity*. Rome: Pontifical Gregorian University
Press, 1977.

Bagnall, Roger S. *Egypt in Late Antiquity*. Princeton, N.J.: Princeton University
Press, 1993.

Balch, David. *Let Wives Be Submissive: The Domestic Code in 1 Peter*. Chico,
Calif.: Scholars Press, 1981.

Banana, Canaan S. "The Case for a New Bible." In *'Rewriting' the Bible: The
Real Issues*, ed. Isabel Mukonyora, James L. Cox, and Frans J. Verstraelen.
Harare, Zimbabwe: Mambo Press, 1993.

Banks, Robert. *Paul's Idea of Community: The Early House Churches in Their
Historical Setting*. Grand Rapids: Eerdmans, 1980.

Baron, Salo. *A Social and Religious History of the Jews*. New York: Columbia
University Press, 1937.

Barr, James. *The Semantics of Biblical Language*. Oxford: Oxford University
Press, 1961.

Barrett, C. K. *The Gospel of John and Judaism*. London: SPCK, 1975.

Barth, Fredrik. *Ethnic Groups and Boundaries: The Social Organization of
Culture Difference*. Boston: Little, Brown and Company, 1969.

Bartlett, David. *Ministry in the New Testament*. Minneapolis: Fortress, 1993.

Baskin, Judith R., ed. *Jewish Women in Historical Perspective*. Detroit: Wayne
State University Press, 1991.

Batstone, David B. *From Conquest to Struggle: Jesus of Nazareth in Latin
America*. Albany, N.Y.: State University of New York Press, 1991.

Baur, Ferdinand C. "Die Christus Partie in der korinthischen Gemeinde, der
Gegensatz des petrinischen und paulinishchen Christentum in der ältesten
Kirche, der Apostel Petrus in Rom." *Tübinger Zeitschrift für Theologie* 5
(1831): 61–206.

————. *Die Epochen der kirchlichen Geschichtschreibung.* Tübingen: Fues, 1852.

————. *The Church History of the First Three Centuries.* Trans. A. Menzies. London: Williams and Norgate, 1878.

————. *Ausgewählte Werke in Einzelangaben.* Stuttgart: Fromann, 1963.

Beckwith, Roger T. *Calendar and Chronology, Jewish and Christian: Biblical, Intertestamental and Patristic Studies.* Leiden: Brill, 1996.

Benoît, André. *Le baptême chrétien au second siècle: la théologie des pères.* Études d'histoire et de philosophie religieuses de l'Université de Strasbourg publiées sous les auspices de la Faculté de Théologie Protestante 43. Paris: Presses universitaires de France, 1953.

Beskow, Per. *Rex Gloriae: The Kingship of Christ in the Early Church.* Trans. Eric J. Sharpe. Stockholm: Almquist and Wiksell, 1962.

Best, Ernest. *Disciples and Discipleship: Studies in the Gospel According to Mark.* Edinburgh: T. & T. Clark, 1986.

Boman, Thorlief. *Hebrew Thought Compared with Greek.* Trans. Jules L. Moreau. London: SCM, 1960.

Borg, Marcus J. "Jesus — A Sketch." *The Fourth R* 7, no. 3 (1994): 10–15.

————. "The Jesus Seminar at Work: The Making of *The Five Gospels.*" *The Fourth R* 7, no. 6 (1994): 3–11.

————. *Conflict, Holiness, and Politics in the Teachings of Jesus.* Harrisburg: Trinity Press International, 1998.

Borgen, Peder. *Bread From Heaven: An Exegetical Study of the Concept of Manna in the Gospel of John and the Writings of Philo.* Leiden: Brill, 1965.

Boring, M. Eugene. *The Continuing Voice of Jesus: Christian Prophecy and the Gospel Tradition.* Louisville: Westminster / John Knox, 1991.

Bosch, David J. *Transforming Mission.* Maryknoll, N.Y.: Orbis, 1991.

Bossuet, James Benign. *The History of the Variations of the Protestant Churches.* Vol. 1. Antwerp: n.p., 1742.

Bourguet, Pierre du. *Early Christian Painting.* Trans. S. W. Taylor. London: Weidenfeld & Nicolson, 1965.

Bousset, Wilhelm. *Kyrios Christos.* Trans. J. E. Steely. Nashville: Abingdon, 1970.

Brandon, S. G. F. *Jesus and the Zealots.* Manchester: Manchester University Press, 1967.

Bréhier, Emile. *The History of Philosophy: The Hellenistic and Roman Age.* Trans. W. Baskin. Chicago: University of Chicago Press, 1965.

Bremen, Riet van. "Women and Wealth." In *Images of Women in Antiquity,* ed. A. Cameron and A. Kuhrt. Detroit: Wayne State University Press, 1985.

Brooten, Bernadette J. *Women Leaders in the Ancient Synagogue: Inscriptional Evidence and Background Issue.* Chico, Calif.: Scholars Press, 1982.

————. "The Gender of Ἰαηλ in the Jewish Inscription from Aphrodisias." In *Of Scribes and Scrolls: Studies on the Hebrew Bible, Intertestamentary Judaism, and Christian Origins Presented to John Strugnell on the Occasion of His Sixtieth Birthday,* ed. H. W. Attridge, J. J. Collins, and T. H. Tobin. Lanham, Md.: University Press of America, 1990.

Brown, Peter. *The Cult of the Saints.* Chicago: University of Chicago Press, 1981.

Brown, Raymond. *The Community of the Beloved Disciple.* New York: Paulist Press, 1979.

Bruston, Édouard. *Ignace d'Antioche: ses épîtres, sa vie, sa théologie*. Paris: Fischbacher, 1897.

Bruun, Patrick. "Symboles, Signes et Monogrammes." In *Sylloge inscriptionum christianarum veterum musei vaticani*, ed. Henrik Zilliacus. Acta instituti romani finlandiae, vol. 1, no. 2. Helsinki: Tilqmann, 1963.

Bryant, Carol, et al. *The Cultural Feast: An Introduction to Food and Society*. St. Paul: West Publishing Co., 1985.

Bultmann, Rudolf. *Theology of the New Testament*. 2 vols. Trans. K. Grobel. London: SCM, 1952.

———. "The Christological Confession of the World Council of Churches." In *Essays Philosophical and Theological*. Trans. J. C. G. Greig. London: SCM, 1955.

———. *History and Eschatology*. Edinburgh: Edinburgh University Press, 1957.

———. "The Eschatology of the Gospel of John." In *Faith and Understanding*. Trans. L. P. Smith. London: SCM, 1960.

———. *The Gospel of John*. Trans. by G. R. Beasley-Murray. Oxford: Blackwell, 1971.

Burkett, Delbert Royce. *The Son of Man in the Gospel of John*. Sheffield: JSOT Press, 1991.

Campenhausen, Hans von. *Ecclesiastical Authority and Spiritual Power in the Church of the First Three Centuries*. Trans. J. A. Baker. London: Black, 1969.

Carcopino, Jérôme. *Daily Life in Ancient Rome*. New Haven: Yale University Press, 1963.

Carson, D. A., ed. *From Sabbath to Lord's Day: A Biblical, Historical and Theological Investigation*. Grand Rapids: Zondervan, 1982.

Chadwick, Henry. "All Things to All Men, 1 Cor. 9:22." *NTS* 1 (1954–55): 261–75.

Chadwick, Owen. *From Bossuet to Newman: The Idea of Doctrinal Development*. Cambridge: Cambridge University Press, 1957.

Childe, Gordon. *The Dawn of European Civilization*. New York: Knopf, 1958.

Childs, Brevard. *Biblical Theology in Crisis*. Philadelphia: Westminster, 1970.

Collins, John. Review of *Jew and Gentile in the Ancient World: Attitudes and Interactions from Alexander to Justinian*, by Louis H. Feldman. *JBL* 113 (1994): 716–18.

Congar, Yves M.-J. *Tradition and Traditions*. Trans. Michael Naseby and Thomas Rainborough. London: Burns and Oates, 1966.

Conzelmann, Hans. *The Theology of St. Luke*. Trans. Geoffrey Buswell. New York: Harper, 1960.

———. *Geschichte des Urchristentums*. Das Neue Testament Deutsch, Ergänzungsreihe 5. Göttingen: Vandenhoeck & Ruprecht, 1969.

———. *History of Primitive Christianity*. Trans. John E. Steely. Nashville: Abingdon, 1973.

Corley, Kathleen E. *Private Women, Public Meals: Social Conflict in the Synoptic Tradition*. Peabody, Mass.: Hendrickson, 1993.

Costa, Ruy O., ed. *One Faith, Many Cultures: Inculturation, Indigenization, and Contextualization*. Maryknoll, N.Y.: Orbis, 1988.

Cremer, Hermann. *Biblischtheologisches Wörterbuch der neutestamentlichen Grazität*. Gotha: Perthes, 1911.

Crossan, John Dominic. *In Parables: The Challenge of the Historical Jesus*. New York: Harper & Row, 1973.

———. *The Historical Jesus: The Life of a Mediterranean Jewish Peasant*. San Francisco: Harper, 1991.

Crouch, J. E. *The Origin and Intention of the Colossian Haustafel*. Göttingen: Vandenhoeck & Ruprecht, 1972.

Cullmann, Oscar. *Immortality of the Soul or Resurrection of the Dead? The Witness of the New Testament*. London: Epworth, 1958.

———. "Parusieverzögerung und Urchristentum," *TLZ* 3 (1958): 2–11.

———. *The Johannine Circle*. Trans. John Bowden. London: SCM, 1976.

Culpepper, Alan R. *Anatomy of the Fourth Gospel: A Study in Literary Design*. Philadelphia: Fortress, 1983.

Daillé, John. *De scriptis quae sub Dionysius Areopagite et Ignatii Antiocheni nominibus circumferunter*. Geneva: de Tournes, 1666.

Dalbert, P. *Die Theologie der Hellenistich-Jüdischen Missionsliteratur unter Ausschluß von Philo und Josephus*. Hamburg-Volksdorf: H. Reich, 1954.

Dalby, Andrew. *Siren Feasts: A History of Food and Gastronomy in Greece*. London: Routledge, 1996.

Davidman, Lynn, and Shelly Tenenbaum, eds. *Feminist Perspectives on Jewish Studies*. New Haven: Yale University Press, 1994.

Davidson, James N. *Courtesans and Fishcakes: The Consuming Passions of Classical Athens*. London: HarperCollins, 1997.

Davies, John Gordon. *The Origin and Development of Early Christian Church Architecture*. London: SCM, 1952.

Davies, Stevan L. *The Revolt of the Widows: The Social World of the Apocryphal Acts*. Carbondale and Edwardsville, Ill.: Southern Illinois University Press, 1980.

———. *The Gospel of Thomas and Christian Wisdom*. New York: Seabury, 1983.

———. *Jesus the Healer: Possession, Trance, and the Origins of Christianity*. New York: Continuum, 1995.

Detienne, Marcel, and Jean-Pierre Vernant. *The Cuisine of Sacrifice Among the Greeks*. Chicago: University of Chicago Press, 1989.

Dhavamony, Mariasusai. "Problematica dell'inculturazione del Vangelo oggi." In *Evangelización de la cultura e inculturación del Evangelio*. Buenos Aires: Editorial Guadalupe, 1988.

———. *Christian Theology of Inculturation*. Rome: Editrice Pontificia Università Gregoriana, 1997.

Dibelius, Martin. *A Fresh Approach to the New Testament and Early Christian Literature*. New York: Scribner's, 1936.

Diel, Paul. *Symbolism in the Gospel of John*. San Francisco: Harper & Row, 1988.

Dillow J. C. "Abiding is Remaining in Fellowship: Another Look at John 15:1–6." *Bibliotheca* 147 (1990): 44–53.

Dinkler, Erich. "Shalom-Eirene-Pax: Jüdische Sepulkralinschriften und ihr Verhältnis zum frühen Christentum." *Rivista Archeologia Christiana* 50 (1974): 121–44.

D'Onofrio, Salvatore. "A las mesa con los muertos." In *Antropología de la alimentación: Ensayos sobre la dieta Mediterranea*, ed. Isabel González Turmo and Pedro Romero de Solís. Almería, Spain: Consejería de cultura y medio ambiente de la junta de Andalucía, 1993.

Douglas, Mary. *Purity and Danger: An Analysis of the Concepts of Pollution and Taboo*. London: Routledge and Kegan Paul, 1966.

———. "Deciphering a Meal." In *Implicit Meanings: Essays in Anthropology*. London: Routledge and Kegan Paul, 1975.

Downing. F. Gerald. *Cynics and Christian Origins*. Edinburgh: T. & T. Clark, 1992.

———. "Deeper Reflections on the Jewish Cynic Jesus." *JBL* 117 (1998): 97–104.

Drower, E. S. *Water Into Wine: A Study of Ritual Idiom in the Middle East*. London: J. Murray, 1956.

Duke, Paul D. *Irony in the Fourth Gospel*. Atlanta: John Knox, 1985.

Dupont, Florence. *Daily Life in Ancient Rome*. Trans. Christopher Woodall. Oxford: Blackwell, 1993.

Durkheim, Emile. *The Elementary Forms of the Religious Life*. Trans. J. W. Swain New York: Free Press, 1965.

Durkheim, Emile, and Marcel Mauss. *Primitive Classification*. Trans. Rodney Needham. London: Cohen and West, 1963.

Dyggve, Ejnar. *Dødekult, Kejserkult og Basilika: Bidrag til Spørgsmålet om den oldkristne kultbygnings Genesis*. Copenhagen: Branners Forlag, 1943.

———. *History of Salonitan Christianity*. Oslo: H. Aschehoug, 1951.

Edwards, Richard A. *A Theology of Q: Eschatology, Prophecy, and Wisdom*. Philadelphia: Fortress, 1976.

Eisenman, Robert H., and Michael Wise. *The Dead Sea Scrolls Uncovered*. Rockport, Mass.: Element, 1992.

Erling, Bernhard. "Motif Research as a General Historical Method." In *The Philosophy and Theology of Anders Nygren*, ed. C. W. Kegley. Carbondale, Ill.: Southern Illinois University Press, 1970.

Esler, Philip F. *Community and Gospel in Luke-Acts*. Cambridge: Cambridge University Press, 1987.

———. *Galatians*. London: Routledge, 1998.

Fee, Gordon. *The First Epistle to the Corinthians*. Grand Rapids: Eerdmans, 1987.

Feeley-Harnik, Gillian. *The Lord's Table: Eucharist and Passover in Early Christianity*. Philadelphia: University of Pennsylvania Press, 1981.

Feldman, David M. *Health and Medicine in the Jewish Tradition*. New York: Crossroad, 1986.

Feldman, Louis H. *Jew and Gentile in the Ancient World: Attitudes and Interactions from Alexander to Justinian*. Princeton, N.J.: Princeton University Press, 1993.

Ferngren, Gary B. "Early Christianity as a Religion of Healing." *Bulletin of the History of Medicine* 66, no. 1 (1992): 1–15.

Fieldhouse, Paul. *Food and Nutrition: Customs and Culture*. London: Croom Helm. 1986,

Filson, Floyd. "Who Was the Beloved Disciple?" *JBL* 68 (1949):83–88.

Finn, Thomas H. "The God-fearers Reconsidered." *CBQ* 47 (1985): 75–84.

Fortna, Robert T. *The Gospel of Signs: A Reconstruction of the Narrative Source Underlying the Fourth Gospel*. London: Cambridge University Press, 1970.

Frankfurter, David T. M. "The Origin of the Miracle-List Tradition and Its Medium of Circulation." In *SBL Seminar Papers 29*. Atlanta: Scholars Press, 1990.

Friedrich, Gerhard, "Die Problematik eines Theologischen Wörterbuchs zum Neuen Testament." *Studia Evangelica (Texte und Untersuchungen 73)* (1959): 481–86.

Frymer-Kensky, Tikva. "The Bible and Women's Studies." In *Feminist Perspectives on Jewish Studies,* ed. Lynn Davidman and Shelly Tenenbaum. New Haven: Yale University Press, 1994.

Funk, Robert W. *Honest to Jesus: Jesus for a New Millennium*. San Francisco: HarperSanFrancisco, 1996.

Funk, Robert, Roy Hoover, and The Jesus Seminar. *The Five Gospels: The Search for the Authentic Words of Jesus*. New York: Macmillan, 1993.

Gager, John G. *The Origin of Anti-Semitism: Attitudes toward Judaism in Pagan and Christian Antiquity*. New York: Oxford University Press, 1985.

———. "Jews, Gentiles, and Synagogues in the Book of Acts." *HTR* 79 (1986): 91–99.

Gallagher, Eugene V. *Divine Man or Magician? Celsus and Origen on Jesus*. Chico, CA: Scholars Press, 1981

Gärtner, Bertil. *John 6 and the Jewish Passover*. Coniectanea neotestamentica, no. 17. Lund: C. W. K Gleerup, 1959.

Geertz, Clifford. *The Interpretation of Culture*. New York: Basic Books, 1978.

Goldstein, J. "Jewish Acceptance and Rejection of Hellenism." In *Aspects of Judaism: Jewish and Christian Self-definition*, vol. 2, ed. E. P. Sanders. 64–87. London: SCM, 1981.

Gooch, Peter D. *Dangerous Food: 1 Corinthians 8–10 in Its Context*. Waterloo, Ont.: Wilfred Laurier University Press, 1993.

Goodenough, Erwin R. *Jewish Symbols in the Greco-Roman Period*. 12 vols. New York: Pantheon, 1953–65.

Goodman, Martin. "Jewish Proselytizing in the First Century." In *The Jews among Pagans and Christians in the Roman Empire*, ed. Judith Lieu, John North, and Tessa Rajak. London: Routledge, 1992.

———. *Mission and Conversion: Proselytizing in the Religious History of the Roman Empire*. Oxford: Clarendon, 1994.

Goppelt, Leonhard. "The Existence of the Church in History According to Apostolic and Early Catholic Thought." In *Current Issues in New Testament Interpretation*, ed. W. Klassen and G. F. Snyder. New York: Harper & Brothers, 1962.

Gore, Charles. *The Church and the Ministry*. London: Rivingtons, 1882.

Gowers, Emily. *The Loaded Table: Representations of Food in Roman Literature*. Oxford: Clarendon, 1993.

Grabar, André. *Martyrium: recherches sur le culte des reliques et l'art, chrétien antique*. Paris: College de France, 1946.

Grant, R. M. *Gnosticism and Early Christianity*. New York: Columbia University Press, 1959.

Grilli, Massimo. *Comunità e Missione: le direttive di Matteo: Indagine esegetica su Mt 9,35–11,1*. Europäische Hochschulschriften, Reihe 23, Band 458. Frankfurt: Peter Lang, 1992.

Gunkel, Hermann. *Die Wirkungen des heiligen Geistes*. Göttingen: Vandenhoeck & Ruprecht, 1888.

Gutiérrez, Gustavo. *A Theology of Liberation: History, Politics, and Salvation*. Trans. Caridad Inda and John Eagleson. Maryknoll, N.Y.: Orbis, 1973.

Guyon, Jean. "La vente des tombes à travers l'épigraphie de 1a Rome chrétienne." *Mélanges de l'école française de Rome, Antiquité* 86 (1974): 549–96.

Haenchen, Ernst. *The Acts of the Apostles: A Commentary*. Trans. B. Noble and Gerald Shinn. Philadelphia: Westminster, 1971.

Hall, Barbara. "All Things to All People: A Study of 1 Corinthians 9:19–23." In *The Conversation Continues: Studies in Paul and John in Honour of J. Louis Martyn*, ed. Robert T. Fortna and Beverly R. Gaventa. Nashville: Abingdon, 1990.

Hamman, A. *Vie liturgique et vie sociale: repas des pauvres, diaconie et diaconat, agape et repas de charité*. Paris: Desclée, 1968.

Harnack, Adolf von. *Die Lehre der Zwölf Apostel*. Leipzig: Hinrichs, 1884.

———. *Marcion: Das Evangelium vom fremden Gott*. Leipzig: Hinrichs, 1921.

———. *The Essence of Christianity*. Trans. T. B. Saunders. London: Benn, 1958.

———. *History of Dogma*. Trans. N. Buchanan. New York: Russell and Russell, 1958.

———. *The Mission and Expansion of Christianity*. Trans. James Moffatt. New York: Harper, 1962.

Harnack, Adolf von, and Wilhelm Herrmann. *Essays on the Social Gospel*. Trans. G. M. Craik. New York: Putman's, 1907.

Harrington, Hannah K. *The Impurity Systems of Qumran and the Rabbis: Biblical Foundations*. Atlanta: Scholars Press, 1993.

Hatch, Edwin. *Die Gesellschaftsverfassung der christlichen Kirchen im Altertum*. Trans. A. von Harnack. Giessen: Ricker, 1883.

———. *The Organization of the Early Christian Churches* London: Rivingtons, 1888.

———. *The Influence of Greek Ideas and Usages upon the Christian Church*. London: Williams and Norgate, 1890.

Hilary, Mbachu. *Inculturation Theology of the Jerusalem Council in Acts 15: An Inspiration for the Igbo Church Today*. Frankfurt: Peter Lang, 1995.

Hill, Craig C. *Hellenists and Hebrews: Reappraising Division within the Earliest Church*. Minneapolis: Fortress, 1992.

Hills, Julian. *Tradition and Composition in the Epistula Apostolorum*. Minneapolis: Fortress, 1990.

Hollenbach, Paul. "Jesus, Demoniacs, and Public Authorities: A Socio-Historical Study." *JAAR* 49 (1981): 567–88.

Holtzmann, H. J. *Lehrbuch der neutestamentlichen Theologie*. Freiburg i.B.: Mohr, 1897.

Hommel, H. "Juden und Christen im kaiserzeitlichen Milet." *Mitteilungen des Deutschen Archäologischen Instituts, Istanbuler Abteilung* 25 (1975): 167–95.

Horsley, R., and J. Hanson. *Bandits, Prophets, and Messiahs: Popular Movements in the Time of Jesus*. San Francisco: Harper & Row, 1988.

Hull, John M. *Hellenistic Magic and the Synoptic Tradition Studies in Biblical Theology*, 2d ser., no. 28. London: SCM, 1974.

Humbert, P. "Maladie et médicine dans l'Ancient Testament." *RHPR* 44 (1964): 1–29.

Idowu, Bolaji. *Towards an Indigenous Church.* London: Oxford, 1965.

Ilan, Tal. *Jewish Women in Greco-Roman Palestine.* Peabody, Mass.: Hendrickson, 1998.

Jeremias, Joachim. "War Paulus Witwer?" *ZNW* 25 (1926): 310–12.

———. *Heiligengräber in Jesu Umwelt (Mt. 23,29; L. 11,47).* Göttingen: Vandenhoeck & Ruprecht, 1958.

Jervell, Jacob. "Daughters of Abraham." In *The Unknown Paul: Essays on Luke-Acts and Early Christian History.* Minneapolis: Augsburg, 1984.

Jewett, Robert. "Tenement Churches and Communal Meals in the Early Church: The Implications of a Form-Critical Analysis of 2 Thess 3:10." *BR* 38 (1993): 23–43.

Johnson, Luke Timothy. "The New Testament's Anti-Jewish Slander and the Conventions of Ancient Polemic." *JBL* 108 (1989): 419–41.

———. *Reading Romans: A Literary and Theological Commentary* New York: Crossroad, 1997.

Johnson, William A. *On Religion: A Study of Theological Method in Schleiermacher and Nygren.* Leiden: Brill, 1964.

Kajanto, Iiro. "Les Noms." In *Sylloge inscriptionum christianarum veterum musei vaticani.* Acta instituti romani finlandiae, vol. 1, no. 2, ed. Henrik Zilliacus. Helsinki: Tilqmann, 1963.

Käsemann, Ernst. *Leib und Leib Christi.* Beiträge zur historischen Theologie, no. 9. Tübingen: Mohr (Siebeck), 1933.

———. "Geist und Geistesgaben im NT." In *Die Religion in Geschichte und Gegenwart: Handwörterbuch für Theologie und Religionswissenschaft.* 7 vols. 3d ed. Tübingen: Mohr (Siebeck), 157–65.

———. "The Canon of the New Testament and the Unity of the Church." In *Essays on New Testament Themes.* Trans. W. J. Montague. London: SCM, 1964.

———. "Ministry and Community in the New Testament." In *Essays on New Testament Themes.* Trans. W. J. Montague. London: SCM, 1964.

———. "The Problem of the Historical Jesus." In *Essays on New Testament Themes.* Trans. W. J. Montague. London: SCM, 1964.

———. *The Testament of Jesus.* Trans. G. Krodel. London: SCM, 1968.

———. "New Testament Questions of Today." In *New Testament Questions of Today.* Trans. W. J. Montague. Philadelphia: Fortress, 1969.

———. "The Beginnings of Christian Theology." *JTC* 6 (1969): 17–46.

———. "On the Topic of Primitive Christian Apocalyptic." *JTC* 6 (1969): 99–133.

Kettler, Franz-Heinrich. "Enderwartung und himmlischen Stufenbau in Kirchenbegriff des nachapostolischen Zeitalters." *TLZ* 79 (1954): 385–97.

Klassen, William. *Judas: Betrayer or Friend of Jesus?* Minneapolis: Fortress, 1996.

Klauck, Hans-Josef. *Herrenmahl und hellenistischer Kult: Eine religionsgeschichtliche Untersuchung zum ersten Korintherbrief.* Münster: Aschendorf, 1982.

———. *Hausgemeinde und Hauskirche im frühen Christentum.* Stuttgart: Verlag Katholisches Bibelwerk, 1981.

Klauser, Theodor. *Die Cathedra im Totenkult der heidnischen und christlichen Antike.* Münster: Aschendorf, 1927.

———. "Christliche Märtyrerkult, heidnischer Heroenkult und spätjüdische Heiligenverehrung." In *Gesammelte Arbeiten.* Münster: Aschendorf, 1974.

———. "Von Heroon zur Märtyrerbasilika." In *Gesammelte Arbeiten.* Münster: Aschendorf, 1974.

Kloppenborg, John. *The Formation of Q: Trajectories in Ancient Wisdom Collections.* Philadelphia: Fortress, 1987.

Knox, Wilfred L. *St Paul and the Church of the Gentiles.* Cambridge: Cambridge University Press, 1939.

Koester, Helmut. "History and Cult in the Gospel of John and in Ignatius of Antioch." *JTC* 1 (1965): 111–23.

Konikoff, Adia. *Sarcophagi from the Jewish Catacombs of Ancient Rome.* Stuttgart: Franz Steiner Verlag, 1986.

Kötting, Bernhard. *Der frühchristliche Reliquienkult und die Bestattung im Kirchengebäude.* Cologne: Westdeutscher Verlag, 1965.

Kraabel, Thomas A. "The Disappearance of the Godfearers." *Numen* 28 (1981): 113–26.

———. "The Roman Diaspora: Six Questionable Assumptions." *Journal of Jewish Studies* 33 (1982): 445–64.

———. "Greek, Jews and Lutherans in the Middle Half of Acts." *HTR* 79 (1986): 147–57.

———. "The God-fearers — A Literary and Theological Invention." *Biblical Archaeology Review* 64 (1986): 47–54.

———. "The God-fearers Meet the Beloved Disciple." In *The Future of Early Christianity,* ed. Birger A Pearson. Minneapolis: Fortress, 1991.

Kraabel, Thomas A., and Andrew R. Seager. "The Synagogue and the Jewish Community: Impact of the Discovery of the Sardis Synagogue." In *Sardis from Prehistoric to Roman Times: Results of the Archaeological Exploration of Sardis 1958–1975,* ed. G. M. A. Hanfmann. Cambridge: Harvard University Press, 1983.

Kraemer, Ross S. *Her Share of the Blessings: Women's Religions among Pagans, Jews, and Christians in the Graeco-Roman World.* Philadelphia: Fortress, 1988.

Krautheimer, Richard. *Early Christian and Byzantine Architecture.* Harmondsworth, England: Pelican, 1975.

———. *Rome: Profile of a City, 312–1308.* Princeton, N.J.: University Press, 1980.

Krentz, Edgar. "Order in the 'House' of God: The Haustafel in 1 Peter 2:11–3:12." In *Common Life in the Early Church,* ed. Julian V. Hills. Harrisburg, Pa.: Trinity Press International, 1998.

Kretschmar, Georg. "Ein Beitrag zur Frage nach dem Ursprung frühchristlicher Askese." *ZTK* 61 (1964): 27–67.

Kysar, Robert. "John's Anti-Jewish Polemic." *Bible Review* 9 (1993): 83–95.

Laeuchli, Samuel. *The Language of Faith.* Nashville: Abingdon, 1962.

Lampe, Peter. *Die stadtrömischen Christen in den ersten beiden Jahrhunderten.* Tübingen: Mohr (Siebeck), 1987.

Leon, Harry J. *The Jews of Ancient Rome.* Philadelphia: Jewish Publication Society of America, 1960.

————. *The Jews of Ancient Rome.* Rev. Carolyn Osiek. Peabody, Mass.: Hendrickson, 1995.

Lessing, Gottfried Ephraim. *Werke.* Ed. H. G. Göpfert. Munich: Hauser, 1973.

Levinskaya, Irina. *The Book of Acts in Its Diaspora Setting.* Grand Rapids: Eerdmans, 1996.

Lévi-Strauss, Claude. *The Raw and the Cooked.* Trans. John and Doreen Weightman. New York: Harper & Row, 1969.

Lévy-Bruhl, Lucien. *The Primitive Mentality.* Trans. L. Clare. London: Allen and Unwin, 1923.

Lietzmann, Hans. *Mass and the Lord's Supper: A Study in the History of the Liturgy.* Trans. Dorothea H. G. Reeve. Leiden: Brill, 1979.

Lieu, Judith M. "Blindness in the Johannine Tradition." *NTS* 34 (1988):83–95.

Lieu, Judith, John North, and Tessa Rajak, eds. *The Jews among Pagans and Christians in the Roman Empire.* London: Routledge, 1992.

Lifshitz, B. "Du nouveau sur les 'Sympathisants.'" *Journal for the Study of Judaism* 1 (1970): 77–84.

Lightfoot, J. B. *St Paul's Epistle to the Philippians.* London: Macmillan, 1868.

Lindemann, Andreas. "The Beginnings of Christian Life in Jerusalem According to the Summaries in the Acts of the Apostles (Acts 2:42–47; 4:32-37; 5:12–16)." In *Common Life in the Early Church,* ed. Julian V. Hills. Harrisburg, Pa.: Trinity Press International, 1998.

Linton, Olaf. *Das Problem der Urkirche in der neueren Forschung.* Uppsala Universitets Årsskrift, Teologi 2. Leipzig: A. Lorentz, 1932.

Lucius, Ernst. *Die Anfänge des Heiligenkultes in der christlichen Kirche.* Tübingen: Mohr, 1904.

Lüdemann, Hermann. *Die Anthropologie des Apostles Paulus.* Kiel: Universitäts Buchhandlung, 1872.

————. *Biblical Christianity.* Trans. M. A. Canney. London: Owen, 1905.

Lundberg, Per. *La typologie baptismale dans l'ancienne église.* Acta seminarii neotestamentici upsaliensis 10. Uppsala: Lundequistska, 1942.

Lundsteen, A. C. *Hermann Samuel Reimarus und die Anfänge der Leben-Jesu Forschung.* Copenhagen: Olsen, 1939.

Maccini, Robert Gordon. *Her Testimony Is True: Women as Witnesses according to John.* Journal for the Study of the New Testament Supplement Series 125. Sheffield: Sheffield Academic Press, 1996.

Macdonald, Alexander B. *Christian Worship in the Primitive Church.* Edinburgh: T. & T. Clark, 1934.

MacDonald, Margaret Y. *Early Christian Women and Pagan Opinion: The Power of the Hysterical Woman.* Cambridge: Cambridge University Press, 1996.

Mack, Burton L. *The Lost Gospel: The Book of Q and Christian Origins.* San Francisco: HarperSanFrancisco, 1993.

————. *Who Wrote the New Testament? The Making of the Christian Myth.* San Francisco: HarperSanFrancisco, 1995.

Mackinnon, James. *From Christ to Constantine.* London: Longmans Green, 1936.

MacRae, George. "Theology and Irony in the Fourth Gospel." In *The Word in the World,* ed. R. J. Clifford and George MacRae. Cambridge: Weston College Press, 1973.

————. "The Fourth Gospel and *Religionsgeschichte.*" *CBQ* 32 (1970): 13–24.

Malina, Bruce. *The Palestinian Manna Tradition: The Manna Tradition in the Palestinian Targums and Its Relationship to the New Testament Writings.* Leiden: Brill, 1968.

————. "Honor and Shame: Pivotal Values of the First-Century Mediterranean World." In *The New Testament World: Insights from Cultural Anthropology.* Atlanta: John Knox, 1981.

Martin, Troy W. *By Philosophy and Empty Deceit: Colossians as Response to a Cynic Critique.* Sheffield: Sheffield Academic Press, 1996.

Martyn, J. Louis. *History and Theology in the Fourth Gospel.* New York: Harper & Row, 1968.

Marucchi, Orazio. "L'ipogeo con i graffiti degli apostoli Pietro e Paolo scoperto sotto la basilica di S. Sebastiano." *NBAC* 27 (1921): 3–14.

Meeks, Wayne. *The Prophet-King: Moses Traditions and the Johannine Christology.* Leiden: Brill, 1967.

Mennell, Stephen, Anne Murcott, and Anneke H. van Otterloo. *The Sociology Of Food: Eating, Diet And Culture.* London: Sage Publications, 1992.

Merton, R. K. *Social Theory and Social Structure.* Glencoe, Ill.: Free Press, 1968.

Meyer, Marvin. *The Gospel of Thomas: The Hidden Sayings of Jesus.* San Francisco: HarperSanFrancisco, 1992.

Milburn, Robert. *Early Christian Art and Architecture.* Berkeley: University of California Press, 1988.

Moberly, R. C. *Ministerial Priesthood.* London: Murray, 1897.

————. *Ministerial Priesthood.* Reprint, with an introduction by A. T. Hanson. London: SPCK, 1969.

Moxnes, Halvor. "Meals and the New Community in Luke." *Svensk Exegetisk Årsbok* 51–52 (1986–87): 158–67.

Mozley, J. K. *The Impassibility of God.* Cambridge: Cambridge University Press, 1926.

Mueller, David L. *An Introduction to the Theology of Albrecht Ritschl.* Philadelphia: Westminster, 1969.

Munck, Johannes. *Paul and the Salvation of Mankind.* Trans. Frank Clarke. London: SCM, 1959.

Mussies, Gerard. "Jewish Personal Names in Some Non-Literary Sources." In *Studies in Early Jewish Epigraphy,* ed. Jan Willem van Henten and Pieter Willem van der Horst. Leiden: Brill, 1994.

Neusner, Jacob. *Symbol and Theology in Early Judaism.* Minneapolis: Fortress, 1991.

Newman, John Henry. *An Essay on the Development of Christian Doctrine.* London: Pickering, 1878.

Neyrey, Jerome. *Paul, In Other Words: A Cultural Reading of His Letters.* Louisville: Westminster / John Knox, 1990.

Niditch, Susan. "Portrayals of Women in the Hebrew Bible." In *Jewish Women in Historical Perspective,* 2d ed., ed. Judith R. Baskin. Detroit: Wayne State University Press, 1991.

Niebuhr, Richard R. *Schleiermacher on Christ and Religion.* New York: Scribner's, 1964.

Nighswander, Daniel L. *Paul's Use of Shame as a Sanction in 1 Corinthians.* Th.D. diss., University of Toronto, 1994.

Nygren, Anders. *Dogmatikens vetenskapliga grundläggning med särskild hönsyn till den Kant-Schleiermacherska problemställningen.* Lunds Universitets Årsskrift, N.F. Avd. 1, Bd. 17, Nr. 8. Lund: Gleerup, 1922.

———. *Agape and Eros.* Trans. P. Watson. London: SPCK, 1953.

———. *Essence of Christianity.* Trans. P. Watson. London: Epworth, 1960.

Overbeck, Franz. "Über das Verhältnis Justins des Märtyrers zur Apostelgeschichte." *ZWT* 15 (1872): 305–49.

Pagels, Elaine. *The Gnostic Gospels.* New York: Random House, 1979.

Patai, Raphael. *The Children of Noah: Jewish Seafaring in Ancient Times.* Princeton: University Press, 1998.

Pedersen, Johannes. *Israel: Its Life and Culture.* Vol. 1/2. Copenhagen: Branner og Korch, 1926.

———. *Israel: Its Life and Culture.* Vol. 3/4. Copenhagen: Branner og Korch, 1940.

Perelmuter, Hayim. *Siblings: Rabbinic Judaism and Early Christianity at Their Beginnings.* Mahwah, N.J.: Paulist Press, 1989.

Petersen, Norman. *Rediscovering Paul: Philemon and the Sociology of Paul's Narrative World.* Philadelphia: Fortress, 1985.

Pfleiderer, Otto. *The History of Paulinism in the Primitive Church.* Vol. 2 of *Paulinism: A Contribution to the History of Primitive Christian Theology.* Trans. Edward Peters. London: Williams and Norgate, 1877.

Piper, Ronald A. *Wisdom in the Q Tradition: The Aphoristic Teaching of Jesus.* Cambridge: Cambridge University Press, 1987.

Plaskow, Judith. "Jewish Theology." In *Feminist Perspectives on Jewish Studies,* ed. Lynn Davidman and Shelly Tenenbaum. New Haven: Yale University Press, 1994.

Pope-Levison, Priscilla, and John R. Levison. *Jesus in Global Contexts.* Louisville: Westminster / John Knox, 1992.

Preuss, Julius. *Biblical and Talmudic Medicine.* Brooklyn: Hebrew Publishing, 1977.

Rajak, Tessa. "Inscription and Context: Reading the Jewish Catacombs of Rome." In *Studies in Early Jewish Epigraphy,* ed. Jan Willem van Henten and Pieter Willem van der Horst. Leiden: Brill, 1994.

Redfield, Robert. *The Little Community.* Chicago: University of Chicago Press, 1955.

Reicke, Bo. *Diakonie, Festfreude, und Zelos.* Uppsala: Lundequistska, 1951.

Reimer, Ivoni Richter. *Women in the Acts of the Apostles: A Feminist Liberation Perspective.* Minneapolis: Fortress, 1995.

Reimarus, Hermann Samuel. *The Goal of Jesus and His Disciples.* Trans. and ed. G. W. Buchanan. Leiden: Brill, 1970.

Rensberger, David. *Johannine Faith and Liberating Community.* Philadelphia: Westminster, 1988.

Reumann, John. "One Lord, One Faith, One God, but Many House Churches." In *Common Life in the Early Church,* ed. Julian V. Hills. Harrisburg, Pa.: Trinity Press International, 1998.

Reynolds, Joyce Maire, and Robert Tannenbaum. *Jews and Godfearers at Aphrodisias: Greek Inscriptions with Commentary.* Cambridge Philological Society Supplementary Volume 12. Cambridge: Cambridge Philological Society, 1987.

Richardson, C. C. *The Christianity of Ignatius of Antioch.* New York: Columbia University Press, 1935.

Riesner, Rainer. *Jesus als Lehrer: Eine Untersuchung zum Ursprung der Evangelien-Überlieferung.* Tübingen: Mohr (Siebeck), 1988.

Ritschl, Albrecht. *Die Entstehung der altkatholischen Kirche.* 2d ed. Bonn: Marcus, 1857.

Robbins, Vernon K. *Jesus the Teacher: A Socio-Rhetorical Interpretation of Mark.* Philadelphia: Fortress, 1984.

Rordorf, Willy. *Sunday: The History of the Day of Rest and Worship in the Earliest Centuries of the Christian Church.* Trans. A. K. Graham. Philadelphia: Westminster, 1968.

Rorem, Paul. *Pseudo-Dionysius: A Commentary on the Texts and an Introduction to Their Influence.* New York: Oxford University Press, 1993.

Rothe, R. *Die Anfänge der Christlichen Kirche und ihrer Verfassung.* Wittenberg: Zimmermann, 1837.

Rothkrug, Lionel. *Religious Practices and Collective Perceptions* Historical Reflections, vol. 7, no. 1. Waterloo, Ont.: Historical Reflections Press, 1980.

Rutgers, Leonard V. "The Interaction of Jews and Non-Jews in Late Antiquity." *American Journal of Archaeology* 96 (1992): 101–18.

———. *The Jews in Late Ancient Rome: Evidence of Cultural Interaction in the Roman Diaspora.* Leiden: Brill, 1995.

Sabatier, Auguste. *The Religions of Authority and the Religions of the Spirit.* Trans. Louise Seymour Houghton. London: Williams and Norgate, 1904.

Sanders. E. P. *Jesus and Judaism.* Philadelphia: Fortress, 1985.

———. "Jewish Association with Gentiles and Galatians 2:11–14." In *The Conversation Continues: Studies in Paul and John in Honour of J. Louis Martyn,* ed. Robert T. Fortna and Beverly R. Gaventa. Nashville: Abingdon, 1990.

———. *The Historical Figure of Jesus.* London: Penguin Press, 1993.

Sanders, Jack. *Schismatics, Sectarians, Dissidents, Deviants: The First One Hundred Years of Jewish-Christian Relations.* Valley Forge, Pa.: Trinity Press International, 1993

Sanneh, Lamin. *Translating the Message: The Missionary Impact on Culture.* Maryknoll, N.Y.: Orbis, 1989.

Schelstrate, Emanuel. *De disciplina arcani contra disputationem Ernesti Tentzelli.* Rome: Sac. Congregat. de Propaganda Fide, 1685.

Schineller, Peter. *A Handbook on Inculturation.* New York: Paulist Press, 1990.

Schleiermacher, Friedrich. *The Christian Faith.* Trans. H. R. Mackintosh and J. S. Stewart. Edinburgh: T. &. T. Clark, 1928.

———. *Life of Jesus.* Trans. S. Maclean Gilmour. Philadelphia: Fortress, 1974.

Schlier, Heinrich. *Religionsgeschichtliche Untersuchungen zu den Ignatiusbriefen.* Zeitschrift für die neutestamentliche Wissenschaft, no. 8. Giessen: Töpelmann, 1929.

———. *Christus und die Kirche im Epheserbrief.* Beiträge zur historischen Theologie, no. 6. Tübingen: Mohr (Siebeck), 1930.

Schneiders, Sandra M. "Women in the Fourth Gospel and the Role of Women in the Contemporary Church." *Biblical Theology Bulletin* 12 (1982): 35–45.

Schottroff, Luise. *Let the Oppressed Go Free: Feminist Perspectives on the New Testament.* Trans. Annamarie S. Kidder. Louisville: Westminster / John Knox, 1993.

Schreiter, Robert. *Constructing Local Theologies.* Maryknoll, N.Y.: Orbis, 1985.
Schüssler Fiorenza, Elisabeth. *In Memory of Her: A Feminist Theological Reconstruction of Christian Origins.* New York: Crossroads, 1983.
———. "Theological Criteria and Historical Reconstruction: Martha and Mary; Luke 10:38–42." In *Colloquy* 53. Berkeley, Calif.: Center for Hermeneutical Studies in Hellenistic and Modern Culture, 1987.
Schwegler, Albert. *Das nachapostolische Zeitalter.* Tübingen: Fues, 1846.
Schweitzer, Albert. *Die Religionsphilosophie Kants von der Kritik der reinen Vernunft bis zur Religion innerhalb der Grenzen der bloßen Vernunft.* Tübingen: Mohr, 1899.
———. *Christianity and the Religions of the World.* Trans. Johanna Powers. London: Allen and Unwin, 1923.
———. *The Mysticism of Paul the Apostle.* Trans. W. Montgomery. London: Black, 1931.
———. "The Conception of the Kingdom of God in the Transformation of Eschatology." In E. N. Mozley, *The Theology of Albert Schweitzer for Christian Inquirers.* London: Black, 1950.
———. *The Quest of the Historical Jesus.* Trans. W. Montgomery. London: Black, 1954.
———. *The Teaching of Reverence for Life.* Trans. R. Winston and C. Winston. London: Owen, 1966.
Schweizer, Eduard. *Geist und Gemeinde im Neuen Testament und Heute.* Theologisch Existenz Heute. N.F. 32. Munich: Kaiser Verlag, 1952.
———. *Jesus.* Trans. David E. Green. London: SCM, 1971.
Scott, Ernest F. *The Spirit in the New Testament.* London: Hodder and Stoughton, 1923.
Shorter, Aylward. *Toward a Theology of Inculturation.* Maryknoll, N.Y.: Orbis, 1988.
Sillistone, Thomas. *Religion, Symbolism and Meaning.* Oxford: Cassirer, 1968.
Smith, Dennis E., and Hal E. Taussig. *Many Tables: The Eucharist in the New Testament and Liturgy Today.* Philadelphia: Trinity Press International, 1990.
Smith, William Robertson. *Kinship and Marriage in Early Arabia.* Cambridge: University Press, 1885.
Snyder, Graydon F. "The Text and Syntax of Ignatius PROS EPHESIOUS 20:2c," *VC* 22 (1968): 8–13.
———. *The Shepherd of Hermas.* Vol. 6 of *The Apostolic Fathers.* Camden, N.J.: Nelson, 1968.
———. "The Literalization of the Apocalyptic Form in the New Testament Church." *BR* 14 (1969): 5–18.
———. "John 3:16 and the Anti-Petrinism of the Johannine Tradition." *BR* 16 (1971): 5–15.
———. *Ante Pacem: Archaeological Evidence of Church Life Before Constantine.* Macon, Ga.: Mercer University Press, 1985.
———. *First Corinthians: A Faith Community Commentary.* Macon, Ga.: Mercer University Press, 1992.
Sohm, Rudolph. *Outlines of Church History.* Trans. M. Sinclair. London: Macmillan, 1895.
———. *Kirchenrecht.* Bd. 1. Leipzig: Duncker & Humboldt, 1892.

———. *Wesen und Ursprung des Katholizismus. Abhandlungen der philologisch-historischen Klasse der königlich sächsischen Gesellschaft der Wissenschaft.* Bd. 27, no. 10. Leipzig: Teubner, 1909.

Soler, Jean. "The Semiotics of Food in the Bible." In *Food and Drink in History.* Selections from *Annales Economies, Sociétés, Civilisations,* vol. 5, ed. Robert Forster and Orest Ranum. Baltimore: Johns Hopkins University Press, 1979.

Song, Soonyeol. *The Portraits of God-Fearers in Acts of the Apostles: Its Historical Background and Literary Function.* Ph.D. diss., Chicago Theological Seminary, 1995.

Stacey, W. David. *The Pauline View of Man.* London: Macmillan, 1956.

Stark, Rodney. *The Rise of Christianity.* San Francisco: HarperSanFrancisco, 1997.

Stern, Menahem. *Greek and Latin Authors on Jews and Judaism.* Jerusalem: Israel Academy of Science and Humanities, 1974.

Strauss, David Friedrich. *The Life of Jesus Critically Examined.* Trans. George Eliot and Mary Hennell. London: Sonnenschein, 1898.

Strzygowski, Josef. *The Orgin of Christian Church Art.* Oxford: Clarendon, 1923.

Subilia, Vittorio. *The Problem of Catholicism.* Trans. R. Kissack. London: SCM, 1964.

Sundberg, A. C. "Isos to Theos Christology in John 5:17–30." *BR* 15 (1970): 19–31.

Swanson, Tod D. "To Prepare a Place: Johannine Christianity and the Collapse of Ethnic Territory. *JAAR* 62 (1994): 241–63.

Talbert, C. H., ed. *Reimarus: Fragments.* Trans. R. S. Fraser. Philadelphia: Fortress, 1970.

Taylor, Vincent. *The Atonement in New Testament Teaching.* London: Epworth, 1940.

Theissen, Gerd. *Sociology of Early Palestinian Christianity.* Trans. John Bowden. Philadelphia: Fortress, 1978.

Tilborg, Sjef van. *Imaginative Love in John.* Leiden: Brill, 1993.

Torjesen, Karen Jo. *When Women Were Priests: Women's Leadership in the Early Church and the Scandal of Their Subordination in the Rise of Christianity.* San Francisco: HarperSanFrancisco, 1993.

Torrance, T. F. *The Doctrine of Grace in the Apostolic Fathers.* London: Oliver and Boyd, 1948.

Townsend, J. T. "The Gospel of John and the Jews: the Story of Religious Divorce." In *Anti-Semitism and the Foundations of Christianity,* ed. Alan Davies. New York: Paulist Press, 1979.

Trebilco, Paul R. *Jewish Communities in Asia Minor.* Cambridge: Cambridge University Press, 1991.

Trésmontant, C. *A Study of Hebrew Thought.* Trans. M. F. Gibson. New York: Desclee, 1960.

———. *La métaphysique du christianisme.* Paris: Editions du Seuil, 1961.

Trigger, Bruce G. *Gordon Childe, Revolutions in Archaeology.* New York: Columbia University Press, 1980.

Troeltsch, Ernst. *The Social Teaching of the Christian Churches.* Trans. Olive Wyon. New York: Macmillan, 1931.

Unnik, W. C. van. "Luke-Acts, A Storm Center in Contemporary Scholarship." In *Studies in Luke-Acts*, ed. L. E. Keck and J. L. Martyn. Philadelphia: Fortress, 1966.

Verner, David C. *The Household of God: The Social World of the Pastoral Epistles*. Chico, Calif.: Scholars Press, 1983.

Vielhauer, P. "Franz Overbeck und die neutestamentliche Wissenschaft." *EvT* 10 (1950–51): 193–207.

———. "On the Paulinism of Acts." In *Studies in Luke-Acts*, ed. L. E. Keck and J. L. Martyn. Philadelphia: Fortress, 1966.

Wahlde, Urban C. von. "The 'Johannine' Jews: A Critical Survey. *NTS* (1982): 33–60.

———. *The Earliest Version of John's Gospel: Recovering the Gospel of Signs*. Wilmington, Del.: Michael Glazier, 1989.

Ward-Perkins, J. B. "Memoria, Martyr's Tomb, and Martyr's Church." *JTS* 17 (1966): 20–38.

Waser, O. "Daimon." In *Paulys Realencyclopädie der klassischen Altertumswissenschaft*. Vol. 4.2. Stuttgart: J. B. Metzler, 1901.

Weiss, Johannes. *Jesus' Proclamation of the Kingdom of God*. Trans. R. H. Hiers and D. L. Holland. London: SCM, 1971.

Werner, Martin. *The Formation of Christian Dogma*. London: Black, 1957.

Westermann, Claus. "Heilung und Heil in der Gemeinde aus der Sicht des Alten Testament." *Wege Zum Menschen* 27 (1975): 1–12.

White, L. Michael. *The Social Origins of Christian Architecture*. Vol. 1, *Building God's House in the Roman World: Architectural Adaptation Among Pagans, Jews and Christians*. Baltimore: Johns Hopkins University Press, 1990. Reprint, Valley Forge: Trinity Press International, 1996.

———. *The Social Origins of Christian Architecture*. Vol. 2, *Texts and Monuments for the Domus Ecclesiae in Its Environment*. Valley Forge, Pa.: Trinity Press International, 1997.

Wiefel, Wolfgang. "The Jewish Community in Ancient Rome and the Origins of Roman Christianity." In *The Romans Debate*, ed. Karl Donfried. Peabody, Mass.: Hendrickson, 1991.

Wilken, Robert L. *The Myth of Christian Beginnings: History's Impact on Belief*. Garden City, N.Y.: Doubleday, 1971.

———. *The Christians as the Romans Saw Them*. New Haven: Yale University Press, 1984.

Willis, Wendell Lee. *Idol Meat in Corinth: The Pauline Argument in 1 Corinthians 8 and 10*. Chico, Calif.: Scholars Press, 1981.

Winter, Bruce W. *Seek the Welfare of the City: Christians as Benefactors and Citizens*. Grand Rapids: Eerdmans, 1994.

Wire, Antoinette. *The Corinthian Women Prophets: A Reconstruction through Paul's Rhetoric*. Minneapolis: Fortress, 1990.

Wood, Roy C. *The Sociology of the Meal*. Edinburgh: Edinburgh University Press, 1995.

Wrede, William. *The Messianic Secret*. Trans. J. C. G. Greig. London: Clarke, 1971.

Zias, Joseph. "Death and Disease in Ancient Israel." *BA* 54 (1991): 146–59.

Ziegler, Heinrich. *Irenaeus der Bischof von Lyon: Ein Beitrag zur Entstehungsgeschichte der altkatholischen Kirche*. Berlin: Reimer, 1871.

Index of Texts

Index of Names

Index of Subjects

Entries to plate numbers refer to photographs
appearing between pages 88 and 89.

Acculturation, 2–3, 86, 187–88
Adam and Eve, 140
Agape meal, 94, 96, 163, 169, 171,
    173–74, plates 26–28
Agape to eros, 73–74
Anchor, 93–94, 101, 135, plate 2
Andrew, 40
Angels, 197
Aphrodisias, 16
Apocalypticism, 20, 60–62
    in Fourth Gospel, 42–43
Architecture, 208–9
    antecedents to built forms, 108–9
    for burials, 112–14
    symbolism in shapes of, 107
    synagogue, 108
    see also Churches
Art, representation. *See* Christian
    art; Jewish art
Assimilation, 2

Baptism of Jesus, 101–2, 135, plates
    13–14
Bar-Jesus, 199
Beloved Disciple, 40–41, 161,
    185–86
Biblical theology, 72–73
Birth of Jesus, 43–44, 125, 127–28,
    plate 24
Bishops, 79, 81, 166
Blood, 130, 137, 140–42, 148, 170
Boat, 94, plate 3
Bread
    in meals, 131–32, 143, 144, 209
    symbolism, 96–97, 131–32, 144,
        205, plates 5–6
Burials
    buildings for, 112–13
    for martyrs, 167

and shrines, 166
vocabulary for, 117–18

Cain and Abel, 140
Calendar, 210
    early Christian, 126–28
    Fourth Gospel on, 125–26, 206
    in Jesus tradition, 202
    Jesus' rejection of, 120–22
    Jewish, 120
    lunar and solar, 119
    martyrs in, 128
    Paul on, 36–37, 122–24, 204
    Roman, 126
Capitolina, Claudius, 16
Catholic church, 57, 81–82. *See also*
    Early Catholicism
Celebrations. *See* Calendar
Cemeteries, covered, 113, 167
Chaos, 133–35, 144
Christian art, 208, plates 23–24
    Daniel cycle, 100, plates 9–11
    healing tradition in, 103–5, plates
        12–16
    miracle catenae in, 105–6
    St. Peter excavations, 127, plates
        21–22
    use of vine in, 137
    water narratives, 101–3
Christian burials, 117–18
Christian calendar, 126–28
Christian inscriptions, 116–17,
    plate 21
Christianity
    calendar of, 36–37
    and other cultures, 1
    symbolism, 93–98
    see also Church transformations;
        Jesus tradition
Christian orthodoxy, 5

242